Y. Z.

Parochial Parleys on the Athanasian Creed

The Inspiration of the Bible, scientific Heresies, and other kindred Subjects

Y. Z.

Parochial Parleys on the Athanasian Creed
The Inspiration of the Bible, scientific Heresies, and other kindred Subjects

ISBN/EAN: 9783337110758

Printed in Europe, USA, Canada, Australia, Japan

Cover: Foto ©ninafisch / pixelio.de

More available books at **www.hansebooks.com**

PAROCHIAL PARLEYS

ON THE

ATHANASIAN CREED

THE INSPIRATION OF THE BIBLE

SCIENTIFIC HERESIES

AND OTHER KINDRED SUBJECTS

BETWEEN THE

REV. HUGH HIEROUS, M.A., M.C.U.

AND HIS PARISHIONER

THEOPHILOS TRUMAN

EDITED BY Y. Z.

'*Force never yet a generous heart did gain;
We yield on parley, but are storm'd in vain*'—DRYDEN

'*Veritatis simplex oratio est*'—SENECA

LONDON
KEGAN PAUL, TRENCH, & CO., 1 PATERNOSTER SQUARE
1886

'Beloved, when I gave all diligence to write unto you of the common salvation, it was needful for me to write unto you, and exhort you, that ye should *earnestly* contend for the faith which was once delivered unto the saints.'—*The Epistle of Jude*, v. 3.

'Reason is the only faculty whereby we have to judge of anything, even revelation itself.'—Bishop BUTLER.

> 'Let knowledge grow from more to more,
> But more of reverence in us dwell;
> That *mind* and *soul*, *according well*,
> May make one music as before
> But vaster.'—TENNYSON, *In Memoriam*.

'I say, that in God's own good time you will know all things.'—*The last words of a most loving and beloved Wife.*

In Memoriam

OF

M. A. H.

THE BELOVED

March 24, 1884

'She opened her mouth with wisdom and in her tongue was the law of kindness'

PREFACE.

To soothe a deep sorrow, to cherish a beloved memory, and to vindicate, within a special circle, a departure from old associations, creeds, and practices, this little book has been written. It lays no claim to literary distinction. The great storehouse of biblical literature and religious biography has been searched for materials to sustain and enforce his arguments, but the writer's obligations are too many and too great to admit of individual references, except, it may be, to Cardinal Newman and the Rev. Thomas Mozley.

To avoid local misapprehension, it may be well to state that the character of the Rev. Hugh Hierous is intended to be generic; and the personality and conversations are wholly imaginary. The aim of the writer has been to state most fully and unreservedly *all* that could be plausibly said in support of religious tenets which he himself has abandoned; feeling assured that such of his readers as are both truth-loving and fearless will, like himself, believe those tenets to be fallacious and untrue, and dishonouring to the Most High God, who hath proclaimed, 'I am the Lord, and there is none else; beside me there is no God: I will gird thee, though thou hast not known me: that they may know from the rising of the sun, and from the west, that there is none beside me: I am the Lord, and there is none else.'—Is. xlv. 5, 6.

Y. Z.

PAROCHIAL PARLEYS

ON THE

ATHANASIAN CREED AND OTHER KINDRED TOPICS.

INTERVIEW THE FIRST.

Vicar. (The Rev. Hugh Hierous.) I am glad to have met you in this cool and secluded spot, for I have been longing to speak to you, on a subject of some delicacy—a topic, indeed, which has given me great anxiety, and which, even now, I would not broach to a person of your age and intelligence were it not that I feel bound by my ordination vows to do so.

Parishioner. (Mr. Truman.) My dear Vicar, you somewhat startle me; but I am sure that your motives are kindly, and as I have found this small and beautiful flower (Parnassia palustris), the object of my search, I have abundance of time before me, and am quite curious to know what in me has given you anxiety.

Vicar. Well, I have been concerned to observe that during the five years I have been the vicar of this parish you have never once attended the Holy Communion, although you are a very regular attendant at church; and my appeals to the parishioners on the vital importance of this sacred rite have been most earnest and frequent. Even these circumstances *per se* would not have caused me to intrude on you, because I feel that my strong appeals from the pulpit exonerate me from responsibility in this matter—*liberavi animam meam*; but an intimate friend of yours has informed me that you absent yourself because you hold erroneous doctrine, and that you cannot enunciate the 'Belief,' which is an essential preliminary to the participation of the Holy Sacrament; that, in brief, you disbelieve in the doctrine of the Blessed Trinity, and are even unwilling to address our Lord Jesus Christ as 'God of God, Light of Light, very God of very God.'

Parishioner. Your informant is correct as to the reasons which preclude my presence, but I am not willing to admit that I hold 'erroneous doctrine;' on the contrary, I think it is the faith which was 'once delivered to the saints,' and that it becomes me 'to contend' for it on those rare occasions when I can do so without danger of wrecking the simple faith of others in still more important particulars; and as this appears to be one of those occasions, I invite you, my dear Pastor, to speak freely, and I assure you that I shall accept with becoming reverence your admonitions. In these solemn matters my one sole prayerful wish is to be guided to what is true, and, when, as the Premier Apostle puts it, I am unable 'to give an answer to every man that *asketh* me a *reason* of the hope that is in me' (1 Peter iii. 15), then will I bow with thankfulness to him who has shown me the better way.

Vicar. Your frankness relieves me of all embarrassment. I felt it to be my duty, at whatever cost, to admonish you, on hearing what I did from Mr. H. B., inasmuch as, with a solemnity equivalent to an oath, I had promised the Bishop 'to use both publick and *private* monitions and exhortations,' and 'to be ready with all faithful diligence to banish and drive away all erroneous and strange doctrine contrary to God's word.' And that these views, which you now acknowledge to me, are so, the Church plainly, strongly, yea, most emphatically, teaches in the grandest of her utterances, and in words which no man living can by possibility mistake. She says: '*Whosoever* will be saved, *before all things* it is necessary to hold the Catholick Faith; and the Catholick Faith *is this*: That we worship one God in Trinity, and Trinity in Unity; that the Godhead of the Father, of the Son, and of the Holy Ghost is all *one*, the glory equal, the majesty *co-eternal*; the Father is God, the Son is God, and the Holy Ghost is God; and yet they are not three Gods, but one God;' and she closes her amplifications of this ancient Creed with the awful words, '*This* IS the Catholic Faith, which except a man believe faithfully HE CANNOT BE SAVED!'

Parishioner. Yes, sir; no honest man can say that it is *not* the teaching of the Church of England. She received this metaphysical creed from her venerable mother the Church of Rome, and has given it a conspicuousness and a power in her services higher than does the older Church, dealing out its damnatory clauses with a frequency and an audacity which her parent seems to regard as imprudent. She, I believe, limits its public utterance to the service of Prime, when the clergy are the special audience. It is, as you say, 'the teaching of the Church of England,' and the teaching is clear, bold, and unmistakable; it is almost her characteristic mark among the three great Churches of

Christendom—the Roman, the Greek, and the Anglican—for she alone proclaims it aloud as a creed in the *public* services of the Church at thirteen great and distinct festivals in the course of one year. The 'Holy Orthodox Eastern Church' never uses it; she could hardly do so, for she, with her tens of thousands of followers in Syria, Palestine, Russia, and elsewhere, falls under the condemnation equally with myself; she also is unable to discover any apostolic authority for the statement that 'the Holy Ghost is of the Father *and* of the Son,' and because of this incapacity, all the myriads who do, or have, accepted her teachings '*without doubt* shall perish everlastingly.' The Church of England decrees this appalling sentence, and every priest in her pay is bound *as an honest man* to sing or say it at Morning Prayer on thirteen distinct and separate Feasts, among which stand out prominently the very greatest and most solemn of her festivals—Christmas Day, Easter Day, Ascension Day, and Whitsunday. Yes, sir, I accept all that you state as to the teachings of your Church; I recognise with full reverence that you are simply performing your duty, as one of her consecrated priests, to bring this fact before me as a parishioner and an attendant at your church. Yet with all this, I fail to perceive that in not accepting such teachings I am espousing 'erroneous and strange doctrines contrary to God's word.'

Vicar. We are distinctly told in God's Word that 'There are three that bare record in Heaven—the Father the Word, and the Holy Ghost; and these three are one' (1 John v. 7). And as to the damnatory clauses so called, which evidently excite your indignation, St.

Athanasius in asserting them is simply following the very words of Scripture, for in Mark xvi. 16, it is stated distinctly that 'he that believeth not shall be damned.'

Parishioner. Certainly your quotations are very clear and explicit, and no one who accepts the Bible, *as we have it*, as the undoubted word of God, can do other than bow with reverence to the statements and be silent evermore. I was once in that happy condition. In common with tens of thousands of my countrymen, I accepted without question all the religious statements made by my teachers. I heard them as others hear them—at an age and under circumstances which caused them to be received as 'a matter of course;' and moreover, they did not rouse sufficient feeling to make it a question of *anxious* enquiry. I am sure that in these particulars I formed no exception to my fellows—that is, I had no doubts, *because* I had no continuous or anxious thought upon the subjects, one way or the other.

Vicar. I hope that I am not to understand that you do not NOW accept the Bible as the word of God, and that those clear statements which I have given to you are no longer esteemed by you as of Divine authority.

Parishioner. The solemnity of your question demands that I should give it the fullest thought, and that my statements should be so simple and clear as to leave no erroneous impression on your mind; and that I may not unduly excite your indignation, or your pity, I should like to give a slight sketch of the history of my opinions, or, to use a well-known sentence, my 'phases of faith.'

Vicar. There is scarcely need for this, and it would occupy too long a time, to the exclusion of more essential matters; and I must frankly tell you that I have no other, and desire no other, arguments in defence of my position than the plain statements of the written Word. The opinions of the Fathers and the decrees of the Church are weighty, most weighty; but, in our respective positions, I shall not refer to them, as I have reason to know that the Scriptures will have greater weight with you than even the decrees of Councils.

Parishioner. Yes. You understand me. Like the Puritans of the Commonwealth, I prefer the opinions of the 'grandfathers' to that of the 'fathers;' and as for 'Councils,' their decrees have been so contradictory, and have been so often influenced by State or secular motives, that they fail to inspire my reverence. Even your great St. Athanasius has been disapproved by Councils at Tyre, Antioch, Milan, Constantinople, and elsewhere. The command of an emperor has more than once decided a dogma or creed, and set aside the statements of bishops avowedly made after study, meditation, and prayer. In the fourth century, even at the great Council of Nice, where, and when, the Nicene Creed itself was fixed, the final issue was dependent on the will of the Emperor Constantine; and by what carnal weapons that incomprehensible Creed was enforced may be seen in his decree, in which he commanded not only that all the treaties of Arius should be burnt, but, further, imperiously, nay ruthlessly, proclaimed that 'if anyone shall be detected concealing a book compiled by Arius, and shall not instantly bring it forward and burn it, the penalty for his offence shall be *death.*' The learned historian Gibbon has written truthfully on this subject—' the decrees of Heaven were enforced by the *sword* of the *soldier* rather than by the *arguments of an apostle*,' and another great historian of Christianity, the pious and venerable Dean Milman, tells us that the Roman world was ordered to believe in ' co-equal Holy Trinity upon the authority of two feeble boys and a rude Spanish soldier.'

Vicar. This is lightly spoken on the part of the Dean; but this is not of much moment, since, by whomsoever it may have been originally enforced, it is NOW emphatically *the creed* of the Church—*the* creed which ' *before all things* ' is necessary to be holden, and of which our Holy Church most solemnly declares, ' which Faith, except every one do keep *whole* and undefiled, *without doubt* he shall *perish everlastingly.*'

Parishioner. You have, my dear Vicar, made a most appalling statement, but, as a consecrated priest of the Church of England, bound by promises, nay by solemn vows, to recite this creed, it would be dishonest in you *not* to do so. Those awful words do not appal me as they once did. In the present age of the world they alarm very few indeed, as they can no longer ' be enforced by the sword of the soldier.' The 'Anathemas' of the Church *now* merely excite a smile among thoughtful and intelligent men in England, Germany, and France, however deterrent they may be among the uneducated classes of these countries. The Church of England blundered (as ecclesiastic bodies usually blunder in their policy when matters of 'faith' are discussed) in 1872, when even so 'orthodox' and pious a man as the seventh Earl of Shaftesbury petitioned in vain for the removal of the 'damnatory clause only'—a petition got up in haste; and yet it contained between five and six thousand signatures, among which were ten judges, two hundred and thirty-six barristers and solicitors, one hundred and eighty justices of the peace, some eighty-one peers, and members of the House of Commons, besides mayors, doctors, officers, and churchwardens 'too numerous to mention.' 'Reformed' Church as she is sometimes called, she yet clings as tenaciously as Rome herself to every word and tittle of this mediæval creed, even to assigning '*everlasting*' perdition to those whose reason and conscience are unable to accept it. It has survived through all the stormy conflicts of the Reformation, and her bishops and clergy resolve that 'it shall be retained, and be in use by the Authority of Parliament.' But, although 'retained,' and although ' in use,' the 'anathema' has become a mere sound, almost resembling

> a tale
> Told by an idiot, full of sound and fury,
> Signifying nothing.

It is received by nearly all, except the illiterate, with indifference, because it is so generally felt that they are not true.

Vicar. Not true! No one who dares to say this ought for a single moment afterwards to call himself a member of the Church of England. She teaches no doctrine so plainly, so unequivocally as she teaches this, and to none other does she as a Church declare with more emphasis that it ' may be *proved* by *most certain warrants* of *Holy Scripture*,'[1] nor can I at this moment recall any other matters of faith which she places so distinctly and categorically before her people in the solemn moments of Divine worship, and declares so

[1] Article viii.

authoritatively, '*which* Faith except every one do keep whole and undefiled, WITHOUT DOUBT he SHALL PERISH *everlastingly.*'

Parishioner. I honour you for your honesty, your consistency, and your courage. This is a time of equivocation, unreality, and untruth. Men tamper with their consciences; and to hide, if possible, even from themselves the falseness of their position, they give to words what is called a 'non-natural' sense; they invent 'theories of development;' they 'darken counsel by words without knowledge;' and after pledging themselves by vows and prayers so to 'minister the *doctrine* and Sacraments and the discipline of Christ as the Lord hath commanded, and *as this Church and realm hath received the same*,' they proceed to explain them away, or, as Archbishop Tillotson said of the Athanasian Creed, they 'wish they were well rid of them;' and as hundreds of the 'Evangelical section' of former days said of the plain words of the Prayer Book in reference to baptismal regeneration and the Supper of our Lord. This treachery to language, this 'mental reservation,' is observable in clergymen to a degree unknown among other classes, and lessens them much in the esteem of the cultured classes. The effeminate puerilities, genuflexions, and millinery of the High Church party are less offensive (and must be less mischievous in their result) than is the subtle perversion of words, terms, and incidents observable in the preachings and writings of the more enthusiastic members of the 'Low' and 'Broad' sections in the Church of England; for widely as these two classes differ on doctrinal points, they resemble each other in giving a 'non-natural sense' to words and a fictitious meaning to plain incidents. Your courage and consistency in adhering to the common sense meaning of the lucid words of the Prayer Book please me much, and I thank you.

Vicar. It would seem that I must accept your praise for courage and honesty at the expense of being puerile in my tastes and formal in my worship; but I do not own the soft impeachment. I belong to no party, for I know *who* it was that said 'Every kingdom divided against itself is brought to desolation, and every city or house divided against itself shall not stand.'

Parishioner. Although you stand apart from party squabbles and profess to have 'no views,' yet it is in vain to disguise the fact that there are at least three distinct 'parties' in the Church of England, with 'views' as divided and distinct as the Wesleyans from the Church of England, or as the 'Independents' in contrast with the 'Baptists,' or as either of these with the National Church. For general purposes, or in defence of the 'Church' in her connection with the State, the clergy may, and do, assemble as one body; but between the respective parties in their daily work, in their ministrations, and in their pulpit teachings, it would seem 'there is a great gulf fixed.' In private intercourse with their flocks each describes the other as 'unsound,' or weak, or wicked. In one day I have heard the good Dean Stanley called 'that wicked man' by a member of the 'Evangelical' section, and, worse still, charged with 'profligacy' by a clergyman of the 'High Church' party; the 'profligacy' consisting in his pleading for a 'hearing' on behalf of an absent bishop charged with 'heresy.' In short, the 'divisions' in the 'Church' are well-marked, conspicuous, nay rampant; and unfortunately for the Church as a national institution, two of these 'parties' have their own *special newspapers* to support and disseminate their special 'views.' The 'record' which these respective 'religious papers' gives of their 'brethren' is as damnatory as the early and closing sentences of the Athanasian Creed itself. If a portrait of the Church of England were drawn from the description given by the 'High Church' division of the 'Low,' or from the description of the 'Low Church' of the 'High,' and the people believed what their clergy said of each other in these rival papers, the National Church would become, like Babylon in the days of Jeremiah, 'an astonishment and an hissing,' yea, 'men would clap their hands at her and would hiss her out of her place.'

Vicar. You speak strongly, but I cannot gainsay your statements. The writings of the so-called religious papers are a disgrace to our age. There is not a trace of practical Christianity in their columns. When writing of a clergyman of opposite views to their own, they seem to read all the instructions of our Lord in a contrary sense, and to rebuke the things He praised, and praise the things which He rebuked. The party spirit of John appears to possess them in a frantic form, and they loudly and proudly proclaim that 'they saw one casting out devils' and 'we forbad him *because he followeth not us.*' I am astonished at their virulence, but not so much astonished at this as at the little effect their writings appear to have on the *public* mind. Party zeal and hate are thereby intensified in the special party, and the 'odium theologicum' is vivified among the priests. But despite all the theological thunders of the 'religious' press each individual parish seems content with its own clergyman, even in places where he has been preceded by an incumbent of opposite 'views.' In a neighbouring parish, where 'Evangelical views' had been preached and enforced in all their gloomy intensity for nearly fifty years, a minister of the opposite school, or rather a clergyman of sound Church principles, holding up the Prayer Book in all its integrity (as I strive to do), fills his church with *the same* congregation which listened with like reverential calm while 'apostolical succession,' 'baptismal regeneration,' and 'priestly absolution' were *denounced* with the same fervour as they are *now* upheld and enforced as the true teachings of the 'Catholic Church' and of their Book of Common Prayer.

Parishioner. As regards the scornful contumely and the reckless assertions of the 'religious' newspapers, it is a fortunate thing for the 'Church of England,' nor less so for the nation, that the secular law enforces that each priest should have his own distinctly defined local area of action, within which no other priest of his own Church can exercise priestly functions except by permission. Hence theological strife is lessened, if not removed, in the individual Church, and the general moral tone of the Incumbent, and his social courtesy, and his friendly interest in the secular affairs of the parish make each one popular, or at least accepted with grace by his own parishioners. Mankind (at least those who dwell in villages) are as a class passive and apathetic on the matters the newspapers wrangle over. They may incidentally hear at their market table that the 'Church Times' or

'The Record,' as the case may be, has painted their respected Vicar in very black colours; but when they learn that it was not because of 'a matter of wrong, or wicked lewdness,' he had done, but that the paper had fiercely assailed him because, as it said, 'this fellow persuadeth men to worship God contrary to law,' they at once conclude that it 'is a question of words and names,' of which they will be no judge; like the prudent Gallio of old, 'they care for none of these things' (Acts xviii. 7). If he preach 'contrary to law' they know that he has been placed over them by the ordinary custom, and 'mos pro lege' is their axiom in all things. He has become '*their parson*'; he occupies the same house or 'parsonage' as his predecessor; they hear the same chimes, on the same day, from the same place, and at the same hour, calling them to prayer; they go to the same church, and to the same spot in the church, as heretofore; the same words are addressed to them at the opening of the service, and the old familiar prayers follow; and provided their *senses* are not appealed to by new robes and new formalities, the old routine will be followed: they will walk contentedly along the old paths to the old church in which their fathers worshipped; and I speak from the accumulated experience of fifty years when I say that, in our small towns and rural parishes, the bulk of the congregation would be equally content whether the sermon preached was taken from the pages of Dr. Pusey, of John Henry Newman, of Charles Simeon, of John Wesley, or of Francis W. Rice. Only let it not be too long, and the Incumbent take care not to wear any robe strikingly distinct from that of his predecessors, and then the slumbers of his hearers will be equally sweet at night, whether he faithfully observed the charter of his Church, and taught them that in baptism 'they were made members of Christ, children of God, and inheritors of the kingdom of heaven,' or whether, deserting this authority, he courageously declared, as did the Rev. F. W. Rice, Vicar of Fairford, that such statements 'lead men to mistake nature for grace, to fancy themselves spiritual whilst they are carnal, and to *assume* that they are the children of God whilst they are in *reality* children of the wicked one.'[1]

As I have already said, it would be all the same to such parishioners. The elder ones, if appealed to, would probably say, 'I be noa scholar,' and conclude that this solved their responsibility, if indeed they thought at all on such a subject. In the secluded villages of the Cotswold Hills, during my youth, few, if any, of the older farm-labourers could read, and I knew not one who was forty years old and could write. As a class, they are apathetic or most passive in religious matters. Religion with them is a sentiment with which the intellect has little to do. They trouble not themselves about 'creeds' or 'doctrines,' but retain a general reverence for the Bible—a kind of 'fetish' worship or awe difficult to describe, but manifest in times of sickness or sorrow; *then* 'The Bible' is resorted to, and, if not read beyond the verse or two which may first fall under the eye, is kept near to them, feeling, if not expressing, that it imparts a protective influence or support, and to have it *near* to them was a good thing, a religious act acceptable to God,

---

[1] *Reply to Mr. Dodsworth on Baptismal Regeneration*, by Rev. F. W. Rice, p. 3.

regarding it, in fact, with the same emotion or sentiment as an unlettered but a devout Papist would regard the presence of a picture of 'the Virgin,' a crucifix, a rosary, or a bottle of holy water. Whenever I found in this class of people any special interest in religion, they were usually 'chapel-folk'—descendants of men who in the long past had suffered from the 'Act of Uniformity,' the 'Mile Act,' and such unwise legislation. They were 'dissenters' by birth, and for the same reason as their more numerous neighbours were Churchmen. It was an hereditary custom, which had become instinctive. As a peasant once said to me, 'Why, zur, it be our way; vathear and granvathear did it afore.' It was a habit which had become confirmed by continuous hereditary transmission, an act prompted by an impulse apart from *mental* convictions of any kind, a habit produced by long-continued antecedents, almost as much as the features of their faces.

Vicar. This is a very dangerous deduction of yours. It strikes at the very roots of moral responsibility and makes men the creatures of circumstances.

Parishioner. It may be a dangerous statement, but the *consequences* of any *truth* should not deter us from seeking it. To broach an 'hypothesis' may be wrong, but it never *can* be wrong to state a *fact* in nature, for God has made it. His word and His works *cannot* contradict each other. We may be in doubt as to his *alleged* word; we may be deceived by the statements of history, more especially when that history comes down to us through long ages, through various nations with all their complexities of language, with all the possible errors of translators, and with all the bias of conflicting religious creeds; but a *natural fact* stands before us in its integrity, and is as new at *this* moment— as *recent*, that is—as the words of Moses were recent when spoken at Sinai three thousand three hundred and seventy-five years ago, or by Paul and Peter one thousand eight hundred and twenty-four years ago.

Vicar. Time cannot affect these statements; and you seem to forget that St. Peter distinctly states that 'holy men of God spake as they were moved by the Holy Ghost' (2 Peter i. 21).

Parishioner. I will not now pause to say that the second Epistle of Peter is one of those epistles whose authenticity is questioned by many pious men and ripe scholars, nor will I espouse wholly the statement of the distinguished biologist Lawrance, or of the great Lord Brougham (who, by-the-bye, edited with much ability an edition of Paley's Natural Theology), to the effect that a 'man was no more responsible for his creed than for the colour of his skin,' but I am not able to forget that one who was as much inspired as Peter (even if the text you quote be genuine) has said, 'Can the Ethiopian change his skin, or the leopard his spots: then may ye also do good that are accustomed to do evil' (Jeremiah xiii. 23); and another (the most distinguished of all the apostles), in an epistle whose authenticity has never been questioned by the most sceptical of historians, distinctly asks, 'Nay, but, O man, who art thou that repliest against God? Shall the thing formed say to him that formed it, Why hast thou made me thus? Hath not the potter power over the clay of the same lump to *make one* vessel unto *honour* and *another* unto *dishonour*?' (Romans ix. 20, 21). And sure am I that I have seen men so organised that in their cranial and facial configurations they appear to approximate the brute creation, and again and again in visiting a prison have I been able to 'pick out' the 'confirmed criminals' from these characteristics alone, and have gone away saddened by the solemnity and the truth of the words spoken amid 'thunders and lightnings, and a thick cloud upon the mount, and the voice of the tempest exceeding loud,' at Sinai some three thousand years ago, to this awful effect: 'I the Lord thy God am a jealous God, visiting *the iniquity of the fathers upon the children* unto the third and fourth generation of them that hate me' (Exodus xx. 5). Here are statements made by Jeremiah, by Paul, and by Moses, more startling in themselves than the statements made by Tyndal, by Darwin, and by Spencer, which have roused the indignation and evoked the censure of many pious divines. That some persons have been distinctly created and specially ordained to be *vessels of dishonour* is affirmed by Paul; that you may as reasonably expect the 'Ethiopian' to 'change his skin' as to think that a certain class of habitual wrong-doers will 'do good,' is implied by Jeremiah, and that *the innocent suffer* not from any iniquity of their own doing, but from the iniquity of their fathers committed before they were born, is pronounced by Moses to be the decree of the Almighty Himself. Moreover, any person of observation may see *proofs*, actual, positive, *living proofs, of the truth* of each one of the statements if he will look for them in the society around him, in the gaols of our land, or in the hospitals and lunatic asylums of the kingdom. It is as true in the nineteenth century after Christ as it was in the seventh century before Him, that 'the fathers have eaten a sour grape and the children's teeth are set on edge' (Jeremiah xxxi. 30).

Vicar. You use that passage very wrongly. The prophet quotes the saying, expressly to declare that it shall be said 'no more.'

Parishioner. The 'Bible' being a collection of many books, poems, histories, and essays, written in different places, in ages far apart, and by people of various positions, differing in age, station, education, and knowledge, it often happens that one statement or 'text' is in flat contradiction to another; **but in this** particular instance there is no discrepancy either as to fact or inference. Ezekiel, who wrote somewhat later than Jeremiah, still called the above saying a 'PROVERB.' Now a proverb is always the fitting record of *experience*, if it be long current as a 'proverb' among an intelligent people. Jeremiah speaks as a prophet (*pro*, before ; *phemi*, to speak) concerning something which is *to come*, and not of what IS. 'Behold the days *come* ;' and then, in reference to that coming time, Jeremiah added: '*In those days* they shall say no more the above proverb.' So that I do not feel that I have used the passage 'wrongly': although the time foretold has not yet arrived in Europe. Moreover, I remember that even when using this figurative language the prophet distinctly enunciates that the event foretold is to be brought about in strict accordance with the same Divine law which had previously ordained that the 'sour grape' *should* produce special results, that the 'iniquity of the father *should* be visited upon the child ; for, as a necessary preliminary to the disappearance of the proverb, a '*new covenant*' had to be made, and 'the house of Israel and the house of Judah had to be *renewed*,' the promised law that 'whatsoever a man *soweth* that shall he also reap' had to be acted upon, and the great Eternal resolved 'to sow' them with 'the seed of man, and with the seed of beast' and that as heretofore they had been surrounded by agencies (environments) 'to pluck up and break down, to destroy and to afflict,' so henceforth should they be watched over 'to build and to plant' (Jeremiah xxxi. 27, 28, 29), to become, in the words of Oriental poesy, figs—'very good figs, even like the figs that are first ripe' (Jeremiah xxiv. 2).

Vicar. These are deep mysteries, into which I do not at this moment desire to enter. I am not able to contradict you as to the unhappy divisions which beset our Church. You have yourself admitted that there are good men who hold each of the various 'views' which you have taken such pains to set forth ; and I think you must admit that when individuals have given their solemn pledge to uphold the teachings of the Church, they are bound as honest men *so to uphold them*, or to cease to take the pecuniary endowments of that Church, and to resign the office the duties of which they have failed to fulfil. 'Scripta litera manet'—the written word remains. The Prayer Book is the charter of the Church. All its formulas are simple, clear, and intelligible, so that 'he may run that readeth it' (Habakkuk ii. 2). Individually I cannot accept the special pleadings and the ingenious subtleties by which many of my fellow-priests attempt to explain away, by 'non-natural' verbiage, the simple and lucid statements of that book. It has come down to us sanctioned and hallowed by the practice of ages ; its creeds and its formulas are the creeds and the formulas of the Church long before it was distracted by divisions—before the monk Luther of Erfurt violated his vows, or the lustful arrogance of Henry VIII., or the imperious will of Queen Elizabeth, or the immature mind of Edward VI., influenced by vile, ambitious, and political priests, had attempted to 'explain,' dilute, modify, and change them, or to nullify their import by 'Acts of Parliament' and by an appendix of 'articles,' which for decency's sake, however, is not intruded into the orders for Morning and Evening Prayer, and which articles are not heard of until the exigencies of party strife drag them into the controversy. That book distinctly tells us that there are two sacraments '*necessary to salvation*,' 'that is to say, baptism and the supper of the Lord'; and it emphatically and unmistakably declares that in the latter 'the Body and Blood of Christ *are verily* and *indeed* taken and received by the faithful.' The Church, as if it prophetically foresaw that in the 'latter days' some doubters or even 'scoffers' may arise, was not content simply to state that the Body and Blood of Christ were taken in that blessed sacrament, but to place her decree beyond all possible honest 'cavil,' *emphasised*, nay reiterated her emphasis, by two of the strongest, clearest, and most unmistakable words our language possesses, and added, 'are *verily* and *indeed taken and received*.' To controvert these words is wilfully to trample her language and her meaning under foot, and practically to affirm that words were meant not to *express* thoughts and wishes but to *conceal* them. It is a crime against the great distinguishing characteristic of humanity, the faculty of speech, and is in its tendency akin to the principle which would rescind the word '*not*' from the commands of the Decalogue; and this brings me to the object of my interview with you, from which we have too long departed, namely, to speak respecting your absence from the Holy Communion, and to remind you that the Church expects, nay demands, your presence, for in one of the most prominent of her rubrics she says, 'and NOTE that every parishioner *shall* communicate *at the least* three times in the year, of which Easter to be one.'

Parishioner. I am glad that you have returned to it, although I do not feel that a sentence has been spoken by either of us which is irrelevant to that subject. I know that as a 'Churchman' I have failed in fealty to her commands; but I have done so in obedience to a *higher* law, and could, I think justify the act—as a very large number of 'Evangelicals,' clergymen even, justify *their* corresponding procedure, in other departments of her liturgy—by quoting the twentieth clause in her 'Articles of Religion,' to the effect that although 'the Church hath power to decree rites and ceremonies' . . . yet it is *not lawful* for the Church to ordain *anything* that is contrary to *God's Word written*, neither may it expound one place of Scripture that *it be repugnant to another*;' but I shall not do so, because I think it is subtle sophistry on their part so to manipulate and parry with her plain instructions, and because, moreover, I regard this particular 'rite' as one clearly commanded to be observed by our Divine Master. My reverence and love for Jesus of Nazareth are sincere and profound, and I remember that on that august occasion when He last partook of bread and wine with His disciples, He said, 'This do ye as oft as ye drink it in remembrance of me' (1 Cor. xi. 25), and in the most tender and touching of all His speeches to His disciples He added, 'If ye love me keep my commandments' (John xiv. 15). I yearn to partake of that hallowed festival, but the Church precludes me by the additions, and conditions, and prefaces with which she surrounds it, and by which she converts the sweet Memorial of a dear Friend and great Deliverer into a theological dogma against which my mind and my conscience alike rebel.

Vicar. I am sorry to hear that you again revert to this difficulty, because I had hoped that the distinct Scriptural authority which I had given to you from the words of the inspired apostle John, that 'there are *three* that bear record in heaven—the Father, the Son, and the Holy Ghost—and that these three are *one*,' would have removed your objection, would have caused you to abandon your position, and compelled you to forsake the vain suggestions of a feeble reason and to bow to the supreme authority of the Divine Word. Moreover, I would add (and the awful consequences involved compel me to forego the shallow amenities of social life) that the entire Christian world, north, east, west, and south, with the exception of a small, cold, and singular sect, numbering units among tens of thousands, adopt this creed, and that it implies something of arrogance and self-conceit in any individual to withstand such a testimony, such 'a cloud of witnesses;' and to think himself *wiser* than the Fathers, wiser than the great Churches of west and east, wiser (although it is certainly lowering the standard) than all the Nonconformist bodies—Wesleyans, Presbyterians, Baptists, Independents—and the shoals of sectaries, who, however schismatic, rebellious, and heretical in *other particulars*, accept *this* Divine tradition, and make the rebellious reason to bow before the sublime authority of the Word of God.

Parishioner. I am almost ashamed to confess to you, my dear Vicar, that the facts mentioned by you in the latter part of your statement kept my reason in thraldom and my judgment in suspense for ten or twelve years ; and that an overwhelming majority of men 'who profess and call themselves Christians' should acquiesce in the Trinitarian doctrine is, even now, to me, one of the most stupendously astounding facts in the history of mental thought and human progress. The thought *did weigh*, and weigh heavily, upon me, as to whether it was not presumptuous in one so unlearned as myself to differ in opinion from the Fathers and the Councils of the Church, from the teachings of the National Establishment of the Church of England, and more especially from the tenets of the tens of thousands of 'Nonconformists' who are so clamorous and so combative in respect to other religious opinions and practices, which appear to me so *small* and *insignificant* compared with this *momentous* question ; for, as the eloquent and learned Rev. Henry Melville once said, in a sermon which became the 'momentum' to my mind, and fixed its conclusions for ever : 'It is a *fundamental doctrine*. It is not a mere abstruse and speculative matter on which your judgment may be safely suspended' ; and he added, 'Take away the doctrine of the Trinity from the creed of Christendom, and there is no resting-place for guilty sinners.'[1]

Vicar. In thus preaching, that learned divine was faithfully enunciating the doctrines of the Church, was honestly fulfilling his ordination vow, was, in simple truth, reiterating the doctrine of that holy, ancient, and august Creed, which, as I have already told you, the Church of England in the solemn moments of Divine worship places so distinctly and categorically before her people, and respecting which she declares more authoritatively than she does of any other belief, or rite, or sacrament, that 'except every one do keep whole and undefiled, WITHOUT DOUBT he shall PERISH EVERLASTINGLY.' The eloquent clergyman expressed no more than the Athanasian Creed does, or ought to do, and would do thirteen times a year, and especially on the high festivals, the great *epochs* of Christian history—the celebrations of the Birth, the Resurrection, and Ascension of our Lord, and the descent of the Great Comforter, the Illuminating Spirit and Guide of the Church: that is, on Christmas Day, Easter Day, Ascension Day, and on Whitsunday—if all her priests did their duty faithfully and fearlessly. But how *could* such a statement as this by Mr. Melville have become a momentum to your mind and have brought about such sad conclusions as those you now unhappily hold?

Parishioner. It *did so.* No enthusiastic Wesleyan is more conscious and more positive of the birth-moment of his 'conversion' and spiritual life than am I of the cause, or 'momentum,' and of the 'start-point' of

---

[1] Preached at Camden Chapel, Camberwell, May 29, 1831. Published by Sherwood, Gilbert, and Piper: 1838.

these readings, researches, and prayers which have ended in *demonstrating the fallacy of my former views*—of those 'teachings' which I accepted in childhood, nurtured in youth, and kept unquestioned in manhood until the moment Mr. Melville's statements aroused my attention and demonstrated the fallacy of my former views, revealing to me the eternal truth as spoken by Moses— ' Hear, O Israel : The Lord our God is *one Lord*' ; and as reiterated, and confirmed by Jesus in one of the latest and most tender and impassioned of His prayers—' And this is life eternal, that they might know THEE, THE ONLY TRUE GOD, AND Jesus Christ, *whom* THOU *hast sent*' (John xvii. 3). Until that memorable day, I had passively received the '*incomprehensible*' statement which declares 'the Father incomprehensible, the Son incomprehensible, and the Holy Ghost incomprehensible : the Father uncreate, the Son uncreate, the Holy Ghost uncreate : the Father eternal, the Son eternal ; the Father is God, the Son is God, and the Holy Ghost is God, and yet there are not three incomprehensibles, nor three uncreated, nor three eternals, nor three Gods, but one incomprehensible, one uncreated, one eternal and one God.' This extraordinary paradox of words had been accepted by me with the same simplicity as a good 'Catholic' accepts the '*fact*' of the flight of the Virgin's house from Nazareth into Dalmatia, from thence to Recanati, and thirdly to Loreto, and all the miracles achieved therein. I had never read a word of controversy on the subject, had never heard a 'Unitarian' preacher. My faith was as serene and orthodox as gross ignorance could make it. I entered Camberwell 'Chapel of Ease' in the same frame of mind as hundreds of my neighbours enter their parish church every Sunday. I repeated the 'Athanasian' Creed with the same intelligent and orthodox appreciation as the children in our parish church repeated the 'Nicene' on the Sunday following their 'confirmation' this summer. But, alas for my 'orthodoxy!' the fervid and eloquent sermon of Henry Melville, B.D., roused the startling thought, If this dogma be '*fundamental*,' if upon it rest such tremendous consequences, that if 'without the doctrine of the Trinity there *is* no resting-place for guilty sinners,' how comes it that it is so seldom referred to in Holy Writ? how comes it that in this Book, which we have been taught to regard as a Revelation of God, from God Himself, the word Trinity is not to be found, or the doctrine anywhere distinctly and lucidly declared? Surely, thought I, I have overlooked large portions of its sacred pages. What could I do if asked to-morrow by anyone for Scripture proof of this solemn, this '*fundamental*' doctrine which alone secures a 'resting-place for guilty sinners'? St. Peter has commanded us to be ready to give an answer to 'everyone that asketh you a *reason of the hope that is in you*' (iii. 15); yet I could not supply even a solitary 'text.' But I felt there *must be many texts*, clear, bold, explicit, but hitherto overlooked. Some power bore in upon my soul the words

ἐρευνᾶτε τὰς γραφάς,

'Search the Scriptures.' Days, and months, and years, I 'searched' prayerfully, searched solitarily, independently searched, with a *strong bias to sustain the idea* associated with all my early antecedents, yet with a stronger bias to accept simply what the Scriptures might teach thereon, be it what it may. The more I read the more was I astonished to find so little that sustained a doctrine of such overwhelming importance—a doctrine which both my pastor and the Church regarded as 'fundamental'; and again and again had I trembled lest my early bias should fade away for want of Scriptural support, lest I should lose that 'faith' 'which except every one do keep whole and undefiled, WITHOUT DOUBT he shall PERISH everlastingly!' No one around me seemed to have enough interest in the subject to discuss it at all. As you have now told me, only a very small sect (and of these I knew nothing) dissented from the doctrine. Noisy polemics, radical Ranters, Baptists, Independents, 'Methodists'— all acquiesced in the decree of the Church on this especial matter. And certainly if any *external authority* ought to decide in matters of faith, here was a case in point, 'per urbem et orbem'; here, if anywhere, was '*Catholicity*'; here Pius IX. and Mrs. Girling the Shakeress, Dr. Pusey and the youngest recruit of the 'Salvation Army,' Dr. Ryle (the Bishop of Liverpool) and the Rev. A. Heriot Mackonochie, Canon Liddon and the Rev. C. Spurgeon were in perfect accord, and it seemed for a *long, long time presumptuous* in me to pause, to hesitate, to doubt, where so many wise and good men were confident and believing, where even the 'Pharisees and Sadducees' were in accord, and the Jews (metaphorically) could have dealings with the Samaritans. Yes, my struggle was long and arduous; but 'light came at eventide' and as Luther at Erfurt, after long prayers and meditations, was suddenly illumined and directed by the words the 'just shall live by faith,' even so has it been mine to know that if we 'ask we shall receive,' that if 'we seek we shall find.' Long did the blessed words sustain me: 'If any man of you lack wisdom, let him ask of God, that giveth to all liberally, and upbraideth not; and it shall be given him' (James i. 5); long was I upheld by the assurance from Jesus that a great 'Comforter' would come 'from the Father, even the Spirit of Truth, who shall *teach you all things*'; ardently did I pray God 'to send out His light and His truth' to lead me; and as to Luther there came like a voice from Heaven the words, 'The just shall live by faith,' even so came to me the words of Jesus to the young man seeking the way to eternal life, 'Why callest thou *me* good? there is *none good but God*,' and also His words to the adoring Mary after His Resurrection, 'Go to my *brethren* and say unto them, I ascend unto *my Father*, and to *your Father*; and to *my God*, and *your God*' (John xx. 17). *Thenceforth* all was calm, clear, and bright. Mists, doubts and perplexities vanished. The 'Great Comforter' *had come* down upon my soul. The Spirit of Truth *had spoken*. The voice alike of Councils and mobs was silenced; they became to me as were the 'familiar spirits, and wizards that peep, and mutter' to Isaiah (viii. 19, 20); and if thousands, nay tens of thousands, clamoured out their dogmas my spirit would remain calm, because, with that great prophet, it could say, 'To the law and to the testimony: if they speak not according to this word, *it is because* there is no light in them.'

Vicar. I have listened with great patience to your long dissertation. I have done so because, however erroneous your conclusions, I plainly see that they have not been hastily and lightly arrived at, and, moreover, they have cost you some thought and research; and when you add that you have earnestly and continuously sought guidance from on High *through prayers in private*, my respect was enhanced; although it would have been better if, at first, when your conscience was unquiet on this subject, and you needed comfort or counsel, you had come to me, 'or to some other discreet and learned minister of God's Word, and opened your grief,' so that by 'ghostly counsel and advice' your 'scruples and doubtfulness' might have been dispersed. I trust, however, that even now you may be delivered from all false doctrine, heresy, and schism, because you have admitted that the great body of Christians and the most ancient of Churches, or rather, I ought to say the 'one Catholick and Apostolick Church,' from the earliest ages has decreed the Trinitarian doctrine to be the 'true faith,' 'which faith except everyone do keep whole and undefiled, without doubt he shall perish everlastingly.' You have said that if ever there was 'Catholicity' it is found on this point, and if '*authority*' could determine a question, *here* was the *unanimous* authority, not only of the Church, but of the numberless schismatics who had separated themselves from her pale; and this being so, I hope you will perceive that you must *necessarily be wrong*. It is *absolutely* imperative that individuals should be guided by authority; it is schism and a sinful thing to neglect to hear and obey the Church; and therefore, my dear friend, you are in the sad position of those of whom St. Paul spoke in writing to his beloved saints in Rome—'I beseech you, brethren, mark them which cause *divisions* and offences *contrary to the doctrine* which ye have learned, and *avoid* them (Rom. xvi. 17); and our Divine Lord himself has declared of such, 'If he neglect to hear the church, let him be unto thee as a heathen and a publican' (Matt. xviii. 17). It pains me deeply to have thus to speak, but I trust that you will be able to see that it is a wicked thing to be at variance with the Church; that it *is* not only unbecoming, but arrogant, in an individual to place himself in a matter of doctrine in opposition to an overwhelming majority. For I need not remind you that in all the momentous questions which spring up, even in matters of life and death, such as trials by jury, decisions of Parliament, and the like, the vote of the majority is final. It is so likewise in spiritual things. The Church at Jerusalem in the early days of Christianity was the final appeal, and St. Paul and St. Jude alike denounced those who despised dominion and who separate themselves. But I am unwilling to think that you have reached so sad a stage. I shudder to think that one whom I so much esteem should become 'a wandering star to whom is reserved the blackness of darkness for ever,' and as you still revere the Scriptures, and say 'to the law and the testimony,' I hope and pray that you may discard the pride of reason, and be led 'to hear the Word, and to receive it with pure affection,' and that it may please God, although you have erred and deceived, to bring you back into the way of truth. And since, my dear friend, you still appeal 'to the law and the testimony,' let me *again* remind you of the words of St. John— 'There are three that bear record in heaven: the Father, the Son, and the Holy Ghost: and *these three are one.*'

Parishioner. I thank you for your tender sympathy,

and I assure you that you do me no more than justice when you say that I have not adopted the opinions I have formed lightly or without much hesitation, and without appealing by prayer to the Great Source of all illumination. I have, indeed, prayed long and continuously. I have pondered most profoundly on the fact that my conclusions *are at variance* with the decrees of Councils, with the writings of the venerable Fathers, who in a dark age were the chief sources of light and truth to the people around them. I have felt, yea, keenly felt, who and what am I that I should presume to differ from the wise and holy men of the olden and the present time? Long, long, have I kept silent under the fear that it was possible that I might be among those who cause 'divisions and offences'; for many weary and anxious months I said, 'I will take heed to my ways, that I sin not with my tongue: I will keep my mouth with a bridle . . . I was dumb with silence, I held my peace.' But there came a time when, like unto David, 'My heart was hot within me, while I *was musing* the fire burned; *then* spake I with my tongue' (Ps. xxxix). Yes. 'Blessed be *God*, even the *Father* of our Lord Jesus Christ, the Father of mercies, and the *God of all comfort*' (2 Cor. i. 3); a moment came to me, yea, even to me, as it did to St. Paul, when 'I conferred not with flesh and blood, neither went I to them which were apostles before me' (Gal. 1). My prayers had been heard. Although 'I lacked wisdom, yet in this matter it was ultimately given.' Most assuredly 'the eyes of the blind were opened.' The path of truth was revealed; was made so plain and so smooth that 'the feeble knees' and 'the fearful heart' could march forward, 'and the wayfaring man, though a fool, could not err therein.' The subject became clear and visible as did the outer world to the blind man whose eyes the beneficent Jesus had anointed with clay and then bade him wash in the pool of Siloam. Like him, I could say : ' One thing I know, that, whereas I was blind, now I see ' (John ix. 25), and to feel with Paul, ' Necessity is laid upon me, yea, woe is unto me, if I preach not the Gospel.' 'Woe unto me' if I do not proclaim with all my feeble powers the sweet, the precious truth that GOD '*will have all men to be saved, and to come unto the* KNOWLEDGE OF THE TRUTH.' For there is ONE God, and one Mediator between GOD and men, the MAN Christ Jesus ; Who gave Himself a ransom *for all*, to be testified in *due* time ' (St. Paul to Timothy ii. 3, 4, 5, 6). That, dear sir, is a statement plain and clear as the sunlight, derived from no uncertain source of oral tradition, coming to us from no doubtful epistle or late gospel imbued with, if not interpolated by, the philosophy of the Schools of Alexandria ; coming from a source more trustworthy even than the ' logia ' or sayings of the synoptic gospels, for no historian has questioned the genuineness of the Pauline Epistles ; they are the most certain, as they are the earliest, writings which have come down to us from the Apostolic Age, and therefore I abandon for ever, as erroneous and heretical, the statement that ' The *God*head of the Father, of the Son, and of the Holy Ghost, is all *one*; the glory equal, the majesty co-eternal,' and *accept* the statement of Jesus (in one of His tender prophetic addresses to His disciples) : ' Let not your heart be troubled, neither let it be afraid. . . . If ye loved me ye would rejoice, because I said, I go unto the Father, for my Father is greater than I' (John xiv. 28).

Vicar. You are becoming somewhat too warm—too impassioned in your arguments—and are forgetting, in the confidence you place in the last text quoted, that there are other texts which seem to clash with it, and have altogether overlooked the very decisive words of John, which I have recited to you as sustaining the ancient and catholic view. Moreover, your Church—if you will allow me to call her so—in her 20th article distinctly states that it is not lawful for the Church (still less for private individuals) 'so to expound one piece of Scripture that it be repugnant to another.'

Parishioner. The words of St. Paul to Timothy belong to that higher 'law and the testimony' to which I steadfastly appeal, and from which I cannot—dare not—depart until a text as clear, as explicit, and as unquestionably authentic can be found to sustain the Athanasian Creed. Nay, it should be more clear and more authentic—if that were possible—for the first enumerates a fact, which is not opposed to all the instincts of common sense and to the conclusions of right reasoning ; while the other can be accepted only by the prostration of reason before a blind faith—faith which finds its best, as it has been its most eulogised, commentary in the devotee who cried, 'Credo quia impossibile est' (I believe because it is impossible).

Vicar. This is hardly respectful to the Church, from which you have not formally and officially seceded ; and I am, therefore, compelled to remind you that the 34th Article of the Church of England decrees that

'Whosoever, through his private judgment' [and it is on this you are acting], 'willingly and purposely doth openly break the *traditions*' [*traditions*, mark] 'and ceremonies of the Church, which be not repugnant to the Word of God, and be ordained and approved by common authority, ought to be rebuked openly (that others may fear to do the like) as he that offendeth against the common order of the Church.' Now, that which you have been considering is most certainly 'ordained and approved by common authority'; and you, in common honesty, have been compelled to admit that as a 'tradition' it is of the most hoary antiquity; that it is all but universally accepted, practically, one might say (to use one of your quoted phrases) 'per urbem et orbem'; that it is one of the most catholic doctrines.' And yet, alas! sad it is that against all these ancient, august, and sacred authorities, you are rash enough, I might say wicked enough, willingly to bring your 'private judgment,' and 'purposely' and 'openly' break its traditions.

Parishioner. 'Openly,' as yet, I have not, and for reasons which I have already described to you; and there is one clause in the Article you cite, which you seem not to have noticed, which robs it of all its sting and its power as far as I am concerned, for I am not desirous of breaking *any* traditions 'which be *not* repugnant to the Word of God.' I *dispute the 'tradition' solely and exclusively because it is* 'repugnant to the Word of God.' You admit St. Paul to be an inspired apostle, and you regard his writings as a most important portion of 'the Word of God'; and his words to the young minister whom he loved, whom he especially wished to train for his successor—'unto Timothy, my own son in the faith'—were those that I have given unto you as the foundation of my faith on this particular matter. He told his young and able disciple not to 'give heed to *fables* and endless genealogies'; he pointed out to him some who, 'desiring to be teachers of the law,' 'have turned aside to *vain jangling, understanding neither what they say nor whereof they affirm.*' (How, very like the teachers who debate and 'jangle' to the effect that 'there are not three incomprehensibles, nor three uncreated, but one uncreated and one incomprehensible!) To this 'dearly beloved son' he appealed, imploring him to 'hold fast the form of sound words' which he had heard from him, to avoid 'profane and vain babblings and oppositions of science falsely so called, and to commit that which he had heard from him 'to faithful men who shall be able to teach others also.' In his dying moments, so to speak, when he was 'ready to be offered, and the time for his departure was at hand,' Paul, in the most impassioned manner, and dreading that the time would come when men 'would turn away their ears from *the truth*, and shall be turned unto *fables*,' besought Timothy to 'preach the word,' and, inasmuch as he 'had fully known his doctrine,' 'to continue thou in the things which *thou hast learned* and *hast been assured of*, knowing of whom thou hast learned them'; and this 'doctrine' and this 'truth'—the cardinal spring, 'the *fundamental doctrine*'—was not the 'jangle' of, 'there is one Father, not three Fathers; one Son, not three Sons; one Holy Ghost, not three Holy Ghosts: in this Trinity none is afore or after other; none is greater or less than another; but the whole Three Persons are co-eternal together and co-equal. So that in all things, as is aforesaid, the Unity in Trinity and the Trinity in Unity is to be worshipped. He therefore that *will be saved: must thus* THINK *of the Trinity.*' No, Paul did not thus address his dearly beloved son in the faith, to whom he bequeathed his noble mission of carrying forward 'the faith once delivered to the saints'; he did not hand down to him the crude metaphysics of the Alexandrian School of Philosophy, 'the *babblings* of *science falsely* so called'; but he bequeathed to him these clear and noble words: 'There is *one God* and one *Mediator* between God and men, *the Man* Christ Jesus; who gave himself a *ransom for all*, to be testified in due time (1 Timothy ii. 5, 6). This statement is so *definite*, so unmistakable, is written *so* 'plain upon tables, that he may run that readeth them' (Habakkuk ii. 5), and the revelation is complete. Henceforward, as I have already said, *crowds, creeds, councils*, and *Churches*, by *whatever name they are called*, have no 'authority' with me upon this topic. They are, as was the decree of Nebuchadnezzar to Shadrach, Meshach, and Abednego—'the law and the testimony' outweigh the clamour of crowds. If priests or prelates proclaim dogmas which are not in accord therewith, I am compelled to say unto them as Peter and John said to 'Annas the High Priest, and Caiaphas, and John, and Alexander,' and other dignitaries, 'kindred of the High Priest,' who 'were gathered together at Jerusalem:—' Whether it be right in the *sight of God* to hearken *unto you* more than unto *God*, judge ye (Acts iv. 19). No, my dear Vicar, from the above statement of Paul there can be no appeal, for it is in harmony with all the teachings of Holy Writ. 'Hear

O Israel, the Lord thy God is *one* Lord' (Deut. vi. 4), was the old emphatic proclamation of the *Old* Dispensation, and 'There is *one* God and *one* mediator between God and men—the Man Christ Jesus' (1 Timothy ii. 5, 6), is the equally positive declaration of the *New* Testament. The words in each case are simple, clear, and definite. No language could by possibility be plainer. No person hearing them *in adult life* for the *first time could* mistake their meaning. It is astounding to the unsophisticated understanding how such a confused and mystic idea as the one embodied in the Athanasian Creed could have been concocted out of the book called the Bible. In truth, it never was derived from that source. It sprang out of the subtle disquisitions of so-called Greek philosophers. One of the 'inspired' writers of the Bible has told us, ' Lo, this only have I found, that God hath made men upright ; but they have sought out many inventions' (Eccles. vii. 29) ; and of all the ' inventions ' and the staggering statements which the subtlety and the sophistry of speculative minds have spun from their 'inner consciousness,' none can possibly exceed in absurdity that paradox of words 'the *Son* is *co-eternal* with the *Father.*' How amazed would the learned Arabian Mohammedans of the seventh century (these philosophers who, even at that early date, had catalogued all the stars in their visible heaven, had determined the true length of the year, and other scientific matters) have been to have heard 'a Christian,' or as they would have called him, ' the infidel,' utter such a statement ! How confirmed would they have been in their superiority, and the superiority of their creed over a race which chose to talk in such a paradoxical manner and elevate into 'a creed,' a 'shibboleth,' a statement which overturned the meaning of words and *subverted the order of nature and of things!* Can it be surprising that the Jews, who reverence their ancient Scriptures, who honour the wisdom of Moses and of Solomon, the piety of David, and the sublime utterances of Isaiah and Ezekiel, should for well-nigh two thousand years turn with disdain from a religion couched in such phrases as these? Is it to be wondered at that the gentle Hindoos and the thoughtful Buddhists in their myriad numbers remain 'unconverted' as a people, despite the hundreds of thousands of pounds and the many noble lives which Christian England and other nations have poured forth for their 'conversion'? Is it a marvel that in the nineteenth century of the 'Christian Era' scepticism swarms in our cities and saturates our literature and our science; that wise and good and illustrious men like Sir Isaac Newton, the discoverer of the law of gravitation, the pious poet John Milton, and the moral and learned philosopher John Locke should consent to be branded as 'heterodox' and 'unsound' rather than accept the idea that *before all things* it was necessary *thus to think* of their Creator, or *without doubt* to '*perish everlastingly*'? The marvel of marvels is, that for this *fundamental doctrine* there is not *one* clear unequivocal verse to be found in the entire range of Scripture! The most painstaking reader will search the pages of the Bible in vain to find even the *word* which has been ingeniously fabricated to express the mystic and 'uncomprehensible' idea. *Not* to express your belief in the 'Trinity,' or rather to *disavow a belief in it*, will cause you to be branded by all the Christian

Churches of the realm as a 'heretic' and a kind of social Pariah ; *and yet from the first chapter of Genesis to the twenty-second and last chapter of Revelation this all-important word which embodies a 'fundamental doctrine' is nowhere to be found!*

Vicar. It is evasive and somewhat 'jesuitical,' as it is often called, that you should lay such emphasis on the absence of the *Latin* word 'Trinity,' which simply means 'three in one,' when you are aware that the same thing is distinctly stated in *English* ; and that in the very early part of our interview I drew your attention to it, and have since repeated it, and had hoped, from the reverence you express for the Scriptures, that it would have reconciled you to the doctrine as being, in the words of the eighth Article of our Church, 'proved by most certain warrants of Holy Scripture.' As you have so long ignored it, and have brought forward other texts with so much confidence, altogether forgetful of the great law of Exegesis, and of the 'twentieth Article of Religion'—not 'so to expound one place of Scripture that it be repugnant to another'—I must remind you for the *third* time that St. John, in the fifth chapter of his first Epistle, distinctly states 'there are three that bear record in Heaven, the Father, the Word, and the Holy Ghost : and these are one.' This verse refutes your very strong statements as to the entire absence of all Scriptural authority for the doctrine, and also your last assertion that the word 'Trinity' (for the words 'these three are one' are more than an equivalent for it) is not to be found from the first chapter of Genesis to the very last chapter of the Book of Revelation.

Parishioner. I had by no means forgotten the quotation in question. When my mind was first directed to this question, under the circumstances I have detailed to you, this Epistle of John came as a great solace to my mind, and for many months sustained my primitive faith. I had heard the especial verse read year after year on the first Sunday after Easter; read, too, from the very altar, as the most sacred spot in the Church, and immediately following the collect in the communion service. It was read also in due course on the 29th of April in the service at Evening Prayer. The words are certainly most clear, most distinct, and they demonstrate the truth of the doctrine of the Trinity, so far as an inspired Scripture stating a fact must be accepted as a demonstration by all (and most certainly I *was then one of those*) who regard it as *the Word of God.* The enunciation ' and these three are one ' leaves nothing to be desired as to explicitness. I bowed with reverence where I could not fully understand. I felt that great was 'the mystery,' but I no more questioned than Abraham questioned when he climbed the mountain of Moriah on his painful errand. God had spoken, and there was no sacrifice, whether the offspring of Reason or the offspring of the body, that could be withheld by one who had a due sense of his creatorship, his omnipotence, and his goodness. It was an unfathomable mystery, but so is the origin of God. Believing the words *to be* the words of God, through the immediate inspiration of his apostle John, my 'doubts' were annihilated, and I listened to the 'damnatory clauses' uttered by the priest on those who did not believe in the 'Catholic Faith' with the same kind of emotion I felt when reading of the curses of Ebal on those who 'setteth light by his father or his mother, who removeth his neighbour's landmark, or maketh the blind to wander out of his way.' For, at that time I had not perceived the tremendous distinction between the two cases—one (Ebal) dealing with overt *acts*, with demonstrable *deeds*; while the other deals exclusively with the subtle and intangible speculations of the mind. One 'curses' wicked *acts*; the other 'curses' *ideas*. Each, however, *appeared to be* the declaration of the Almighty One, and to HIS command the response could only be as it was at Ebal—'Amen!' Imagine, then, my dear sir, if you possibly can, the awful revulsion of my feelings when the time came, as *come it did*, when the words you have recited to me turned out to be the *interpolations*, the forged utterances of some enthusiastic copyist of MSS. in the fourth century, who, seemingly, not finding any verses sufficiently distinct and clear to uphold the hypothesis of the 'Trinity,' deliberately invented and added the one you have quoted to me; but, whatever may have been its origin, it was wholly *unknown* to the followers of Jesus until some hundreds of years after the 'inspired' apostle had 'slept with his fathers!' Such a discovery overwhelmed at once all my reverence for the doctrine. It was the only spot of ground on which I could rest my faith; the one sole atom of Scripture which seemed to demand that reason should be prostrated to the requirements of 'faith'; the only verse which lifted the mystery from the dogmas of priestcraft into the requirements of the Gospel; and, lo and behold, it was worse than a broken reed on which I was leaning! It was no more the word of God than were the words 'Zedekiah, the son of Chenaanah,' when he made him horns of iron, and, standing before Ahab and Jehoshaphat in their royal robes, sitting on their respective thrones as the Kings of Israel and Judah, he said unto the King Ahab, ' *Thus saith the Lord*, With these shalt thou push the Syrians until thou have consumed them ' (1 Kings xxii. 11). In that case, it is sad to know that the lying statement was repeated by *all the prophets* of Israel, and that honest Micah, who protested against the statement, was smitten on the mouth by the false Zedekiah, without a word of remonstrance raised either by kings or prophets; and yet it is *sadder still* to feel that for centuries in the Christian era words equally false, *and alike imputed to the Most High*, have been repeated and enforced by *Christian* priests; nor have many (if any) hesitated to smite on the mouth (nay, some have not hesitated to burn slowly to death at the stake, as Calvin did Servetus at Geneva) those who have gainsaid their statements. It is a most damaging fact against the Church in England that her priests and her prelates have *known* for years that verse to be a spurious introduction into the chapter; and yet to sustain a theory to uphold a Church dogma, they have read it to the people, even to this very Easter, as ' the Word of God '! From the lowliest curate through all the ranks of the priesthood up to the loftiest archbishop, not one in the United Kingdom has had the simple honesty and fealty to the truth to pause in their public reading of the chapter, and to say of this verse,' Here is something false and wrong; this verse does not occur in any of the earliest manuscripts;' no, not one. If anything were wanting to prove its spuriousness it would be found in the fact that it was never once quoted by the partisans of ' orthodoxy ' in the great Arian Controversy, A.D. 325. To me, this reticence—no, not reticence, but wilful acquiescence in a fraud—this public use of a falsehood (for 'Church' purposes) in the very 'House of God,' and in an act of adoration and worship, is revolting, and would of itself repel me from a creed in defence of which such nefarious practices were resorted to.

Vicar. I do not think that I am acting rightly in listening to such strong condemnation of the bishops and pastors of the Church, with whatever leniency I may be disposed to treat the censure which has been indirectly passed upon myself. I wish, however, to state that the grammatical construction of verses 7 and 8 in the chapter to which you refer would seem to *need* the presence of the disputed passage; for what can the article τὸ ἕν at the conclusion of verse 8 have reference to if not to the former 'ἕν' in the preceding verse? Moreover, the learned Erasmus prints the clause in the third edition of the Greek Testament, 1522; and our own learned Bishop Burgess, as also Horsley, and Bull, and Stillingfleet, and Pearson, are unwilling that the passage should be considered spurious. In a bishop or a priest to have done as you suggest, and to have proclaimed the passage *untrue*, would *have been to shake the* confidence of the common people altogether *in the whole* Bible; or probably have caused them to execrate the bishop in question for himself daring to doubt the truth of anything within the pages of that book, which from their childhood they had been taught to reverence, and which many, if not most of them, considered to be sacred, yea, as sacred as the consecrated elements of the Blessed Sacrament.

Parishioner. My dear Vicar, you astound me! Practically considered, what is this conduct but the embodiment of the great sin which Protestants allege continually against the Church of Rome? What is it but carrying out to the full the daring maxim of the fourth century—'that it is an act of virtue to deceive and lie when it could promote the interest of the Church'? It is the upholding of the very spirit of forgery. You have often spoken with indignation of the shameful 'Decretals of Isidore'—documents said to be written by the early pontiffs, containing grants to the Holy See from Constantine, upholding the supremacy of the Pope, and the like—which were proved by the clearest evidence to have been forged. In what does it differ from the degrading tricks of the olden time, such as the showing of a coloured fluid for many, many years at Hales in this county of Gloucester as the very Blood of Christ brought from Jerusalem? except, indeed, that it was worse inasmuch as the 'Decretals' were only alleged to be the productions of *men*, whereas the blood *was* something *visible* to the senses which *could* have been tested and determined by experiments, but here, here, 'horresco referens,' was the daring impiety of giving the words of *men* as the utterances of the *Almighty and Eternal God*; and you, sir, indirectly justify it as being useful in sustaining the faith of the people in a dogma and in a book! Oh, this is pitiful—most pitiful!

Vicar. I did not admit that this important verse was forged; on the contrary, I gave grammatical reasons to show that it might not have been, and then pointed out the mischief which might arise from the utterances of a contrary opinion. Moreover, I told you that the passage is to be found in an edition of the Greek Testament issued by the learned Erasmus in 1522, and also that good and learned divines like unto Bishop Burgess, and Horsley and Bull, and Stillingfleet supported its authenticity.

Parishioner. Pardon me when I say that it amazes me to observe how education, a special profession and training, and party zeal can blind even a man of good intentions and a pure purpose. It saddens me to find what very shallow arguments will satisfy a mind full of preconceived notions and anxious to uphold a system to which it is attached. On any other subject apart from your priestly office and its relations, you, my dear Vicar, would smile at the simplicity of the person who quoted as an authority for a disputed statement that the statement was contained in a book published, as was Erasmus' Greek Testament, one thousand years or more after the alleged forgery had taken place! Moreover, Erasmus himself prevaricated much and varied his words from time to time. As to your other remarks, in a matter of Greek scholarship can Bishop Burgess be compared for a moment with Porson, who maintained the spuriousness of the verse in question? The other names given by you appear very weak on such a subject, when the learned Michaelis and the great investigators of Greek MSS. Griesbach, Scholz, Lachmann, Tischendorff, Tregelles, Alford, and Jowett have shown that it is spurious, and opposed to the authority of all authentic Greek MSS., of all ancient MSS., of the Latin Vulgate, and of the Greek, Latin, and Oriental Fathers. But what is perhaps of more weight to the ordinary English mind is the fact that an assembly of the most learned Greek scholars and devout divines of the *nineteenth* century have unanimously agreed that it *is* spurious and ought no longer to appear in the pages of our Bibles.

Vicar. I did not at all expect that our interview would end in this manner, nor was I in the slightest degree prepared to enter into so elaborate a discussion as you have opened up. Moreover, you have used expressions which I hope, upon reflection, you will feel to be unjust towards myself personally, for I should scorn to use a forged document for the purpose of argument if I had known it to be so. After your statement to the effect that it *is* excluded from the Revised New Testament by such ripe scholars and pious men as Bishop Ellicott and Bishop Lightfoot—or, as I ought rather to say, by the Bishops of Gloucester and Durham—and others possessing profound Greek learning, I must admit it henceforth *to be spurious*, and consequently not of the transcendent value in support of the Athanasian Creed as I had supposed. However, the doctrine does not rest exclusively on the passage in question; although I know of no other that directly refers to and declares it in the lucid, positive, and explicit manner as does St. John in that Epistle.

Parishioner. I should be sorry indeed to hurt your feelings, for I have great esteem, nay, affection, for you, and will at once withdraw the implication of folly in reference to your quotation of Erasmus as an authority on this subject, and will consider it an inadvertence, drawn forth by the exigencies of your position at the moment. You have certainly been unfortunate in your Scriptural quotation in defence of the Trinitarian Creed, nor less so for the one given to justify the *damnatory* clauses of the Athanasian Creed, for I am sure that I have only to mention it and you will remember that the passage you quoted from Mark xvi. 16, to the effect 'he that believeth not shall be damned,' is *also an interpolation*, and was *not* written by St. Mark. It was appended as early as the time of Irenæus, but was still absent from the majority of codices so late as Jerome's day.

Vicar. I have been conversing far too long, and urgent duties call me away. I was reading that chapter in Valpy's Greek Testament this morning, and he gives the passage in full, and makes no reference in his copious notes to any doubt of the kind you refer to. Moreover, it is certain, as you say, that Irenæus, who was acquainted with Polycarp, and is thus, through Polycarp's knowledge of St. John, linked with apostolic times, quotes from this portion of Mark without hesitation ; and I am not, therefore, willing at this moment to admit that the verses are an unauthorised addition to the writings of the Evangelist.

Parishioner. I myself appealed to Valpy on this point, but obtained no information ; and also to Wilkinson and Webster in their more recent edition of the Greek Testament, with no satisfactory result ; but Griesbach, Tregelles, Tischendorff, and even Alford, declare that the verses from the 9th are *not* written *by Mark* ; and I think that this would be conclusive to any mind, unbiassed by antecedents and thoroughly *judicial* in its nature, who would carefully read the verses from the 9th to the 20th in that chapter, and compare them with the preceding verses ; for he would find in those twelve verses at least *sixteen* words which are *not* to be found in the other parts of this Gospel.

Vicar. I am not prepared at the present moment to say that you are wrong as to the introduction of the said new words; but, even admitting that the concluding verses were *not* written by St. Mark, it does not destroy their *authenticity.* And as you refer to Dean Alford, he, I am sure, regards the verses as an *authentic* fragment, placed as a completion of the Gospel in very early times, and that it has strong claims on our reception and reverence. Moreover, everyone receives the Epistle to the Hebrews as *authentic* and part of the inspired Word; although all Biblical scholars agree in stating that it was *not* written by St. Paul.

Parishioner. Most true, does Alford write so; but he also states that the verses are absent from the majority of codices as late as Jerome's day, and that the internal evidence is against the authorship of Mark, and that the real author is unknown; and I hold that when the author of a statement is *not* known, and when the date or first appearance of the statement is also *uncertain*, or *unknown*, although it may be accepted *provisionally* as to *unimportant* matters, yet, when 'INSPIRATION' is claimed for it, and it contains solemn, nay, awful statements, involving the damnation of souls, and is quoted in *defence* of the damnatory clauses in *other* works and treatises, *then* I could not accept it as an *authority*, or admit that on *such* a *point* 'it has strong claims on our reception and reverence.' In fact, strict justice demands that it should *not* be accepted as *evidence.* It would *not* be accepted as evidence in any of our courts of law. If a witness should say of any statement, 'I do not know *by whom* it was said, or *when* it was said,' he would be requested to withdraw, and the statement in question would be set aside, unless supported by some other direct, positive, and personal testimony. These facts compel me to repeat what I have already said : that it is a moral delinquency on the part of the bishops, priests and deacons of the 'Catholic Church' (and I say 'Catholic' to include all who read the 'Bible' in public places of worship) that they practically hand on a falsehood from generation to generation, and salve their consciences under the idea that it is better for the Church to do so *lest 'the people' should have their 'faiths' disturbed*. I hold that every man who in God's House reads the entire sixteenth chapter we have been discussing as 'the sixteenth chapter of the Gospel *according to St. Mark,' believing* at the same time that more than half of it was written by *someone else*, is guilty of a falsehood, has committed a wilful sin ; for St. Paul himself declares, whatsoever 'is not of faith is of sin.' As Jeremiah said of Judæa, so may it be said of England in our day—'A wonderful and horrible thing is committed in the land ; the prophets prophesy falsely, and the priests bear rule by their means, and my people love to have it so : and what will ye do in the end thereof?' (v. 30, 31). It is a painful thought, and a fact dishonourable to the clerical profession, that from the time of Edward VI.—to go no further back—the priests and prelates of the Church of England, and nearly all the Nonconformist ministers, have been preaching *as the words of St. John* that 'there are three that bear record in heaven, the Father, the Son, and the Holy Ghost : and these three are one' ; and further, have also been preaching *as the words of St. Mark*, 'He that believeth and *is baptized* shall *be saved*, but he that believeth not shall be damned'; *knowing all the time that neither St. John nor St. Mark wrote or spoke the words!* This have they done, deeming it politic or 'expedient' to give the sentences as they had received them, *because* there were no other words in the Bible which gave such immediate, direct, and lucid support to the doctrine of the Trinity in the one case, and to the teachings of the Church in respect to baptism in the other! This broad historic fact is in itself damnatory of the theory, and justifies scepticism on other seeming corroborative testimony given by the clergy as the testimony of Holy Writ.

Vicar. Neither the one nor the other doctrine is dependent on the texts quoted. They rest on the authority of the Church, on the decrees of Councils, on the universal acceptance of the great majority of Christians, and on the words of our blessed Lord, his Evangelists, and his Apostles. Moreover, as you have yourself admitted, we have the majority of professing Christians of nearly all sects with us, besides the ancient Fathers, and therefore THE DOCTRINES MUST BE TRUE. But, I cannot parley longer: important duties call me. Moreover, the sun is going down, and a storm is springing up in the east.

Parishioner. Farewell, and many thanks for your time and attention. Yet, my dear Vicar, kindly remember that I did not open the discussion, but have been all along on the defensive, and giving my *humble reasons why* I have hitherto been unable to accept your pastoral invitation to be present at the Holy Communion.

Vicar. That is indeed a vital matter; a matter so solemn, so deeply affecting your eternal welfare, that I must see you again, and that soon, upon the subject. In the meantime I commend to your prayerful consideration the solemn facts I have placed before you. Remember *you stand alone!* The great Churches of Christendom condemn you, and, let me remind you again, that tens of thousands of men who are *schismatics* and Dissenters on *other points* of Church doctrine and discipline are in accord with the National Church on this vital point of the Athanasian Creed, and have no sympathy with your opinion.

Parishioner. I have very long and very painfully felt this, but, as I have said, *it has now* ceased to affect me. The minority is often right: Jesus had not many to sustain and carry forward his doctrines when in the Garden of Gethsemane, 'All his disciples forsook him and fled.' The Christians were not in the 'majority' when they returned from Olivet, and sought an 'upper chamber' for council and prayer. Paul, as he stood before the crowd of Greeks, philosophers, and others on Mars Hill, would not have obtained a show of hands in his favour. Necessarily, in the history of truth, there is a period when its supporters are in a minority. Therefore *mere numbers do not influence me.* Christianity itself is in a minority yet among the religions of the world. The 'Bible' has not displaced the 'Koran,' the 'Vedas' of the East, or the writings of Confucius. *Facts,* and the conclusions derived from them by the reason honestly and logically applied, are of greater weight with me than the opinion of the multitude. 'Vox populi' is *not* 'Vox Dei.' Barabbas was preferred to Jesus. Ecclesiastic authority has almost invariably condemned that which was true and just. Witness the Protestant

Reformation, witness the condemnation of Galileo, the abolition of slavery, and the improvements in our 'Criminal Code.' Please accept my little flower; it is very rare in this neighbourhood. I shall look forward anxiously for your promised visit. Good-bye.

INTERVIEW THE SECOND.

Vicar. (The Rev. Hugh Hierous.) I am very glad indeed to see you, for although only a week has elapsed, yet have you been constantly in my thoughts and in my prayers. Moreover, I have felt the solemn responsibility which rests upon me, as your pastor, in respect to the views you hold; they are so heterodox, so contrary to Scripture and to the teachings of the Universal Church, that I must, to *free my own soul* from guilt, again recur to the topic of our late discussion, and implore you to abandon your dangerous errors. Believe me, dear sir, it is no matter of form that I am anxious about. It is a vital question, for on it hinges your eternal salvation. The words of St. John, or rather of Jesus, as reported by St. John, are absolute, and they are so lucidly given that there is no escape from their meaning. The Jews were, as you now are, doubtful and disputatious, saying, 'Can this Man give us his flesh to eat?' Jesus therefore said unto them, 'Verily, verily, *except* ye eat the flesh of the Son of man, and drink his blood, ye have not life in yourselves. He that eateth my flesh, and drinketh my blood, hath eternal life; and I will raise him up at the last day' (John vi. 54). This being so, I bid you in the name of God, I call you in Christ's behalf, I exhort you, as you love your own salvation, to come and be a partaker of the Holy Communion.

Parishioner. (Mr. Truman.) I am sorry to have caused you so much anxiety, and grateful indeed do I feel towards you for your friendly interest in my welfare. After this warm and solemn appeal to me you will be able to say, with a clear conscience, '*Liberavi animam meam.*' You have done your duty as a 'watchman,' you have 'blown the trumpet,' you 'have warned the people,' you can comfort yourself with the words recorded by Ezekiel, chapter xxxiii.: 'If thou warn the wicked of his way to turn from it, if he do not turn from his way, he shall die in his iniquity; but thou hast delivered thy soul.' I repeat that *all* the solemn responsibility rests upon my own head. If 'eternal life' *depends* exclusively upon partaking of this holy rite in the manner and method and with the preliminaries enjoined by the Church of England, I am in a most perilous position. As I have already told you, these things have weighed heavily upon my soul; it was with no light heart that I ceased from the practice of many years, from that 'communion' which once brought peace and consolation, and which recently I have been invited to share with one who was dearer to me than life itself. But a more imperious voice has spoken; and as Christ said, 'He that loveth father or mother, brother or sister, more than me is not worthy of me,' and remembering that whatsoever 'is not of *faith* is of *sin*'; and as St. Paul said, respecting a far inferior matter, namely, that of partaking of a special kind of food, under special circumstances, 'He that *doubteth is damned* if he eat, because he eateth not of faith,' it is not possible that I should partake of so solemn a feast as that to which you invite me.

Vicar. But *why* should you doubt?

Parishioner. Because, as I told you, I could not repeat the words, 'God of God, Light of Light, very God of very God, begotten not made, being of one substance with the Father,' and I *might* have added that I could not 'acknowledge one baptism for the remission of sins.'

Vicar. Your state of mind grieves me much. I had hoped that reflection upon the statements I made at our last interview had dispelled your doubts; that 'increase of grace' had been imparted to you; and that you were now prepared 'to hear meekly the Word, and to receive it with pure affection,' and that it would have been my joy to learn that my prayer had been in some measure answered; and that if not '*all* such as have erred and are deceived had been brought into the way of truth,' yet that *one* I esteemed *had* been brought into that happy condition.

Parishioner. I assure you, Mr. Hierous, that although my views of inspiration are wholly changed, and I am no longer a Bibliolater, yet am I still disposed 'to hear meekly the Word, and to receive it with pure affection'; for, as I said at our former interview, my convictions as to the nature and character of Christ have been derived wholly from the Bible; and at the time when my faith in the Trinity began to be unsettled I was as complete a believer in the verbal inspiration of the Scriptures as you are at this moment; but I have described this so fully that I need not, and hope not to enter upon this phase of the subject again. *It was the Bible, and the*

Bible alone, that shattered my early opinions, and even now I repeat, ' to the law and the testimony'; and if you can show me that the *balance* of scriptural evidence in favour of the Athanasian belief is such as to outweigh its logical and intellectual difficulties I shall at once succumb. Most gratefully then should I accept your invitation, and in your own 'communion service' partake of 'bread and wine' in remembrance of him 'who grew in favour both with God and man'; who spake as never man spake'; 'who went about doing good'; and who was 'obedient unto death, yea, the death of the cross.'

Vicar. I am gratified to hear you thus speak, and especially as, I must now admit, you have shown the untrustworthiness of the powerful passages that I placed before you at our former conversation from 1 John v. 7, and from the concluding portions of St. Mark's gospel. Happily, as I said before, this essential doctrine does not hinge on these strong texts, nor yet wholly on the authority of the Church and of the early fathers, but upon clear and indisputable statements of Holy Writ; in truth, upon the very words of Jesus himself, who said, 'I and my Father are one' (John x. 30).

Parishioner. Almost anything can be proved by individual texts isolated from their contexts; but your quotation, even if it stood distinct and separate from all circumstances whatever as an enunciation by Jesus of his relationship with the Father, would fail utterly in the purpose for which you have used it; for it would prove only ' two in one,' a duality and NOT a TRINITY. But as I remember the circumstances under which it was spoken I should only have to ask you to read *all the details* in order that it should prove to an *absolute demonstration* the position I have taken up, namely, the entire *distinctiveness* between Jesus and God. Here, if ever, a truthful man would have spoken the truth (and Jesus was of all men the *most* truthful). The irate, bigoted, and vindictive Jews, catching at this sentence, took up stones to stone him, although not a moment before he had announced the supremacy of God in the words, 'My Father which *gave them* me is *greater* than *all*;' and when *they* charged him with blasphemy because, as THEY SAID, 'thou being a man makest thyself God,' he showed them that *he had done nothing of the kind*—that he had not even called himself by so high a title as their forefathers and they themselves had called others. With that wisdom, that gentleness, that God-like forbearance which at all times characterised him, Jesus did not 'render railing for railing,' but instead, placed before them calm argument, the practice of their forefathers, and the words of their own law. Although they had furiously assailed him, and said 'he had a devil and was mad,' he gently replied, 'If he called them *gods*, unto whom the word of God came, and the scripture cannot be broken; say ye of him whom *the Father hath sanctified*, and *sent* into the world, Thou blasphemest; because I said' [not 'God the Son'—not even 'God'], 'I am the Son of God?' (John x. 36). Nowhere in this episode of Christ's history is there the slightest attempt to claim the Godhead; indeed the very opposite to this is everywhere *implied*. He claimed no *inherent* power on this occasion, he is everywhere the *recipient* of the Father's bounty, the *delegate* of his Father's will. 'My Father which *gave* them is *greater* than all';

'Many good works have I *shewed* you *from* my Father. For which of those works do ye stone me?'—*here is scathing irony*, but no arrogant claim. Again, 'Say ye of him, whom the Father *hath sanctified*' [the sanctity has been imparted and is not inherent], 'Thou blasphemest; because I said, I am the Son of God?' In your ancient histories even your Judges were termed 'gods' (Exodus xxii. 28) and your Psalmist, speaking in the name of God, said of those 'who should die like men': 'I have said *ye are gods and all of you are* CHILDREN *of the Most High*.' Seeing all this, Jesus practically said, Why charge me with blasphemy because I too said, 'I *am* the *Son* of God?'

Vicar. Still Jesus never recalled his utterance; he added 'I am the Son of God,' and—the words remain—'I and my Father are one.'

Parishioner. They remain because they embody a truth which no honest reader of the New Testament can gainsay. They were *one*, but in no Athanasian sense. They were 'one,' but in no mystic or mysterious manner. They were 'one,' even as in a later period of his history Jesus prayed that *all* his disciples may be *one*. In that tender prayer, when 'he knew that his hour was come,' Jesus revealed his whole nature to his disciples, and the words of the prayer throw a flood of light on the words which you have quoted and *settle for ever their meaning*. There is nothing more lucidly stated in the whole range of Holy Writ than is the nature of that unity, that *oneness*, to which you have referred. To me the exposition is complete—so complete that loyalty, fealty to Jesus would compel me to disregard all other statements, come from whom they may. Popes, Councils,

Doctors, Athanasius or Augustine, Church Articles, Prayer Books, and 'creeds' clamour in vain. *The Master has spoken*, and his words are 'a lamp unto my feet and a light unto my path' (Ps. cxix. 125). All so-called 'authorities' who speak at variance with these words are to me 'as sounding brass or a tinkling cymbal.' To repeat what I said at our former interview, Christ has spoken and all other voices are futile. I feel as Paul felt (without using the maledictory phrase) when, writing to the churches of Galatia, he said, ' Though we, or an angel from heaven, preach any other gospel unto you than that which we have preached unto you, let him be accursed. . . . For *I neither received it of man, neither was I taught it*, but by the revelation of Christ' (Galatians i. 8–12). Christ has been to me the expositor of the words you have quoted, and *therefore* all else becomes, as I have said, 'as sounding brass or a tinkling cymbal.'

Vicar. Some words have, indeed, impressed you strongly, but you have not given them; and really, at this moment, I cannot recall anything—that is, any words of Jesus—which so clearly define and explain the nature of the unity existing between himself and the Father, as could in any degree divest it of that mystery which appertains to the Nicene or Athanasian Creed. Indeed, as St. Paul said to Timothy, 'without controversy great is the *mystery* of godliness; God was manifest in the flesh, justified in the spirit, seen of angels, preached unto the Gentiles, believed on in the world, received up into glory.'

Parishioner. I said they explained the *meaning* of your text quoted. They unfold the nature of the unity which existed between him and the Father, and they do this so completely that not a single word needs to be added to or taken from them to enhance their lucidity. They occur in the impassioned prayer which towards the close of his ministry he offered up for his disciples, and they are these: '*Sanctify* them through thy truth: thy word is truth. As *thou hast sent me* into the world, even so have *I* also sent THEM into the world. Neither pray I for these alone but for them also which shall believe on me through their word; THAT THEY ALL MAY BE ONE; as *thou, Father, art in me*, and I in thee, *that they also may be one in us*; that the world may believe that thou *hast sent me*. And *the glory* which *thou gavest me* I *have given them*; THAT THEY MAY BE ONE, EVEN AS WE ARE ONE: I in them, and Thou in me, that *they* may be made *perfect in one*; and that the world may know that *thou hast sent me*, and hast *loved them*, AS thou hast loved me' (John xvii. 17–23). Such are the words, my dear Mr. Hierous. They require no ingenious explanations, no verbal sophistry, to elucidate their meaning; they stand out plain, clear, luminous, yea, as incisive and distinct as the command of the Decalogue, 'Thou shalt not kill.' These words are not plainer or more clear to the simple mind than are the words, 'that *they* may be *one, even as we are one*.' It is a moral unity, a spiritual affinity, to be understood by everyone, and having no relation to the 'substances,' 'the co-equalities,' and 'co-eternities' of a mystical creed. It is a 'unity' of thought, feeling, and purpose such as the disciples might possess in relation to each other as fully and as completely as Jesus with the Father—'THEY MAY BE ONE, EVEN AS WE ARE ONE.' Moreover, that nothing should be wanting in Christ's revelation to men as to his true relationship with the Father, and the dignity and power which respectively belonged to them, in this tender address to his disciples (which possesses all the pathos of a final farewell) Jesus said to them : ' If ye *loved* me, ye would rejoice, because I said, I go unto the Father: FOR MY FATHER IS GREATER THAN I.' I base my faith on these clear strong words of Jesus himself. As Luther said on a great occasion, ' Here I stand.' Henceforth it matters not to me what Paul, or Apollos, or Cephas, or 'even an angel from heaven ' may say. All the Athanasiuses the world has ever known, and all the priests of Baal, of Rome, of Russia, of England—Pagan, Papal, Eastern, and Anglican—may shout until they are hoarse, 'Heretic! and may say of me *because of this*, ' Without doubt he shall perish everlastingly.' I should remain fearless and calm. Jesus has spoken. His words are graven on my soul deeper and more indelibly than ' with an iron pen.' Wherever from high altars and from priestly lips the words go forth—' In this Trinity none is afore or after another ; none *is greater* or less than another ; but the whole three Persons are co-eternal together, and co-equal : so that in all things, as is aforesaid, the Unity in Trinity and the Trinity in Unity is to be worshipped. *He, therefore, that will be saved must thus think of the Trinity*'— ' a voice from heaven ' seems simultaneously to say, ' My Father is greater than I,' and, as a sweet antidote to the anathema, there come the comforting words, ' These things I have spoken unto you, that in *me* ye *might have peace*. In the world *ye shall have tribulation* : but be of good cheer ; I have overcome the world.'

Vicar. I am almost embarrassed by your earnestness, by the zeal and confidence with which you express yourself. And indeed the words you quote are emphatic and lucid; but you forget that when Jesus said, 'my Father is greater than I,' he meant in reference to his manhood—in the words of our Creed 'inferior to the Father as touching his manhood.'

Parishioner. I have often heard clergymen say this, but I have never met with one who could give the slightest *Scriptural* authority for the statement that Christ was in the habit of speaking *in two characters*. I have heard it said of one who claimed to be his vicegerent on earth—the infamous Pope Alexander VI.—that, when he was swearing and cursing in a passionate rage, and was reminded by a pious attendant of the 'holiness' of his office, he exclaimed, 'I am not swearing as Pope, but as Rodrigo Borgia,' to which came the natural enquiry, 'When Rodrigo Borgia is in Purgatory, where will the Pope be?' No, sir, this 'double nature' is the subtle invention of a later time, a sophistry to mystify, an expedient to explain the 'inexplicable.' Zealots, and creed-makers, and creed-believers, and other enthusiasts have not hesitated to *introduce words* into the early MSS. of the Gospels to serve their theories; nay, *whole verses*, as I have already shown; so have subtle scholars and platonic philosophers of Alexandria, Egypt, and Athens *invented* a 'double nature' and a 'god-man' to explain their scholastic schemes and 'theosophies.' Popes, like unto Alexander VI., may find it convenient to have a 'double nature,' but not so Jesus. He could say, 'Which of you convinceth me of sin? And if I say the truth, why do ye not believe me?' (John viii. 46.) Of him it could be said, in the words of the prophet

Malachi, 'Saith the Lord of Hosts. My covenant was with him of life and peace ; and I *gave them* to him *for the fear wherewith he feared me,* and was afraid before my name. *The law of truth was in his mouth,* and *iniquity was not found in his lips* : he walked with me in peace and equity, and did turn many away from iniquity' (ii. 5, 6). No, sir ; sophistry and subterfuge did not belong to Jesus. At all times, and on all occasions, he uttered the simple truth ; he never once claimed to *be God*, and even when simply called 'good' by a young man earnestly seeking guidance and information as to eternal life, Jesus at once exclaimed, 'Why callest thou me good? *there is none good but God.*' On another occasion, when the Jews, furious and vindictive on the subject of their descent from Abraham, were ready and anxious to destroy him, he calmly said, 'Now ye seek to kill me, a MAN *that hath told you the truth,* which I *have heard of God: this* did not Abraham' (John viii. 40).

Vicar. As I have said before, so must I repeat now, that all these words were spoken by Jesus in his character as a man, and not as God : he had not at that time revealed himself as God.

Parishioner. Most true, he had not at *that time* revealed himself as *God*, nor at *any other time did he do so.* Being no impostor, but an honest man, 'a teacher sent from God,' as Nicodemus called him, he told the people 'the truth, which he had heard from God.' He was no dissembler, but the fearless truth-bearer and great revealer, and in that capacity he said, 'I can of *mine own self* do nothing : as I hear, I judge : and my judgment is *just, because* I seek not *mine own will,* but the *will of the Father which hath sent me*' (John v. 30). If Christ had been the Almighty God, could he have thus spoken? could he have so *dissembled* as to say, '*I can of mine own self do nothing*'? would he have so misled the Jews as to have veiled his deity, nay, to have denied and *falsified* his real character by uttering the words, 'Ye seek to kill me, *a Man* that hath *told you the truth*, which I have heard of God'? It is a moral impossibility! such a wild idea as that of the 'double nature' would never occur to any person who read the New Testament BEFORE his mind had been saturated with the scholastic inventions of divines and pedants. We learn from intelligent travellers that this mystic theory of the Trinity repels from 'Christianity' the pious Jew, the thoughtful Brahmin, and myriads of Mohammedans and Hindoos who bow to the sovereignty of our Queen, the Empress of Hindostan.

Vicar. If Christ had not been God how could he have possibly said, 'That all men should honour the Son, *even as* they honour the Father'? (John v. 23).

Parishioner. Surely the mystic dogma of a Trinity cannot be based upon so slender a foundation as this. It is impossible that the very plain statements which I have just given from the speeches of Jesus can be nullified by the phrase which you have just quoted. Why, a corresponding incident occurs every day in the political actions of all European nations. Has not our own beloved Sovereign on more than one occasion during the current year requested that the nobility and gentry attending the Court levees should honour the Prince of Wales *even as* they honour her by attendance on the said ceremonials? and has she not affirmed that introductions to the Prince should *in all respects convey the same honours* and *privileges* as if they had been made to herself personally? Are not the myriads of her subjects in Hindostan and the empire of India requested 'to honour the Viceroy *"even as"* they honour the Queen?' Are not all those who attend the levées at Dublin Castle requested to honour the Lord Lieutenant 'even as' they honour the Queen? This is done, but the homage given and received do not make the Lord Lieutenant the King of Ireland, or the Viceroy the Emperor of Hindostan. It has according to the Epistle to the Hebrews pleased God to elevate and dignify Jesus above 'all his fellows.' The writer of that book, whether Paul or Apollos, or whoever the 'inspired' author might have been, records the fact thus: 'Thou hast loved righteousness, and hated iniquity; *therefore* GOD, even THY GOD, hath anointed thee with the oil of gladness above thy *fellows*' (Heb. i. 9). It was thus, you see, a *delegated honour*, precisely as were those honours of the Viceroy, and of the Lord Lieutenant to which I have referred, and the verse I have quoted (if there were no other in the whole range of the inspired writings), is sufficient to confute your statements and to justify me in asserting the sole and supreme Godhead of the Father, and reiterating emphatically the clear unclouded statement of our Divine Lord: 'This is life eternal, to know Thee THE ONLY TRUE GOD, and Jesus Christ, whom Thou hast sent (John xvii. 3).

Vicar. Let me remind you further that Jesus claimed to be able to forgive sins, as when he cured the sick man of the palsy; as recorded by St. Matthew, ix. 2, he said, 'Son, be of good cheer; thy sins are forgiven thee.'

F

Surely, this is arrogating a power surpassing all mere human capacities.

Parishioner. Mr. Hierous, you astound me. 'To forgive sins!' Was not this a power possessed even by his disciples? Did he not say to them, 'Whose soever sins ye remit, they are remitted; and whose soever sins ye retain, they are retained'? (John xx. 23). Why, upon this principle, and if I am to take these words as a demonstrative proof that the person speaking them is God, is the Almighty, I should have to prostrate myself in reverence before you; for not a week since, in the cottage of Job Thresher, when visiting him in his sickness, I distinctly heard you say to him, 'I absolve thee from all thy sins.'

Vicar. But you omit the very important words that I used preceding these. I told him that 'our Lord Jesus Christ had *left power to his Church* to absolve all sinners who truly repent, and by his authority committed to me I absolved him from all his sins.'

Parishioner. Precisely so; the cases are exactly parallel; as I have already said, the power was a DELEGATED POWER; the honour claimed in the words 'even as' was a delegated honour: and as the Lord Lieutenant of Ireland and the Viceroy of India could by the authority committed to them absolve from certain political penal sins, so could Jesus 'forgive sins.' He *has himself declared this*—declared it so emphatically that it cannot be gainsaid. It is among the marvels, it is among the stupendous facts which amaze the unsophisticated and philosophic mind, that any other idea should have been formed respecting it; and it never could have been formed by the tens of thousands who have acquiesced in it had it not been enforced by powerful authority in the ages of barbarism and ignorance by potentates in State and Church to serve their own purposes. Children were trained up to accept these inventions as truths, and this system having been carried on for generations, Error has usurped the place of Truth, and the minds of many are become so enfeebled and timid, speaking generally, that they are no more capable of investigating facts and drawing correct and logical conclusions in *matters of religion* than are domestic geese capable of flying in high air and for long distances as their ancestors did. Just as man has so modified the organisations of these creatures that they can now only waddle on the surface, instead of winging their way through the clouds, as did their remote forefathers, so has he, by early training carried on through a long series of years, so moulded the plastic minds of his children that they are now receptive of any absurdity in one special direction. Their minds have become as incapable of healthy and vigorous action in theological matters as the domestic goose in the matter of flying to high altitudes. This training and its hereditary influence carried on for ages have dwarfed the intelligence and its perceptive power, so that it can now acquiesce in the wildest phraseology and the most absurd paradox. It cannot soar into the high and clear regions of ratiocination. It 'waddles' and paddles in the muddy paradoxes of 'logomachy'; can accept the proposition that one is three, and three are one, and that Jehovah is God, Christ is God, the Holy Ghost is God, and yet that there are not three Gods, but one God! This is a curious phenomenon in psychology, more especially when there is no statement in history, there is no fact in science, placed more clearly on record than is the true nature of Jesus in the following words of his biography by his disciple John: 'But Jesus answered them, My Father worketh hitherto, and I work. Therefore the Jews sought the more to kill him, because he not only had broken the sabbath, but said also that God was his *Father*, making himself equal with God. *Then answered Jesus* and said unto them, VERILY, VERILY, I say unto you, THE SON CAN DO NOTHING OF HIMSELF, but what he seeth the Father do: for what things soever he doeth, these also doeth the Son likewise. *For the Father* loveth the Son, and *showeth him* all things that himself doeth: and *He will show him* greater works than these, that ye may marvel' (John v. 18-20). Nothing can be more plain than these words, and yet there are tens of thousands of persons who do not accept them in their integrity. To repeat a former illustration, they are become like the ducks described by Darwin, which by special environments and hereditary transmission of habits have lost the capacity of ducks, dread the water, and cannot swim. In like manner and from like causes many Christians seem incapable of accepting plain words in their plain meaning, and in 'matters of faith' have the same dread of honest research and truthful investigation (which to a natural and healthful mind are genial and pleasant) as the aforesaid ducks have of water.

Vicar. I am distressed to observe from your remarks how rapid and how deep is the descent into infidelity, when the conscience has once abandoned the traditions and the authority of the Church. Not content with bringing scriptural texts in support of your own individual opinions, you now daringly bring in 'material' conditions to explain national characteristics, and give to 'circumstances' or, as you call them, 'environments,' a potentiality which is startling to listen to. I never in my life heard so bold — I may say so rash — a statement as that the reason why the mass of Christians accept the doctrine of the Blessed Trinity is that the doctrine having been handed down through many generations, and inculcated by authority on the plastic minds of children, it has become a kind of *instinct* to acquiesce in it; and that were it not so the mind would be staggered by its incongruity, and, aided by the facts you have quoted, would expel it from the Christian Creed.

Parishioner. It may be all that you call it, but it *is nevertheless* TRUE. It is observable in other 'religions.' How otherwise can be explained the fact that for many *centuries* tens of thousands in China and elsewhere, when too poor to have a special *wheel* to themselves, make fatiguing journeys to temples where wheels are kept — '*praying wheels*' — whose every revolution is considered as a prayer, and where man's favour with Buddha or God is in exact proportion to the number of prayers he can wheel off — the prayers consisting of a shibboleth of these words 'Aum-mi-to fuh'?[1] If reason had

---

[1] Sometimes given as O-mi-to fu. In Thibet travellers affirm that the words 'Om-Mani Padme Hrum' are regarded as a holy mystic charm of special sacredness, and are to be found roughly carved on slabs of stones piled on high mountain passes, or the faces of rocks, and on pillows and terraces of stones built especially for their accommodation; as also, of course, in temples and monasteries. To utter these words three hundred thousand times gives the devout Buddhist a high place in the favour of Buddha. 'Om' is the equivalent of the Hebrew Jah; 'Mani,' the Jewel; 'Padme,' Lotus; 'Hrum' Amen, or, So be it. The Japanese cry, 'Namu Amida Butzu,' 'Save us, O Buddha.' The Chinese as given above. Millions of Foists cry hourly, 'O-mi-to-fu.' The rosary is com-

not been perverted into an 'instinct,' how could such things go on for centuries among people otherwise intelligent? I did not obtain the notion of hereditary *instinctive* ideas from the illustrious Darwin, but I was glad to have the support of so accurate and acute an observer of *facts*, who has written, ' It is worthy of remark that a belief constantly inculcated during the *early years of life whilst the brain is impressible* appears *to acquire almost the nature of an instinct* ; and *the very essence of an instinct is that it is followed independently of reason*' (' The Descent of Man,' p. 100).

Vicar. It is a wicked and dreadful idea.

Parishioner. It is quite easy to apply the words 'wicked and dreadful' to anything. The entire Christian world applied them to Galileo in the seventeenth century (1634), when he said that the earth moved round the sun. He 'recanted' to save his life, but in private he was heard to mutter, in his own Italian language, ' e pur si muove ' (the earth does move). They were applied to Latimer, and he was burned to death because he could not recognise and would not acknowledge that ' bread and wine ' had been transformed by the utterances of a priest into

---

mon to the worshippers of East and West, to the Foists and to the Papists ; and Gordon Cumming alleges that four hundred and fifty millions of Buddhists find solace in counting such beads. Mohammedans use it also. After the funeral of a friend they cry, ' Allah el Allah !' three thousand times, and check the number by beads. Hindoos follow the example of the Buddhists, and the various sects have varying rosaries ; among the very wealthy the beads are formed of various precious stones.

The *wheel* had a mystic meaning from early times. In the sixth century before Christ they formed a very prominent item in the Visions of Ezekiel, such as, ' The wheels were full of eyes round about, even the wheels that they four had. As for the wheels, it was cried in my hearing, O wheel ' (Ezekiel x. 12, 13).

the Body and Blood of his Redeemer. Your favourite theory of numbers of the vast majority of mankind as a test of truth was fallacious in these and countless other instances. Sir Isaac Newton, John Milton, and John Locke, the learned expositor Samuel Clarke, and the pious Dr. Watts—five Englishmen of great renown and moral worth—no more accepted the Nicene Creed than I do. And as a matter of 'AUTHORITY,' I would rather bow to them than to five thousand of the ordinary people who throng church and chapel, and utter phrases no more intelligible to themselves or to others than the mystic words, 'Aum-mi-to fuh,' babbled by the Buddhists of Asia, or whirled as a printed prayer by rapid gyrations of the ' praying wheels.'

Vicar. The test of numbers may not be always infallible, but, as I have already said, it is the only possible practical way of deciding disputed matters.

Parishioner. And, as I have also shown, has, on the most important occasions, *decided* them *wrongfully.* It was a very decided majority that shouted on a solemn occasion, ' Not this man, but Barabbas!' ' Now Barabbas was a robber.'

Vicar. That was certainly an unjust decision, but it was necessary to the scheme of salvation.

Parishioner. I will not believe it—you must pardon my being thus abrupt. My whole nature revolts against the supposition that, in the councils of the Eternal, it was a *necessity* that *injustice* should be perpetrated in order that God ' might be just, and the Justifier of him that believeth in Jesus ' (Rom. iii. 28).

Vicar. That unfortunate axiom of the 'right of private judgment,' so much insisted on at what has been unfortunately called the 'Reformation,' is leading you into sad errors, and is imbuing you with a spirit most unfavourable to true piety. But, as your spiritual pastor, as the priest appointed to this parish, I must wrestle with your errors; and I must call back your mind from the new and *dangerous* speculations of hereditary influence.

Parishioner. Pardon me for interrupting you, but I must protest at once against the appellation 'new,' for they are not 'new,' and against their being called 'speculations,' for they are not '*speculations*,' but *facts*. As to the word 'dangerous,' it is the old cry of selfishness and ignorance when any truth new to them is brought forward which apparently clashes with their interest. It was old when, eighteen hundred years ago, Demetrius shouted as against Paul in the streets of Ephesus, 'Not only this our craft *is in danger* to be set at nought; but also that the temple of the great goddess Diana should be despised, and her magnificence should be destroyed, whom all Asia and the world worshippeth' (Acts xix. 27). It has been repeated ever since by the timid, the superstitious, and those who adhere to old habits and custom instinctively (that is, as Darwin says), 'independently of reason'; and it is especially clamoured forth when any humble individual like myself presumes to enquire into the truthfulness of any mystic 'double nature,' or Trinitarian God, or goddess, 'whom *all Asia* and the *world* worshippeth.'

Vicar. Your interruption is embarrassing, and I hope that you will give me the same patient hearing as I have always given to you, even under circumstances of considerable provocation. My thread of thought has been broken, but show me in what sense your theory is not '*new*,' and that it is not a '*speculation*,' but a fact.

Parishioner. Yes, from a source more acceptable to you than from Tyndal, or Huxley, or Spencer, or the great and truth-loving Darwin; from no less a person than your charming Horace, whose Odes are so dear to you, that you will be surprised that the striking lines have not leaped into your memory during this discussion.

> *Fortes creantur fortibus et bonis:*
> Est in juvencis, est in equis patrum
> Virtus : neque imbellem feroces
> Progenerant aquilæ columbam.
> *Carminum*, Lib. IV. IV.

That statement is at least nineteen hundred years old. That young ducks, newly-hatched ducks, descended from ducks of natural habits, rush into the water and swim merrily on its surface from an *inherited* impulse, even if hatched by *a hen*, who calls them in maternal terror from the dangerous element ; that the said ducks do not attempt to fly, although the wild-duck, their remote ancestor, does ; that young pointers who have never seen their parents ' point,' do themselves point— are *facts, and not speculations.* And that posthumous children often repeat in their own lives the *habits* of their parents whom they have never seen are also *facts*, and *not speculations* ; and although the first stated 'facts' are taken from the ' lower animals,' and not from the habits of mankind, they are not the less germane to the subject ; for, as Pope has said, and it bears repeating—

> The first Almighty cause
> Acts not by *partial*, but by *general* laws.

Vicar. We have dwelt too long on those 'general laws' in your desire to find a physiological explanation for what you conceive an anomaly—viz. that tens of thousands believe in a faith which has been handed down to them for ages, but from which you, in your intellectual pride, recoil. *Reason*, remember, was the 'goddess' raised to honour when France, mad with crime and blood, deserted all that was holy, and appalled the nations by her demoniac frenzy. You must place 'reason' in the secondary place, and approach the 'mystery of godliness' in the spirit of faith if you desire to profit by it. 'Verily, I say unto you, Whosoever shall not receive the kingdom of God *as a little child*, he shall not enter therein.'

Parishioner. The French Revolution of 1789, most horrible as it was, has long ceased to be a bugbear to religious enquirers, because its true origin is now well known. It has been the policy of all priestly powers to decry 'Reason,' and they do so with an intensity corresponding to the unworthiness and rottenness of the system they espouse. The system MUST be a bad one that requires the prostration of the highest attribute of man. On this subject I can quote the words of one—whom you reverence—whose 'orthodoxy' you, at least, will not question, and for whose personal morality and worth I myself have a great esteem. *William Ewart Gladstone*, in his controversy with the Vatican, said, 'Authority can only be defended *by reason* ; it is a part of what reason sanctions and recommends. But there is no escape from this, *that it must be tried by reason*; as even the being of God, with reverence be it spoken, must be tried by reason—tried by reason under a great responsibility, but under no external coercion either physical or moral.'[1] Moreover, Bishop Butler himself has written, 'Reason is the only faculty whereby we have to judge of anything, even revelation itself.'

Vicar. I revere Gladstone and Butler, but a greater than Gladstone or Butler, even St. Paul, has said, ' The world by *wisdom* knew not God.'

Parishioner. And a greater than St. Paul has said, ' Be ye *wise* as serpents '; and the ' wisest of men ' has written, ' Fools despise wisdom,' and added, ' Wisdom is better than rubies ; and all the things *that may be desired are not* to be compared to it ' (Prov. viii. 11). Still, without stopping to determine whether ' wisdom ' and 'reason' mean the same, I maintain that reason, illumined by the Spirit of God, is man's sole guiding star amid the perplexities of the Churches and Creeds of Christendom.

Vicar. I hold, on the contrary, that God has appointed his Church to be the interpreter of his Word, and that it becomes you and me to bow to her authority.

Parishioner. Had there been but one Church and, therefore, one authority, what you have said may have carried weight ; but as there are two Churches on the Continent and one in this island, that is, the Western, the Eastern, and the Anglican, issuing conflicting decrees, the honest man has still to call in his individual reason to decide between their respective claims.

Vicar. We have made a considerable ' excursus ' from your last quoted text, in which you endeavoured

---

[1] *Contemporary Review.* Article, Sixteenth century arraigned before the nineteenth.

to prove the humanity of Christ, to the loss of his Godhead ; but that Christ was superhuman was proved by the fact that he had no human father, and by the circumstance that this miracle was distinctly and unequivocally foretold by Isaiah some seven hundred years before, viz. 'A virgin should conceive, and bring forth a son, and that his name should be called Immanuel.'

Parishioner. I have not, as yet, stated that Jesus was not 'superhuman,' and was simply 'co-equal' with all men ; on the contrary, I have quoted a text to show 'that *God*, even his *own God*,' had 'anointed him with gladness *above* his fellows' ; but this is at an ineffable distance from showing that he was 'co-equal' and 'co-eternal' and 'co-almighty' with God.

Vicar. It shows him to be the Son of God, with whom, we are assured, 'God was well pleased.'

Parishioner. This has never been in dispute between us ; what I maintain is, that there is no fact and no statement in the whole range of well-authenticated Scripture, which would justify you in calling Him 'God the Son.'

Vicar. Yes ; the text quoted by me from Isaiah, to the effect that the Child of the Virgin should be called 'Immanuel,' 'which being interpreted is God with us.'

Parishioner. I am not concerned at this moment to discuss the facts in relation to the miraculous incidents which, according to St. Matthew, preceded and accompanied the birth of Jesus. All that I desire to say now is that the circumstance of the Child being called 'Immanuel' as a *name* is by no means equivalent to the declaration that he was *God* ; for among the Jews it was not an uncommon thing to give their children names which should associate them with the God of Abraham, of Isaac, and of Jacob. Thus we have 'Elizabeth' 'which being interpreted' is 'the oath of God'; 'Elijah,' 'which being interpreted' is 'my God is Jehovah'; 'Elidad,' 'which being interpreted' is 'whom God loves,' and so on, with a number of names like unto Elisha, Elkanah, Elihu, and others. In connection with what you have said, it appears to me a most astonishing circumstance that in neither of the *synoptic* gospels is the name 'Emmanuel' applied to Christ, and equally astonishing is the fact that the angel which appeared to Joseph, and the angel also who came to Mary, directed that he should be called by a very different name than 'Emmanuel,' Jesus; and more extraordinary still that Matthew himself, leaving the prophetic record, and becoming the historian of the circumstances, writes of Joseph, that when his first-born son was brought forth 'he called his name' (not Emmanuel, but) 'Jesus.'

Vicar. You pass by the stupendous fact, the holy mystery of the incarnation. You omitted the circumstance which preceded and gave all significance to the request that the Child should be called 'Emmanuel'—namely, that the prophet said, 'A virgin should conceive and bear a Son.'

Parishioner. I intentionally avoided it, as I did not wish to introduce matters affecting the credibility of St. Matthew's gospel. It is well known that the word 'Virgin' in the Hebrew language, and as used by Isaiah, does not convey the same meaning as it does to us. It is a curious fact that none of Christ's disciples appear to have been aware of the 'miraculous conception.' St. John, referring to the early mission of Jesus, writes: 'Philip findeth Nathaniel, and saith unto him, We have found him of whom Moses in the law and the prophets did write, Jesus of Nazareth, the son of Joseph.' It is equally surprising that St. Paul never once in all his energetic epistles to Rome, Corinth, Ephesus, Galatia, and Thessalonica, refers to the miracle, although it would have been useful to him, probably at Mars Hill in Athens, as being in harmony with much of Greek mythology; and the Jews might have welcomed it as an analogous incident to that which raised the name of 'Sarai' to 'Sarah.' Moreover his 'brethren' and the townsmen of Nazareth appear unconscious of the stupendous miracle. There are several curious anomalies in relation to it, for even St. Matthew, who with Luke records the incident, writes thus naïvely on another occasion, respecting Jesus, 'When he was come *into his own country*, he taught them in their synagogue, insomuch that they were astonished, and said, Whence hath *this man* this wisdom, and these mighty works? Is not this the carpenter's son? is not his mother called Mary? and his brethren, James, and Joses, and Simon, and Judas? And his sisters, are they not all with us? Where then hath this man all these things? And they were offended in him. But Jesus said unto them, A prophet is not without honour save in his own country, AND IN HIS OWN HOUSE' (Matthew xiii. 54–57). In this narrative there is not the slightest indication that the writer was conscious of the supernatural circumstances attending the birth of him whose 'wisdom and mighty works' filled the minds of his townsmen and neighbours with wonder and astonishment. No one reading this description by itself could have thought that the historian was fully aware 'whence' the wisdom and the power came, and that the Teacher was *not* the 'carpenter's son,' unless, indeed, the earlier portion of the gospel was a detached portion of the 'loggia,' or 'sayings,' from which the gospel as a whole was subsequently compiled. The annunciation resembles those angelic communications in the Old Testament which related to extraordinary births in this, that the angel commanded that the child be called Jesus, as the respective angels which visited Hagar and Sarai commanded special names to be given to the children who were promised ; and as the angel who appeared to the barren wife of Manoah declared that the child to be born should 'deliver Israel out of the hand of the Philistines,' so was Jesus to 'save his people from their sins.'

Vicar. There is a dangerous tone in all that you have just said to me. It certainly implies that St. Matthew is not trustworthy so far as the supernatural facts are concerned, and that you are inclined to regard St. Mark and St. John as the more historic, and that the narrative of the first Gospel has been tampered with or added to by the legendary fancies of a later time. I do hope that this is not so. I have been particularly struck—nay, I might truly say that I have been pained—by your implying that Matthew had strained the facts to accommodate them to *prophecy* ; that in doing so he had mistaken the meaning of the word 'virgin' ; and that all in connection therewith may be regarded as a myth.

Parishioner. I will not disguise from you, my dear Vicar, that such thoughts *have* crossed my mind (although I purposely withheld them from our discussion), for I cannot forget that what we call the 'Inspired Word' has in the progress of ages been wickedly tampered with. I have shown—and you have (reluctantly, I admit) acquiesced in my statement—that the words 'there are three that bear record in heaven, the Father, the Son, and the Holy Ghost: and these three are one,' are practically a forgery—that is, they were *not* written in the original Epistle; and I maintain that they were *so* inserted to support the Church's doctrine as to the Trinity. This being so, I now frankly admit that *I am* suspicious of the truth of the history of the 'Miraculous Conception.'

Vicar. How is it possible that such an irreverent, such a wicked doubt could have been suffered to dwell in your mind? I say *dwell*, because transient doubts, possibly suggested by the powers of darkness, will occasionally intrude upon our souls; but, unfortunately, you now say, 'I *am* suspicious.'

Parishioner. I say so because the narrative partakes so largely of the character of the legendary myths of the widespread 'religions' which you and I regard as false. I will mention only a few. In the vast empire of China it is universally alleged and universally believed of the birth of Fohi, or Fow, that three nymphs descended from heaven to bathe, that a lotus-plant adhered to one, and that thus she became pregnant and gave birth to a son, who became the founder of a religion, and a law-giver. The birth of one person is said to be the result of a *virgin* having haunted a forest expecting the advent of a god long predicted, and that she became pregnant by the sunbeams; and the great, almost unpronounceable, Huitzilipochtle in Mexico was born of a woman who caught in her bosom a feather-

ball which descended from heaven; and Ellis, in his
'Polynesian Researches' (good missionary as he was),
published in 1829, gives one or two most beautiful legends of a like kind. One is especially striking, namely,
that Taaroa, the creator of the earth, sent forth *Oro* to be
the medium between celestial and terrestrial things. Now
the birth of Oro was in this wise: the *shadow* of a bread-
fruit leaf, shaken by the power of the arm of Taaroa,
passed over Hina (as we read in St. Luke of Mary—'the
power of the Highest shall *overshadow* thee'), and she
afterwards became the mother of Oro. Hina, it is said,
abode in Opoa at the time of his birth; hence Opoa
was honoured as the place of his nativity, and became
celebrated for his worship (p. 194, vol. ii.). The parallel
is so striking that Hina certainly suggests Mary, and
the village of Opoa brings to mind the village of Bethlehem, which the angel called the City of David.

Vicar. Is it not more than probable that these
islanders have confused a true narration which centuries
ago may have reached them though some travellers;
and that this historical truth became converted into
legend, and subsequently, by continuous tradition and
fancy, became a 'myth;' imagination or poetry substi-
tuting the beautiful bread-fruit tree with which they are
so familiar, and the shadow of its leaf shaken by the arm
of Taaroa, for the sober facts of the Gospel narrative?

Parishioner. I do not think it probable that those
beautiful islands of the Southern Seas were ever visited
by Europeans until the discovery of Captain Cook in
1778; and even admitting the possibility of such a visit,
I think it still more impossible that such visitors knew
the language of the Sandwich Islanders, or that the Sand-

G

wich Islanders knew theirs. That the marvellous story of St. Matthew should have been treasured up by these simple idolaters through the rolling centuries passes belief. But that the facts of sober history *do* get transformed, magnified, and blended into the mystic legends of fancy, has been abundantly proved. Certainly the most serious attack on the credibility of the supernatural facts of the Gospel has been based on a theory of this kind. The history of Jesus by the German David Strauss has never yet been satisfactorily answered, and, followed as it has been by the brilliant writings of the Frenchman Renan on corresponding lines, has done more injury to Christianity on the Continent than have the writings of the scientists in this country. But neither, nor both combined, has done so much to disturb men's faith and create distrust as the extravagant statements of the Church herself, and the audacity with which her most zealous servants have declared that those who cannot accept her statements 'shall *without doubt* perish everlastingly.'

Vicar. I am ignorant of the writings of the persons to whom you refer. I have heard of them from time to time, but, knowing from the writings of Jude that there 'should be mockers in the last time,' I have most scrupulously and conscientiously avoided them. I wish that you had been equally prudent, for I fear greatly that you have read them, and that they have influenced your opinions. Let me beg of you to read the Epistle of Jude at your earliest possible opportunity.

Parishioner. At our last interview I had occasion to quote this very Epistle. Its contents are impressed on my memory, and the writer Jude is one among many whose statements have tended to overthrow and dissipate my early faith in that awful creed upon which we are conversing.

Vicar. How is that possible? I had relied on its startling statements to check you in your downward way and to bring you back into the paths of truth.

Parishioner. I am glad, my dear pastor, that all the reserves of mere courtesy have been set aside between us. The subject we are discussing is too solemn, too momentous, for etiquette. You have from time to time spoken with warmth, and I must plead guilty of having overlooked in some moments our respective positions. My path may—nay, *must*—appear to you *downward*, and your solemn oaths and your naturally kind disposition would alike make you desirous to bring one 'who had erred and was deceived' back again 'into the path of truth.' But I *feel* that my progress is not 'downward,' but *upward*, and that I *am* 'in the path of truth.' Still more am I confident that I am further removed even than yourself from the condition of those whom Jude has described with such graphic power; inasmuch as those upon whom he poured forth his indignation were those who were 'denying the ONLY Lord *God*' AND 'our *Lord* Jesus Christ'; and all my feeble efforts are devoted to affirming instead of denying 'the ONLY Lord GOD,' and to recalling the solemn asseverations of Jehovah (as recorded by Isaiah)—'there is *no God* else beside me; a just God,' and 'there is none beside me. Look unto *me*, and be ye saved, all the ends of the earth: for I am *God*, and there is *none else* (Isaiah xlv. 21, 22).

Vicar. These words were spoken under the Old Dispensation, before 'the fulness of time' had come, i.e. before the ' appearing of our Saviour Jesus Christ, who hath abolished death, and hath brought life and immortality to light through the Gospel' (2 Timothy i. 10). And you seem to forget that, while the Creed states that Christ is God, yet it states also that there is 'not three Gods, but one God'; and that Christ *was* God is distinctly proved by two great facts: he raised the dead, and he was distinctly seen to 'ascend into heaven.' Surely you do not mean to assert that a *man* could raise the dead, and be seen bodily to ascend into heaven?

Parishioner. Personally, I should not dare to assert anything so contrary to all modern experience. But, most certainly, the Scriptures, which you hold to be verbally and in their entirety (at least, did hold) the inspired and infallible Word of God, tell us of *men* who have raised others from the grave, and also of a man who, with great pomp, visibly ascended into the heavens. Moreover, as regards the power of raising the dead, they tell us that even the *dead bones* of a man sufficed to do this; for we read: 'they were burying a man . . . they cast the man into the sepulchre of Elisha: and when the man was let down, and *touched the bones* of Elisha, he revived, and stood up on his feet' (2 Kings xiii. 21). One is not surprised that the holy prophet, whose dead bones effected such a miracle, had previously raised to life again the dead child of a Shunammite woman (2 Kings iv. 34, 35). As to the ascension into heaven, Mark tells us of our Lord that after he had spoken unto his disciples 'he was *received* up into heaven.' Luke tells us that 'he was parted from them, and carried up into heaven.' Now, in neither of these accounts—and they are *all* we possess from the Evangelists themselves—is there that distinctiveness, that absolute freedom from all possible optical illusion, that explicit clearness of detail, which marked the ascension of one whom, I think, you will not claim to have been God. Mark tells that Jesus was received up into heaven. May that not be said of any true Christian dying in the faith? St. Luke tells us 'that he was carried up to heaven.' This is a more striking statement than that of Mark, but it has not the detail or the splendour of description which has been given us of the ascension of Elijah, of whom we read: 'And it came to pass, as they still went on and talked, that, behold, there appeared a *chariot of fire*, and *horses of fire*, and parted them both asunder, and Elijah went up by a whirlwind into heaven' (2 Kings ii. 11). So that we have in these records instances of the dead being raised by men. Moreover, in your eager desire to establish the Divinity of Jesus, you have not only overlooked these remarkable incidents in the history of Elijah, but have also forgotten for a time the fact that Peter raised Tabitha from the dead; that Paul performed a like act on the person of the young man Eutychus at Macedonia, who went into a deep sleep while Paul was 'long preaching,' and 'fell down from the third loft, and was taken up dead.' Thus, neither the circumstance of the ascension nor the raising of the dead to life again suffices so to mark off Jesus from all other prophets and saints of God as to justify us in addressing him as 'very God of very God.' And, moreover, even apart from this circumstance, we have, as I have again and again shown, the

distinct and unmistakable words of Jesus himself—
'the Son *can do nothing* of *himself*, for, as the *Father
hath life in himself*, so *hath he given to the Son* to have
life in himself'; and St. Paul is emphatic in his testimony
to the Romans, to the effect that, 'if thou shalt confess
with thy mouth *the Lord Jesus*, and shalt *believe in thine
heart that God hath raised him* from the dead, thou *shalt
be saved.*' How consolatory is such a clear apostolical
statement as this to one who, like myself, has been
awed by the maledictions of 'the Church'; who, for long,
distrusted his 'private judgment' because of the thousands who *appeared* to acquiesce in the creed which, in
that 'judgment,' appeared contrary to the Scriptures
and to common sense! Before I *knew* that the said
thousands were apathetic, passive, and uninquiring as to
religious theories and dogmas, such a clear, lucid text
was a consolation and support. To *all* the Churches
St. Paul has spoken with equal plainness, and in so many
places, that I have *now* no awe from the maledictions of
'the Church'; and the fact of thousands *acquiescing* in
the 'Creed' gives me no more personal spiritual anxiety
than that thousands and tens of thousands of 'Christians' acquiesce in the doctrine of the 'Immaculate
Conception of the Blessed Virgin,' and in the absolute
'Infallibility of the Pope'!

Vicar. Your familiarity with the Scriptures shows
me that you have sought earnestly their counsel. From
the tones of your voice, from the expression of your
countenance, and from my knowledge of your life, I am
assured that this is no mere polemic wrestle on your
part. Never having had a transient doubt myself, and
never having in the whole course of my ministry been

consulted upon it before, I have not given the subject the minute attention which you appear to have done, and am therefore somewhat surprised at the number of quotations from the Scriptures you have produced in relation thereto. It is in my power, however, through the advice of a learned brother in the Church, to name to you a most orthodox work, which fully sustains the Nicene and Athanasian Creeds in all their integrity. Pray read it. It is the Bampton Lecture by Canon Liddon ' On the Divinity of our Lord.' I am assured on the highest authority that it is wholly unanswerable. I *hope* and *believe* that it will bring you the intellectual satisfaction you need, and that we shall soon have you in spirit, as in body, within the pale of the Church, among the true believers, and thus removed far, far away from the consequences of those anathemas which you condemn so strongly as unscriptural and unjust.

Parishioner. I thank you very, very much for your kind words and good wishes; but, alas! your hope cannot be realised. The remedy you prescribe has *long since been tried*, and found *impotent*. I saw that a dignitary of the Church had called the Canon a great champion of the truth, and his book an invulnerable bulwark against the encroachments of infidelity. I hastened with joy to obtain it. My 'views' at that time were 'nebulous,' or rather like the first stage of a transformation scene in a magic-lantern; the old convictions were become hazy and dim, and no definite ones had taken their place. I longed for light and guidance. I yearned for some support to the cherished beliefs of my earlier life. General report as to the power and brilliancy of the lecturer made me hope that in Canon

Liddon I should find a Joshua to conduct me from the wilderness of doubt into a bright land of certainty and repose. In a sense, he did this, for he convinced me that the *subject* ' doubted ' *was* a mirage, an illusion, a baseless vision. He helped me to reach a region of light and peace, but he did this by unintentionally revealing to me that, stript of all subtlety, and read in a simple sense, with the aid of fit scholarship, the Scriptures negative the Athanasian theory, and lucidly proclaim ' *One God* and Father of all, who is *above all*, and through all, and in you all ' (Ephes. iv. 6).

Vicar. What can you mean? Surely you do not dare to gainsay the scholarship or the sincerity of the eloquent Canon?

Parishioner. Neither. The first thing that disheartened me was, in cutting open the book, to find no less than five hundred very closely printed pages, together with some thirty or forty others in the form of notes, and an appendix of texts. Five hundred pages— equivalent in the number of words to a thousand pages of some books—to prove what Melville, another eloquent Canon, called a *fundamental doctrine* of the Christian faith, were, *à priori*, a very suspicious circumstance. However, the fascination of the style, the dogmatic assurance of the lecturer, and the thrilling importance of the question discussed made me read on with avidity, although with lessening ardour at every page, until at length I closed the book, my mind and my conscience uttering, ' Unproven and unprovable.'

Vicar. As you are the first person I have heard speak of the work except in praise, and certainly the first that has intimated that the Canon has not demonstrated to every candid mind the Divinity of our Lord, I will ask you in what particular you were disappointed?

Parishioner. If brilliant diction: if eloquent, poetic, and impassioned appeals to the sentiments and preconceived notions and feelings of his hearers: if subtle scholarship and bold assumptions: if the concealment of negative evidence, the skilful marshalling of facts, and the dazzling display of forced inferences: if extravagant eulogy of the Church and the Fathers as exponents of and authorities in determining doctrine: if the consummate skill of a forensic advocate (with such scanty materials as the Scriptures supply) *could* have proved the Godhead of our Lord, *then* would Canon Liddon have proved it. He reminds me of a very distinguished special pleader—the late Serjeant Scarlett. It requires the calm and the coolness of a judicial mind, 'the clear cold light' of the intellect, and a firm grasp of the *evidence* of *all* the witnesses, to withstand his personal fascination and his wealth of words: but, possessing these, the verdict of every honest mind will be, ' Not proven.'

Vicar. Give me some instance or instances of what you call special pleading, the concealment of negative evidence, or the 'subtlety' of a forensic advocate.

Parishioner. A very conspicuous example occurs at page 250, where the Canon writes, ' Accordingly Jesus *never* calls the Father *our* Father, as if he *shared his Sonship with his followers.* He always speaks of "my Father."' Can you suppose that this master of dialectics had *forgotten* the instructions given by Jesus to Mary Magdalene after his Resurrection—' go to my brethren, and say unto them, I ascend unto my Father, and *your* Father; and unto *my God*, and *your* God' (John xx. 17). 'Ex uno disce omnes.' Further, the Canon heads a page with the words 'Our Lord *reveals his Godhead explicitly*'; and then, after the mind of his reader has been dazzled and dazed by a series of brilliant interrogatories, he is informed that 'although the solemn sentences in which he (Jesus) makes that *supreme* relationship' [that of this 'Godhead' and that *explicitly*] '*are* comparatively *few*, it *is clear* that the truth is *latent in the entire moral and intellectual posture* which we have been considering'; then follow the marshalling of the confessions of Nathaniel, of Peter, and the words of Nicodemus; and at length comes (to me) the long-wished-for fact or utterance by or in which 'our Lord *reveals* his Godhead *explicitly*'; and, lo! behold the circumstance! 'Philip preferred to our Lord the peremptory' [sic] 'request, "Lord, shew us the Father, and it sufficeth us."' Well might the answer have thrilled those who heard it. 'Have I been so long a time with you, and yet hast thou not known me, Philip? he that hath seen me hath seen the Father, and how sayest thou then, Shew us the Father. Believest thou not that I am in the Father, and the Father in me?' (p. 178). Thus it stands, with all the enforcement which capital letters to the pronouns can give, although the capital letters are not given in the received text of the Gospel. The concealment of negative evidence and the subtlety of the advocate are shown in the fact that the Canon *closes* the speech of Jesus at this especial point. Had he prolonged it, its metaphorical character would have been *intimated* by the words 'the words that I speak unto you I *speak not* of *myself*, but the Father that dwelleth in me, *he doeth the works*'; had the speech of Jesus been continued to its end, it would have '*explicitly*' demonstrated that he had been speaking *metaphorically*, by the statement, 'At that day *ye shall know* that I am in my Father, *and ye in me*, and *I in you*.' In these words are the proof that the truthful historian had been converted into a subtle advocate of a special theory. This shallow elucidation that our Lord had '*explicitly* revealed his Godhead' disappointed me much, after the bold and promising prologue. Despite the sacredness of the theme, the pungent lines of Phædrus obtruded themselves on my mind, and I could not refrain from uttering

> Mons parturibat gemitus immanes ciens,
> Eratque in terris maxima expectatio;
> At ille murem peperit.

The final result left upon me after the study of this book was admiration of the Canon's scholarship, his diction, and his ingenuity as an 'advocate.' I felt that all that *could be said had been said*; but that facts were too stubborn to be welded into *such* a theory, even by his titanic energies. The truth emerges and shines forth *when* the *Canon* writes, 'Certainly our Lord insists very carefully *upon the truth that* the *power which he wielded* was *derived originally from the Father*' (p. 181). Surely no rhetoric can enable the mind of a sane thinker to conceive of a supreme God 'wielding a power' *derived originally* from a power apart from himself.

Vicar. I deeply regret that you have remained unconvinced even by Canon Liddon's eloquence and fervid arguments; but never shall I forget you in my prayers, and when, in our daily service in the sanctuary our sublime Litany is read, I shall have you especially in my mind and heart as I utter the words, "That it may please thee to bring into the way of truth all such as have erred and are deceived.'

Parishioner. No words of mine can sufficiently thank you for your pure, and kind, and loving motives; and believe me, my dear Vicar, when I say that I too shall breathe out that prayer with equal ardour, and that my response, 'We beseech thee to hear us, good Lord,' will be in every way as earnest and as loving as your own.

Vicar. *Then* your case is not so hopeless as I feared. So long as you feel the need of guidance, so long as your conscience whispers that *all is not well*, there is hope; and, remember that our blessed Lord himself has said, 'If ye *do* my will, ye shall know of the doctrine.'

Parishioner. My responsive prayer will be for others rather than for myself. My troublous doubts on this especial subject are quite gone. I no longer 'sit in darkness'; the 'true light now shineth.' In *this* particular matter, as I have already said before, I resemble the blind man whose eyes Jesus had opened, and who, when catechised and upbraided by the Pharisees for his convictions respecting Jesus, answered,' *One thing* I know; that, whereas I was blind, *now* I see ' (John ix. 25).

Vicar. Although I do not know any theologian who could guide you into the truth more surely than Canon Liddon, yet would I wish to suggest that you read 'Pearson on the Creed.'

Parishioner. Happily, I know a far more illuminating guide than either Liddon or Pearson. But that you may know that I have not neglected any source of information within my reach, I will tell you that before I ventured to speak in the positive manner I am now compelled to do, I have diligently sought counsel from the pages of Pearson, Ellicott, Neander, Jeremy Taylor, Yonge, Hannah, Chalmers, Paley, Farrar, Bengel, Delitzsch, Davidson, Alford, Melville, Newman, Milman, Pressensé, Robertson, Lange, Schleiermacher, Thompson, Westcott, Plumptre, Edersheim, and, last though not least, Geikie, whose 'Life of Christ,' on the orthodox side, is worthy of comparison with any of the others which I have named.

Vicar. It is a goodly array for a layman to have studied ; but I fear that along with these, and perhaps preferred before them, were many of a heterodox character.

Parishioner. I have read some of the writings, which are so called, of such as Matthew Arnold, Baur, Strauss, Renan, Channing, and Martineau ; but never with so strong a bias as I read the writings of those you deem 'orthodox.' Not *one* of these writers *originated* in my mind a *conviction previously unheld.* My lapse into 'heresy,' as you call it, is wholly due, as I have already said, to Mr. Melville's sermon enforcing a belief in the Trinity, or rather the impulse which that sermon gave me to 'search the Scriptures daily' in order to ascertain 'whether those things were so' (Acts xvii. 11), and before that incident I had never read a page of any Socinian writer whatever.

Vicar. Your last words painfully remind me of a sentence in St. Paul's Epistle to the Corinthians, which asserts that there is a 'godly sorrow which worketh repentance,' and also a 'sorrow of the world which worketh death (2 Cor. vii. 10); and so I perceive that there may be *a* reading of the Scriptures themselves which leads to heresy and all its fearful consequences. Had these holy Writings been read in a proper spirit you could not have failed to learn that *the doctrine* you dispute ought (in the words of the eighth Article of Religion of our Church) thoroughly to be received and believed; for they may be proved by *most certain warrants* of Holy Scripture.

Parishioner. Your esteemed champion of the faith, Canon Liddon, in his third sermon, speaks of the Rev. John Keble as 'the boast and glory of his university, great as a poet, greater still, it may be, as a scholar and *theologian*, greatest of all as a Christian saint; and yet, if my memory does not greatly deceive me, he in his sermon on tradition implies that this doctrine is *not* anywhere distinctly and clearly enunciated in Holy Writ, but that it has been handed down to the Church *by tradition*; and in the writings of his friend and admirer Cardinal Newman the same fact is enunciated. If this be so—and I feel assured that it is so—I cannot be blamed for *not finding* it there; and as to 'tradition,' I regard it as a most unsafe guide, and, as Jesus said to the 'Scribes and Pharisees which were at Jerusalem,' so am I—with reverence be it spoken—inclined to say of the Councils and 'Fathers' and dignitaries of the Church—'Thus have ye made the commandment of God of none effect by your tradition' (Matt. xv. 6).

Vicar. You have descended deeper into the depths of doubt and of heresy than even I had feared! You have abandoned not only the Creed—which had given

(I must now admit) some perplexity and pain to more than one bishop and archbishop of our Church, and which perplexity, therefore, was in some measure to be excused in a layman—but you disregard the Church's authority, and even dare to place 'private judgment' on an equality with her decrees! This is a sinful act of schism, which calls for my reproof. The thirty-fourth Article of the Church directs and declares that 'Whosoever, through his *private judgment, willingly* and *purposely* doth openly break the *traditions* of the Church, which be not repugnant to the Word of God, and be ordained and approved by common authority, *ought to be rebuked openly*, for he thus offendeth against the common order of the Church, hurteth the authority of the magistrate, and woundeth the consciences of the weaker brethren.' Moreover, to reject the 'traditions' of the Church is in itself a sin. Had the early Christians done so we should not have possessed the Gospels themselves, inasmuch as for several decades they were *traditions only*, handed down orally by faithful men of one age to those who followed them, until they became embodied in manuscript, and have since reached us as the Gospels of SS. Matthew, Mark, and Luke.

Parishioner. And having been so embodied, the authority of 'tradition' has ceased, as far as *Protestants* are concerned. I am aware that this term 'Protestant' is *now* disdained by 'Anglicans'; but it is the most explicit term still to describe the countless Christians who are without the pale of the Catholic, or perhaps I ought to say the Roman Catholic, Church. Moreover, the sixth Article of your Church has another aspect, for the said sixth Article of your Church distinctly affirms that 'Holy Scripture containeth *all things* necessary to salvation ; so that whatsoever is *not read therein*, nor may be proved thereby, is *not* to be required of any men that it should be believed as an article of the faith, or be thought requisite or necessary to salvation.' Therefore, on the point we are debating I decline to accept as an 'article of the faith' anything which has tradition only for its support ; and this, I maintain, is the case with the Trinitarian doctrine, as has been affirmed (as I think) by Keble and by Newman ; but, whether or not, I challenge you to show any Scriptural authority for the Creed. There may be scattered here and there a 'text' or so which may *appear* to indicate a *duality*, but not one to affirm *a Trinity* save the forgery in St. John's Epistle, which has *now* been thrust out of the New Testament as it stands revised by the greatest Greek scholars of the present century.

Vicar. The Church places the doctrine of the Trinity in the very first front of her Articles as the one primary fundamental doctrine which she expects and demands that her children should accept ; and here, even if nowhere else, her Article and her Formula, the first and second Articles of Religion, and the dogmatic statements of the Athanasian Creed are in perfect accord. To dispute this doctrine, then, and to affirm that it cannot 'be proved by most certain warrants of Holy Scripture,' is an act of rebellion against the Church, is treating with disdain her 'authority in controversies of faith,' and rendering yourself liable to be 'excommunicated,' and to be regarded by 'the whole multitude of the faithful as an heathen and publican' until you 'be openly reconciled by penance and received into the Church by a judge that hath authority therein.' This is the admonition of the thirty-third of the Articles of our religion.

Parishioner. All that you have now said is most true ; and I must remind you that I emphatically stated at our first interview that no honest man—and I claim to be honest—could pretend to affirm that it was *not* the clearest teaching of the Church. And I went much further than you have now done in showing how she publicly anathematises *all* who *do not accept* her teachings in this particular. But here, as in some other matters, the Church of England is a paradox ; her *theories* and her practice often contradict each other, and her ' authority ' is weakened thereby. Her ' trumpet gives an uncertain sound ' ; nay, ' her pipes and her harps ' are not only out of tune, but are made to give out *different tunes*; and the priest of one parish is ready to ' anathematise ' the priest of the adjoining one. It has been my lot to hear the author of ' The Christian Year ' described by the vicar of his own parish as ' a blind leader of the blind,' instead of being, as Canon Liddon calls him, ' great as a poet, greater still, it may be, as a scholar and theologian, greatest of all as a Christian saint.' Indeed, the vicar of the parish and the ' Christian poet ' mutually regarded each other as ' unsound in the faith,' although both were ordained priests of the Church of England. It is not pleasant to think that the good John Keble (good in purpose, but intensely bitter towards 'dissent and dissenters') was not regarded by all as a prophet ' in his own country.' Thus, during the Agricultural Riots of 1831 the reverend poet kindly endeavoured to dissuade the agricultural labourers of his neighbourhood from breaking threshing-machines belonging to the farmers and others. Their leader, a 'local preacher' belonging to the Primitive Methodists, confronted him with a Scriptural harangue—a 'bit of the Gospel,' as he called it—and invited discussion, which Mr. Keble most wisely declined. The 'Primitive,' who had lived many years in the same parish with Mr. Keble, then acting as curate at Coln St. Aldwin's, had much to say respecting him, his opinion of the learned 'parson' being akin to that which William Taylor, the 'Model Preacher' of America, is said to have expressed respecting the philosopher Emerson—' He may be a good man, but he is as "*ignorant of the Gospel*" as Balaam's ass was of the Hebrew grammar.' But to return to our subject. The Church of England suffers in authority because of the conflict between her liturgy and her catechism and her 'Thirty-nine Articles,' her avowed 'Protestantism' and her dogmatic creeds. Her sixth Article, which makes the Scriptures the final appeal, goes far to nullify her 'anathemas' in other directions. It is this sixth Article which has enabled me to continue a worshipper within her material fabric and to accept with composure your intimation of 'excommunication.'

Vicar. I hope to be spared so painful a procedure; and it is somewhat ungenerous in you thus (at least indirectly) to taunt her for the reverence and deference she manifests towards the Holy Scriptures—those Scriptures which you have heretofore so warmly espoused, as transcending in authority the decrees of Councils and the statements of the Fathers.

Parishioner. And still do. What I have said is in illustration of the Church's inconsistency in speaking so dogmatically in her 'Creeds,' and, like Saul, 'breathing out threatenings and slaughter against the disciples of our Lord' who cannot accept them, and then, elsewhere, putting another authority—the Holy Scriptures—on the same plane, or higher than herself, to declare what is or what is not required 'to be believed as an article of faith.' She thus provides an 'imperium in imperio,' which leads to vacillation and conflict even among her priests themselves.

Vicar. You surely would not have the Church of England proclaim herself as being superior to God's Word?

Parishioner. Heaven forbid! I wish to see her in *fact*, as in *name*, *the National Church*—a Church, not of catechisms and creeds and of articles, but a Church that could receive within the amplitudes of her love *all who loved God*, all who could 'worship HIM in spirit and in truth,' all who could say, or desire to say, 'O God, thou art my God; early will I seek thee: my soul thirsteth for thee, my flesh longeth for thee in a dry and thirsty land, where no water is; to see thy power and thy glory, so as I have seen thee in the sanctuary. Because thy loving-kindness is better than life, my lips shall praise thee' (Ps. lxiii. 1–3). At present she is far from this. In fact, logically she is a paradox; her practice, in many particulars, is better than her creed (the very opposite of too many of us); but still she is not '*national*'; nay, more, she has much of the exclusiveness and arrogance of the Romish Church, with none of her consistency, her discipline, and authority. She is a house divided against herself. She has no unity of creed (practically) or purpose; and, while frowning on 'dissent,' dissentience and strife are rampant within her own borders. In large cities there is positive rivalry between sister churches—not as to which shall best serve God, but which shall obtain the larger congregation. The very tricks of trade are employed to effect this unworthy purpose; choice music, floral decorations, gorgeous robes, pompous processions, with banners and all the resources and fascinations of song and of choral harmonies, are brought into play to achieve this end. The *words* of a hymn or a psalm are secondary to the beauties and charms of its musical composition. 'Singing with grace in your hearts to the Lord' can be cheerfully dispensed with, provided only that your voice be sweet, powerful, well-cultured, and well-controlled; for the scenic attractions of the theatre and the sensuous sounds of the opera are blended at these sabbath festivals, to attract the fashionable, the idle, the wealthy, and the crowd. Music, colour, and song are evoked to constitute 'a bright service' which should move

> Softly sweet in Lydian measures,

to lull the soul into luscious repose or 'dissolve it into ecstasies,' and make it dream, 'with sweetness through the ear,' that it was treading a flowery path to heaven. Churches crowded with fair women, and coloured dresses glittering with crosses of gold and gems, are the crowning result to human vision. But if the utterance of the name of the Most High in a thoughtless way, and only with regard to musical notation, be practically (as I believe it to be) a violation of the third commandment, then is it a scene upon which the angels of heaven must look with dismay, and One, higher than all angels, may some day say, 'Who hath required *this* at your hand, to tread my courts? Bring no more vain oblations; incense is an abomination unto me; the new moons and sabbaths, the calling of assemblies, I cannot away with; *it is iniquity, even the solemn meeting*' (Isaiah i. 12, 13).

Vicar. I am really embarrassed to understand you. At one moment you seem to me to belong to the 'Rationalists,' and to set aside the high mysteries of our most holy religion and the supernatural facts and miracles of the Gospel, or to explain them by the material or physical laws which science reveals, as, when at our first interview, you implied that there were men of such cerebral organisation that they could not grasp and carry out the highest teachings of the Gospel—men whom you termed in the language of Paul 'vessels of dishonour'; and still lower down in the materialistic or necessitarian scheme, as when you implied that religious habits were contingent on hereditary influence; then you seem to have gone off to the very opposite pole of thought, as if you wished the Church to possess such an autocratic power that there should be no marked difference between the preachings of a priest in one parish and the preachings of the priest in another—that all should be bound in the same iron and inflexible rule as in the Romish Church; and then at the close of your remarks you exhibit all the fiery zeal of the Puritan and condemn all ornate service, forgetting the practice of the olden time, when the church or temple was, so to speak, under the immediate direction of Jehovah—the people were invited to 'praise him with the sound of the trumpet: praise him with the psaltery and harp. Praise him with the timbrel and dance: praise him with stringed instruments and organs. Praise him upon the loud cymbals: praise him upon the high-sounding cymbals. Let every thing that hath breath praise the Lord' (Ps. cl.). Yes, disregarding the command 'Let everything that hath breath praise the Lord' would limit worship to a chosen few, and, like John Knox in the time of the Stuarts, would condemn music itself, and even banish the organ 'as a kist of whistles.'

Parishioner. I deeply deplore my incapacity to place my convictions in so lucid, logical, and consistent a form as they appear to myself. Nothing could possibly be farther from my wishes than that the worship of God should be restricted to a few persons. The Psalmist himself could not be more ardent in his desire than I am that 'everything that hath breath should praise the Lord.' My regret is that the trumpets, and cymbals, and stringed instruments are sounded by men who have no special desire to 'praise the Lord'; by many who 'are lovers of pleasure more than lovers of God'; by some men, indeed, who even deny his existence, but who sound the stringed instruments for mere pay—others do so 'to oblige the Vicar,' or some female friend, or to gratify their love of music and to win praise as accomplished musicians. My objection was that this ornate service should be employed *ostensibly* 'to praise the Lord,' but really to attract a congregation to a special church. It was not the reality that I objected to, but the 'simulacrum,' the 'sham,' the formality of worship! I fear that of too many of the singers and of the musicians it may be truthfully said, ' This people draweth nigh unto me with their mouth, and honoureth me with their lips ; but their *heart* is far from me ' (Matt. xv. 8). My wish is that employers and employed would remember that 'God is a spirit, and they who worship him *must* worship him in *spirit and in truth*' (John iv. 24) ; and as to binding all in an iron and inflexible rule you must know that this is the very exact opposite of my wishes, for no one living can be more thoroughly impressed with the belief that, 'Where the Spirit of the Lord *is, there* is *liberty*' (2 Cor. iii. 17), and my remarks as to a 'national' Church should have caused you to refrain from hinting it.

Vicar. Why, then, draw such a picture of the trumpet, and its uncertain sound, and of the conflicting parties you say exist in the Church?

Parishioner. To show the inconsistency and the fallacy of your urging upon me to accept of a paradoxical creed (a creed irreconcilable with the reasoning faculty) upon the *authority* of the *Church*, when, in fact, she has no controlling 'authority' over the preachings of her ministers and the conflicting deductions they draw from her creeds and formulas. Her inconsistency and weakness in this particular I have already pointed out, and they are almost the 'gibes' of her foes. The eloquent Cardinal Newman, in one of his 'Discourses to Mixed Congregations,' says, 'Attachment is not trust, nor is to obey the same as to look up to and to rely upon ; nor do I think that any thoughtful or educated man can simply believe or confide in the *word* of the Established Church. I never met any such person who did or said he did, and I do not think that such a person is possible.' This is severe, but not more severe, and certainly not more true, than when, in again speaking of the Church of England, he proceeds: 'Does not its *essence* lie in its recognition by the State? is not its establishment its very *form*? What would it be, would it last ten years, if abandoned to itself?' In the same address he said: 'Strip it of this world, and you have performed a *mortal operation* upon it, for it has ceased to be. You know that, did not the State compel it to be one, it would split at once into three' [High, Broad, Low, he means] 'several bodies, each bearing within it the elements of further division. It moves because the State moves; it is an appendage whether weapon or decoration of the sovereign power; it is the religion, not even of a race, but of the ruling portion of a race.'

Vicar. Well may you call the Cardinal eloquent; he exceeds all men in the smoothness, the rhythm, the poetry of his sentences; and his silvery voice adds to their fascination and charm. It was a great, a deep misfortune to lose him from our midst—for who could have foreseen the depths into which he has fallen! 'O what a noble mind is here o'erthrown' by credulity and superstition! How little did any of us deem that the slashing critic of the Church of Rome, the puissant pamphleteer, the trenchant 'tractarian,' the chieftain of the 'British Critic,' should become the abject slave and sycophant of the Church he censured! The man of all others who exercised his mind, who applied the teachings of history with such energy and power to the intellect and reason of his fellows, now, alas! pours scorn on the noblest attribute of man, accepts with reverence the wildest credulities of the 'dark ages,' and clothes the silliest superstitions with all the graces of poetry! 'Great wit to madness nearly is allied.' Who could have thought it possible that the man who drew crowds of the most learned members of one of the most renowned universities in the world to listen to his sermons in St. Mary's, Oxford, would live to write such eloquent nonsense as the following: 'The store of relics is inexhaustible; they are multiplied through all lands, and each *particle* of *each* has in it at least a *dormant*, perhaps an *energetic*, virtue of *supernatural operation*. At Rome there is the true Cross, the crib of Bethlehem, and the chair of St. Peter; portions of the crown of thorns are kept at Paris; the holy coat is shown at Treves; the winding-sheet at Turin; at Monza the iron crown is formed out of a nail of the Cross; and another nail is claimed for the Duomo of Milan; and pieces of our Lady's habit are to be seen in the Escurial. The Agnus Dei, blessed medals, the scapular, the cord of St. Francis—*all are the medium of Divine manifestations and graces.* Crucifixes have bowed the head to the suppliant, and madonnas have bent their eyes upon assembled crowds. St. Januarius's blood liquefies periodically at Naples, and St. Winifred's Well is the scene of wonders even in our unbelieving country!' ('Present Position of Catholics,' p. 290.) Is it not most sad? does not this very record of the signs and wonders of the Popish Church bring to mind with irresistible force the prophetic words of St. Paul: 'Then shall that Wicked be revealed whom the Lord shall consume with the spirit of his mouth, and shall destroy with the brightness of his coming: *Even him, whose coming is after the working of Satan with all power and signs and lying wonders*'? (2 Thessalonians ii. 8, 9). Since the Fall and the Crucifixion I know nothing more sad, more appalling in the spiritual history of man than this spectacle! Does it not shock you?

Parishioner. I am grieved, but not shocked; that is, I am not surprised, because it is the *practical* outcome of dogmatic teachings upon an inquiring, honest, and devout spirit. By inheritance, by disposition, by training, and every social surrounding, John Newman was from his earliest years imbued with a spirit of devout reverence. He has undergone three stages; but the *first* and *last* are *analogous* in this respect, that they are based on the *feelings* and sentiments alone, and hold the intellect and the reasoning powers in aversion and dread. At a time when society around was cold and worldly his home was the abode of piety and of fervid belief in the 'doctrine of grace' and 'of the new birth.' His literary guides were Venn, Simeon, Milner, Scott; and the person who was the human means of his 'conversion' and the beginning of 'divine faith in him' was Walter Meyers of Pembroke College. Of this 'conversion' he has said he 'was more certain than that he had hands and feet.' Under these influences he went to the University of Oxford; while there he became acquainted with Whately (afterwards Archbishop of Dublin), who, he says, 'emphatically *opened my mind and taught me to think and use my reason*; and thus he soon became dissatisfied with the narrowness, the fanaticism, the sour creed, and the mental mediocrity of the 'Evangelicals,' and abandoned them as a party, although their early influence on his nature abides to this hour. He then became distinguished as a polemical preacher and an ardent critic, making vigorous onslaughts on Dissent, Protestantism, and the Papacy; and as upholding

Church principles (Anglican) against Papacy and 'Dissent' alike—his great dialectic work on 'The Prophetical Office' being then thought a certain bulwark against the encroachments of the Papal power, as it certainly was destructive, generally speaking, in the Church of England of the 'low' views of Evangelicalism—this middle stage of his thought, like his 'Via Media,' soon merged again into abject submission to dogma and authority. Whately's influence passed away; and 'to open the mind,' 'to teach to think,' '*to use the reason*,' again became as repellent to him as to any 'Evangelical.' The *fanaticism* of feeling and sentiment regained its ascendency. Hereditary influence and the plastic mouldings of childhood reasserted themselves, and the saying of Horace 'Naturam expelles furcâ, tamen usque recurret' was realised. The Pope usurped the place of the Bible. This last 'conversion' (regarded psychologically) was simply a recurrence to the emotions and feelings of his earlier days. In Cardinal Newman we observe one of those impassioned souls which become 'possessed' with an idea, which thenceforth dominates over 'common sense' and every judicial attribute. His fanaticism is absolute. His judgment is as feeble as that of a child. Were the Pope to issue an 'Encyclical' to-morrow declaring that the sun went round the earth, and that the theory of gravitation was sinful, the Cardinal would bow to it with abject submission, like as the Jesuits, when issuing an edition of Newton's works in 1742, stated that they did not accept his description of the movement of the earth *because* the Pope had pronounced it false. In him emotion and sentiment are supreme, and therefore mystic rites and ceremonies become the joy of his existence. 'To me,' he writes, 'nothing *is* so consoling, so piercing, so thrilling, so overcoming as the Mass. I could attend Masses for ever and not be tired' ('Loss and Gain,' p. 290). 'Masses' have become to Newman what wild hymns and rapturous exclamations are to the 'Salvation Army'; or the 'unction' sermons of Spurgeon on 'predestination,' 'special election,' and the like are to 'God's elect' who throng the 'Metropolitan Tabernacle.' Still, with this mental defect, John Henry Newman is an honest man, and as such to be respected. In violating his vows and in abandoning the Church of his Fathers and in going over to the Church whose doctrines he once described as 'impious, heretical, and damnable,' he has consistently carried out the teachings which in these interviews you have earnestly impressed upon me.

Vicar. When have I ever impressed upon you, or upon anyone else, such absurdities as that 'the iron crown at Monza had been formed out of one nail of the Cross,' 'that crucifixes have bowed the head to suppliants, and madonnas had bent their eyes upon assembled crowds'? Your statement as to my teachings is preposterous and most unjust.

Parishioner. You may not intentionally have wished for such results, but the acceptance of such fables as truths is the necessary corollary of your teaching. Whenever the '*reason*,' or discerning power in man, is forbidden to be exercised; whenever it is demanded that the intellect should bow to 'tradition' and to the dogmatic 'authority'; whenever *material* things are represented as the special media 'of Divine manifestations and graces'—it does not matter much whether it be 'an iron nail,' 'a bit of wood,' 'a piece of our Lady's habit,' 'a blessed medal,' or 'a piece of bread and a drop of wine'—when, in short, a man is assured, amid all the holy solemnities of public worship, that, except at the command of the 'Church,' he implicitly believes and holds a faith which *to him* is absurd and incomprehensible, '*without doubt* he shall perish everlastingly': then, there can be no limit to credulity. I myself could more easily believe in any one of the so-called miracles recited by Newman, and in its spiritual potency, than I could comprehend and believe in the phraseology, or, as it might be called, the 'logomachy,' of the Athanasian Creed.

Vicar. It is almost—nay, quite—profane to compare the facts and the circumstances. In the Holy Creed only Divine Persons are referred to, not even the Virgin Mary herself, much less ' a portion ' of her ' habit.'

Parishioner. On this fact we are at issue. You regard Jesus as God, and the Holy Ghost as God; and to these propositions I demur, and am not more willing to accept and use these words than I am to receive and reverence the term ' mother of God,' by which the more venerable, more powerful, and larger Church designates the Virgin. No, sir, Cardinal Newman is more consistent, and infinitely more frank, than any bishop or priest I know of in the Church of England. He is anxious to preserve the traditions, the creeds, and the authority of his Church, and he very wisely writes:
'*Avoid, I say, inquiry; for it will but lead you thither, where there is no light, no peace, no hope; it will lead you to the deep pit, where the sun, and the moon, and the*

stars, and the beauteous heavens are not, but chilliness and barrenness and perpetual desolation' ('Discourses to Mixed Congregations,' p. 283). I regard these eloquent words as most wise, sagacious, and shrewd from *his standpoint*; wise as was the advice of the monk who, soon after Gutenberg's printing-type came into use, said, 'We must root out this press, or it will root out us.' There is, there can be, no alliance between the *principles* of Protestantism, which suggest 'enquiry,' and the principles of a Church which demands that all the reasoning faculties should succumb to her dogmatic 'faith'; hence the consistency of strictly forbidding all 'enquiry,' and demanding absolute submission, without any of the qualifying circumstances which, verbally, the articles of our Church admit. As I have already stated, these qualifying circumstances are illusory and out of place so long as the 'Commination Service' and the 'Athanasian Creed' form important parts of the public worship.

Vicar. There is a bitter perverseness in your frequent comparison between the two Churches, Anglican and Roman, and their respective modes of maintaining their tenets, to the disadvantage of the former. If we had an audience, few would admit that you were sincere in affecting not to see more difficulty in accepting and believing the childish puerilities of Newman than in accepting and believing the sublime mysteries of the Creed of St. Athanasius; and I could recognise no more puerile credulity in accepting and believing the wild legends of the 'coat of Treves,' 'the iron nail' of Monza crown, and such-like follies, than in accepting and reverencing the ineffable dogma that in the Trinity none is afore or after other, none is greater or less than another, but the whole three Persons are co-eternal together and co-equal ; that in all things, as is aforesaid, the Unity in Trinity and the Trinity in Unity is to be worshipped.

Parishioner. Probably, in an audience ' few ' *would* sympathise with me. The audiences I have known have preferred that others should think for them rather than they should think for themselves, and have always been ready to accept of platitudes, if they were only clothed with propriety and grace. But to myself, there is less difficulty in believing the Romish miracles than in accepting the Athanasian mystery. The miracles appear *most improbable*, but still within the *extreme* limits of the possible ; and the other is not. Take the iron crown of Monza, made out of one nail of the Cross, for instance. The iron nail may have been very large, and the crown may have been small and thin, and we all know that iron is a very ductile material. But be this as it may, it certainly does not appear so difficult to believe as if had been said : ' There were three pieces of iron, and each piece of iron was made into a nail : the first was a nail, the second was a nail, and the third was a nail ; and yet there were *not* three nails, but *one* nail.' And even such a proposition or statement is more simple and more easily to be understood than the statement which you have given as *necessary* for a man to believe if he ' will be saved ' ; because there is *not* superadded to the genesis of the nails that the first nail was made of *none*, that the second was derived from the ore of the first, and that the third ' proceeded ' from the other two ; and yet ' none of the nails is afore or after other,' that ' none is greater or less than another, but the whole three nails are co-eternal together and co-equal.' The reverence and awe which have been transmitted to us, and the religious training of childhood, prevent us from laughing at this paradox of things; but if we had *never heard it* until our manhood, we should have been more inclined to smile than we should at the opening of the eyes of a painted madonna in the Roman States or at the wild flight of the 'coat of Treves' over the waters. I cannot, however, conceive that the salvation of an immortal soul is contingent upon the belief of all or any of these absurdities.

Vicar. I am so distressed by your statements that I know not how to treat them. Your enthusiasm, or I might have said party spirit, seems to carry you away so as to cause you to palliate the errors of an apostate from his ordination vows, and actually to place the spurious miracles of the Church of Rome on a plane with the holy verities of our Church; nay, worse, even to prefer them, and to regard the 'iron crown of Monza' as less of an intellectual paradox and 'stumbling-block' to an inquiring mind than the mysteries of the Catholic Faith. This is most perplexing and painful. As respects the late Vicar of St. Mary's, much as I admire his marvellous mastery over the English language, and often as I have been fascinated by his poetry and power, I cannot but feel that his 'Egoism' has been excessive, and chiefly in consequence of the profound reverence we all at one time paid him; that his self-conceit has become great; and that, in the language of St. Paul, 'for this cause God has sent him strong delusion, that he should believe a lie.' I confess that I sometimes tremble for his destiny.

Parishioner. That is strong language. The silly

liquefaction of the so-called blood of St. Januarius at
Naples, the bowing heads of the crucifixes, and the
opening, beaming eyes of the madonnas are indeed
dismal 'delusions'; and in all of these the celebrated
convert has publicly proclaimed he '*believes.*' *Still*,
credulity, however crass and childish, so long as it does
not injure the community, or culminate in an act which
is likely to do so, and remains simply as a 'crotchet' of
the individual, ought, I think, to be treated with com-
passion. I know of no instance in Holy Scripture
where credulity or creed has been condemned. In the
great prophetic panorama which Jesus portrayed (as
recorded by Matthew) of the Judgment Hour, the one
thing, *and the one thing only*, which called forth the
censure and the sentence of the Judge was, that the
hungry, and the thirsty, and the naked, and the captive
had been neglected; no creeds were called for, no
doctrines denounced or applauded. Not even the
'prophesying in *his name*,' or 'casting out devils,' or
doing 'wonderful works in his name, whether at the
font, confessional, or altar, availed anything, but simply
beneficent acts and a pure life; and therefore, I have no
anxiety respecting the ultimate destiny of one so pious
and good. Moreover, St. Peter, under special illumination, declared, 'I perceive that God is no respecter of
persons, but in every nation he that feareth him, and
worketh righteousness, is acceptable with him.' These
conditions the renowned Oratorian certainly fulfils, yet
is he an unsafe guide in all religious perplexities. My
praise, such as it was, had reference to his astuteness
as a partisan, like unto the astuteness of the 'unjust
steward' in the parable. I have shown by quotations

from his published sermons that he is no longer a safe teacher under religious perplexity. He is the slave of dogmatic authority, and his instruction in the words 'Avoid, I say, inquiry,' are in direct contradiction to the teachings of his august Master, who said, '*Search* the Scriptures,' do not accept any pretensions without inquiry; you have confidence in the Scriptures, 'search,' 'inquire and see whether they do not testify of me.' Newman is also practically opposed to the historian of the Acts, who declared that the people of Berea 'were more noble than those in Thessalonica,' in that they 'searched the Scriptures daily, *whether those things were so.*' It is an abject philosophy which inculcates the closing of the eyes that you may not see. And the *consequences* of 'inquiry,' 'the leading into the deep, where there is no light, no peace, no hope, no beauteous heavens, no sun, moon, or stars, but chilliness, barrenness and desolation,' have no foundations except in the poetic and romantic mind of the writer. We know that by 'inquiry' all the material blessings of the world have been obtained, and that sun, moon, and stars were never seen in half their greatness, their grandeur, and effulgence until the telescope of 'inquiry' had been directed towards them. The writings of Isaiah and of Paul prove to us that God desireth to be honoured not with the heart only, but with the '*understanding* also,' and Hosea even declares: 'My people are destroyed for lack of knowledge: because thou hast rejected knowledge, I will also reject thee, that thou shalt be no priest to me (iv. 6). This blind, uninquiring, passive piety, this piety of priests and ritualists, has been well described by a divine (who is as great a master of logic, rhetoric, and style as Newman himself, and far more profound in the domain of philosophy and science) as 'a refuge for the weakness, not an outpouring of the strength, of the soul; it takes away the incubus of darkness, without shedding the light of heaven; lifts off the nightmare horrors of earth and hell, without opening the vision of angels and of God' (Martineau, 'Studies of Christianity,' p. 39).

Vicar. Dr. Martineau certainly gives us a very graphic contrast between spiritual and formal worship; but his remarks are applicable only to superstitious phases of religion, or to those abject forms of Christian devotion seen in some parts of Ireland, and in other countries where the people are very ignorant, poor, and superstitious, and where religious services are conducted in an 'unknown tongue,' as our Article states—in 'a tongue not understanded of the people.' In places and churches where this wise resolution of Paul is disregarded—'I will pray with the spirit, and I will pray with the understanding also: I will sing with the spirit, and I will sing with the understanding also. Else when thou shalt bless with the spirit, how shall he that occupieth the room of the unlearned say Amen at thy giving of thanks, seeing he understandeth not what thou sayest?' (1 Cor. xiv. 15).

Parishioner. I am sorry, my dear Vicar, that the resolve of St. Paul is overlooked and unpractised not only in the wild districts of Connaught, and in Basque provinces, but much nearer home; for practically there is little to choose between 'a tongue' described as 'unknown'—or, as we may say, a 'foreign language'—and native words so connected together in sentences, and having such mystic meanings attached to them, that they cease to convey a comprehensible idea to the mind. When you, in your official robes, and in the performance of your holy office, tell your people that '*whosoever will be saved, before all things* it is necessary that he hold the Catholic Faith,' and you proceed to define that faith in the well-known manner, 'how shall he that occupieth the room of the unlearned say Amen, seeing he *understandeth* not what thou sayest?'

Vicar. I do not admit the applicability of your remarks. Every statement made by me under such circumstances is as plain and as easily to be understood as the nature of the subject admits.

Parishioner. Perhaps it might equally have been said of the shouting of 'unknown tongues' in the Church at Corinth, that it was made as easy 'to be understood' as the 'nature of the case' admitted. Nevertheless the nature of the case was such that St. Paul has himself recorded that 'he that speaketh in an unknown tongue speaketh not unto men . . . for no man understandeth him; howbeit in the spirit he *speaketh mysteries.*' The cases appear to me to be parallel. Certainly when you are reciting the 'mysteries' of the faith one of your audience feels assured 'no man understandeth him.' Leaving myself, however, out of the question, and taking a single sentence only of that detailed 'faith' which 'except everyone do keep WHOLE and undefiled, *without doubt he shall perish everlastingly,*' how many, think you, of your congregation *understandeth* you when you admonish them 'that we worship one God in Trinity, and Trinity in Unity, neither confounding the *Persons* nor dividing the *substance*'? Even removing the incomprehensible first clause, how many 'understandeth' 'confounding the *Persons*,' or 'dividing the *substance*'? They have learnt from the Articles that 'there is but one living and true God, everlasting, without *body*, *parts*, or passions.' What, then, is their perception of 'Person' as applied to the Almighty Father? And as to *substance*, they have read in Genesis that 'every living *substance* was destroyed,' and in Deuteronomy that 'the earth opened her mouth and swallowed Dathan and Abiram up, and their houses, and their tents, and all the *substance* that was in their possession'; and in twenty other places in the Old Testament they have seen the word; but never once in that venerable Book have they read it except in a sense contrary to that in which, I presume, it is used in the above instance. In the philosophic sense, 'substance is that which underlies the attributes by which alone we are conscious of existence,' or 'the unknown, unknowable substratum on which rests all phenomena.' Thus viewed, *substance* is difficult to 'understand.' Methinks, 'trinity, person, and substance,' as they stand in your creed, with their 'confounding' and 'dividing,' may be classed among the 'unknown tongues' of the Pauline Epistles. Most certainly, as 'one that occupieth the room of the unlearned,' I am unable to say Amen, 'seeing I understand not what thou sayest'; and I think my condition would be represented by the greater portion of your congregation.

Vicar. Neither is it necessary that they should understand it. It is enough that they receive it with reverence and godly fear, and with becoming submission to their 'teachers and spiritual pastors and masters.'

It is the meek and lowly who are accepted of God. Our Lord has told us that unless a man receive the Kingdom of God in the same simple spirit of trust as a little child, 'he shall not enter therein'; and the bold inquiring Thomas, who wanted such full proof, both from his senses and his understanding, of the resurrection of his Master, did not receive any special praise, but the Lord said, 'Blessed are they that have *not seen*, and *yet* have believed.' God looks at the motive, accepts the intent, and blesses the deed which springs from a loving and a grateful heart, however futile, or even silly, it may appear in the eyes of the scornful. 'She has done what she could' may be the record and the trophy in heaven of many a deed which on earth has met only with scoffing smile or stern rebuke.

Parishioner. Most true: thrice blessed are the 'poor in spirit,' and the 'pure in heart,' and the 'humble and contrite,' and all 'the weary and heavy laden' ones who pour out their sorrows before a merciful God; yea, much to be envied are those meek and lowly 'babes' to whom has been 'revealed' these 'things' which 'the wise and the prudent' have failed to perceive and to grasp. They may not be able to syllable a prayer, and yet, with a deep consciousness of need and an unfaltering faith and trust in some great Helper of the helpless, may 'count their beads' even in the poor mud huts on the wild moorlands of Connaught or elsewhere, as a religious and prayerful act acceptable to the Great Spirit 'in whom they live and have their being,' and *not count them in vain.* But then what becomes of your previous remarks which called forth mine? St. Paul never said, and I am sure I never thought, that *prayer* in an 'unknown tongue' was unheard by the great Hearer and Answerer of prayer; but it became the *teacher* to speak with 'understanding,' and *not* in an *unknown tongue*, lest 'he who occupieth the room of the unlearned should not be able to say Amen, seeing he understandeth not what thou sayest.' Moreover, there is no possible contact, *there is no semblance of similarity between the acceptance of a paradoxical creed as a condition of salvation, and the outpourings of a ' broken and a contrite spirit' seeking pardon and solace from its Maker and its God.* No, sir. I feel that your antipathy to Roman Catholicism, your mental vision of 'relics' and all the paraphernalia of superstitious worship, coupled with a sense of desertion and wrong inflicted by a once powerful advocate of your own Church, caused you to confound creed and prayer, and to obtrude upon and to censure me for notions which I never entertained. Most heartily do I accept and adopt all that you say respecting the meek and the lowly; and I will go further and say that a bold and arrogant spirit never *can* learn the lore of 'the kingdom of heaven.' It is the humble mind and the loving heart to which are revealed things hidden from the wise and prudent. It was to shepherds in the field rather than to the philosopher in his study to whom the 'good tidings of great joy' first came. I think there is a divine truth, as well as sweet poetry, in the lines of Coleridge—

> He prayeth best who loveth best
> All things both great and small;
> For the great God who loveth us
> Hath made and lovéd all.

Vicar. You brought forward two distinguished

clerical authors to sustain your assertion that in the whole range of Canonical Scripture there was not a verse which *per se* clearly established the doctrine of the Trinity; proved it, that is, in an unequivocal manner, such as might be expected in a book pronounced to be 'a *revelation*,' and 'the New Testament of our Lord and Saviour Jesus Christ'; therefore I felt it my duty to point out to you that one of these divines was untrustworthy and to be avoided, inasmuch as, although he was once 'numbered with us, and had obtained part of this ministry,' yet had he forsaken that 'ministry,' become a 'false teacher,' 'bringing in destructive heresies,' and otherwise proving himself an apostate from the true faith.

Parishioner. Yet, nevertheless, as he was, and *is*, like Apollos of Alexandria—'an eloquent man and mighty in the Scriptures'—his authority for the purpose I quoted remains unimpeached, and is *the more* weighty and 'mighty' from the fact that he, Newman, of all persons, is the most determined opponent of the views I hold. On this especial subject he is severely indignant. It accords with the character I have assigned to him that he should be so. As the Athanasian Creed is the most mystic and incomprehensible of the creeds of the Church, it becomes *ipso facto* the subject of his most rapturous praise. He tells us that 'it is a hymn of *profound self-prostrating homage*; it is the war-song of faith. *For myself*, I have ever felt it as the *most simple* and sublime, the *most devotional* formulary to which Christianity has given birth, *more so* even than the Veni Creator and the Te Deum' ('Grammar of Assent,' p. 128). But, Newman and Keble aside, I repeat that with the exception of the verse which the revisers of the New Testament have thrust out as spurious, there is no verse, or consecutive verses, which in their plain, grammatical, and vernacular sense show forth a Trinity. It is this fact which emboldens me to declare that it is presumptuous audacity in any man or priest to declare that whosoever doth not accept that creed, '*without doubt shall perish everlastingly.*' I maintain that so '*fundamental*' a doctrine would have been—nay, *in accordance with the eternal principles of justice, must have been*—made as plain as the decrees of the Decalogue; made as emphatic, unequivocal, and explicit as were the words of Jesus when he 'lifted up his eyes to heaven, and said, Father, the hour is come; glorify thy Son, that thy Son also may glorify thee: as *thou* hast GIVEN HIM power over all flesh, that *he* should *give* eternal life to as many as thou hast given him. And THIS IS life eternal, that they might know THEE the ONLY TRUE GOD, and Jesus Christ, whom THOU *hast SENT*' (John xvii. 1, 2).

Vicar. I am not surprised at your bringing forward that verse or verses of Scripture again, with the same emphasis as at our former interview; for, standing alone, it would compel even me to fall back *exclusively* upon the authority of the Church and the Fathers for the grounds of my Faith. Indeed it would be well, perhaps, if we all possessed the deferential spirit of St. Augustine, who said, 'I should not believe the Gospel were I not moved by the authority of the Catholic Church.' This, moreover, is the safer guide amid the conflicts, the discrepancies, the deficiencies, and the errors of the Scriptures as we now possess them. But in respect to the especial matter before us, I have only to remind you that our Lord, on finally leaving his disciples, commanded them, 'Go ye, therefore, and teach all nations, baptising them in the name of the Father, and of the Son, and of the Holy Ghost.' This of itself is a complete refutation of your position on Scriptural grounds ; and the command has been carried out through all the Christian centuries to this hour, so that it reaches us with the combined authority and weight *of the Scriptures* and *of the Church.*

Parishioner. I have heard that a distinguished Unitarian—I dislike the term as I do that of Quaker, Baptist, Methodist, and the various other nicknames under which many so-called Christians carry on their petty strifes and warfare—should say that this was the only statement in Holy Writ that gave him any anxiety. Why this in its isolated peculiarity should have done so I know not, even if it had been more distinctive of the three-in-one and one-in-three theory than it is. The record comes down to us with some suspicious circumstances. 'Some' of the disciples who were present on the occasion '*doubted*' ; and further, there is no distinct record (that I know of) of the formula having been used by the immediate disciples of Christ ; and neither Mark nor Luke, in describing the Ascension, reports the words ; and John, I need not say, omits the circumstance of the Ascension altogether from his narrative. It would have been much strengthened as an authoritative statement if in the early baptisms recorded by Luke in his 'Acts of the Apostles' the formula had been repeated. On the Pentecostal occasion, however, when 'about three thousand souls' were added to the Church, we read only that they had been called upon to 'repent' and to be 'baptised, every one of you, in the *name of Jesus Christ* for the remission of sins.' The name only of Jesus appears to have been used. The baptism of Simon the sorcerer, and also those of the people of Samaria to whom Peter and John were sent, appear to have been conducted solely 'in the name of the Lord Jesus.' The special condition which Philip enacted from the distinguished officer of great authority under Candace, Queen of the Ethiopians, in order that he might be baptised was that he should 'believe that Jesus Christ is the Son of God.' When Ananias restored Saul's sight we learn that Paul arose and 'was baptised,' but we have no detail of the ceremony. When under the preaching of Peter the 'Holy Ghost fell' upon many people in Cæsarea, the apostle commanded them 'to be baptised in *the name of the Lord.*' In none of these primary baptisms have we the triple combination of 'Father, Son, and Holy Ghost.' Again the people at Ephesus whom Paul baptised 'in the name of Jesus' had not so much as heard that 'there be a Holy Ghost.' These three names do not prove the theory of three-in-one, still less a 'Trinity' as defined in the Athanasian Creed. No great Act of Parliament is valid – that is, it does not become a part of the statutory laws of the realm—until it has been passed 'in the name of the Queen, the Lords, and the Commons'—analogous to the form you have given as necessary for the due fulfilment of the baptismal rite; but this fact does not prove the *equality* of each body or determine anything beyond the fact that the *consent* of the three powers which constitute the one government is necessary for the permanent ordination of a law. The parallel seems to me to be complete. The argument is powerless for the purpose you quote it, inasmuch as the words Jesus used immediately preceding this parting instruction set aside wholly and absolutely all pretensions of an inherent, underived, co-eternal and co-equal Godhead. His precise words were: 'All power *is given unto me* in heaven and in earth'; thus forcibly reiterating at the very close of his ministry what he had told some of his disciples at its commencement—'as the Father hath life in himself, so *hath he given the Son* to have life in himself; and hath given him authority to execute judgment also, because he is the Son of man' (John v. 27).

Vicar. The manner in which you, and others, bring one passage of Scripture into collision with another, and thus, as it were, throw a suspicion on both, convinces me that Luther and the so-called reformers erred greatly in giving the Scriptures precedence over the authority of the Church; and never was a more unfortunate aphorism than that of Chillingworth, which became almost a war-cry among the 'Evangelicals'—'The Bible, I say, the Bible only is the religion of Protestants,' for in tens of thousands of instances it has caused that Book to become, as it were, a charm, a 'fetish,' and as much an object of superstition, as you have already stated, as a relic of St. Peter, or a 'rosary,' or a cup of 'holy water'; but still, where its enunciations are clear, and harmoniously sustained throughout, they must be authoritative with all professing Christians. I must therefore again impress upon you this clear statement of St. Matthew, and correct you in your notion that it is isolated or unsupported, for we have a corresponding statement in many places, and especially in this striking passage of St. Paul in his second Epistle to the Corinthians: 'The grace of our Lord Jesus Christ, and the love of God, and the communion of the Holy Ghost.'

Parishioner. There is an aspect in which I can sympathise with you in your remarks as to the supremacy given by Protestants to what they call the Bible; but to 'the law and the testimony' is my *present* appeal, and I must not be carried away by a side issue. You have quoted, in vindication, or rather, I ought to say, as an *enforcement* of the 'Athanasian Creed,' the baptismal formula as given by St. Matthew; and I admit that it is, among weak ones, the most weighty text for its authority that I am acquainted with; but, as I have already said, not so overwhelming as to crush the numerous 'texts' which have a different issue, and more especially as the precise words are not again repeated; and, so far as we know, every baptism reported in the Scriptures was performed without them. Baptism was certainly the initiatory rite into many forms of religion; was, in fact, the outward seal that the special faith or religion had been adopted, as when John baptised. But that it had *not* the full significance and vital importance with which the Church of a later age has invested it, becomes, I think, clear, from the fact that Paul even '*thanked God*' that he had *baptised none* of them except Crispus and Gaius and the household of Stephanas. Moreover, the Jews, 'all our fathers,' as Paul called them, were 'baptised unto Moses.' This baptism *unto Moses* shows, with other things, that being baptised in the name of a person does *not establish the divinity of that person.* On the contrary, it brings forcibly to mind the prophecy recorded by Moses of the coming Christ, which *nullifies* the idea you wish to enforce by the text; for the Lord said unto *Moses*, 'I will raise them up a Prophet from among *their brethren, like unto thee*, and will *put my words* in *his* mouth; and he shall *speak unto them* all that I shall command him.' Thus Jesus was to be '*like unto Moses*,' selected from the brethren, and what he should speak was to '*be put into his mouth*,' and he would speak all that *God* should *command* him, *and no more*; and then, after centuries had rolled away, and the prophet, Jesus, had been raised up, we hear him saying, in exact fulfilment of the above prophecy : ' Then shall ye know that I am he, and that I *do nothing of myself*; but as my *Father hath taught me*, I *speak* these things' (John viii. 28). This, I think, is *demonstrative* evidence that the verse *cannot* sustain the doctrine you wish to inculcate. The order of the names may signify the distinctive precedence of the Holy Beings named — the Father first, as the primary source of all power; the Son and the Holy Ghost following, as the recipients and dispensers of that power. Be this as it may, it is to me a most impressive fact that although Peter must have been present on the occasion referred to by St. Matthew —and it is almost morally impossible that *he* should be included in the phrase 'some doubted'—yet did he not use the formula on the memorable occasion at Cæsarea, but '*commanded* them to be baptised in the name of the Lord.' This circumstance cannot be otherwise than most weighty to any honest and discriminative person. It would, I firmly believe, be *conclusive* to any judicial mind before which the question came, untainted by previous education. Ponder, reflect! There is the chief of the apostles, the one especially selected by Jesus to build up his Church, to whom the very 'keys of heaven' had been given, performing or directing the rite of baptism soon after the alleged utterance of the command and the Ascension of his Lord. Is it in the least degree probable—I had almost said, Is it morally possible—after his marvellous experiences, after his thrilling ecstasy of joy on the Mount of Transfiguration, and his anguish and remorse in the palace of the high priest, that he should in his very first official administrative act as chief of the apostles fail to carry out faithfully, implicitly, and exactly the instructions of his beloved Master? Utterly improbable! Moreover, what he did subsequent to their conversion was in exact harmony with his speech which 'pricked their heart'—a speech which nullifies all the subtle dogmas and all the 'damnatory' creeds of the after ages of the Church—a speech which sets forth in simple yet graphic and lucid language the real nature of 'Jesus of Nazareth,' his mission, and his destiny. 'Ye men of Israel, hear *these* words; Jesus of Nazareth, *a man approved of God among* you by miracles and wonders and signs, which *God did by him* in the midst of you, as ye yourselves also know: Him, being delivered by the determinate counsel and foreknowledge of God, ye have taken, and by wicked hands have crucified and slain: *whom God hath raised up*, having loosed the pains of death: because it was not possible that he should be holden of it' (Acts ii. 22-24). I must ask you to pardon this long disquisition; the *apparent* force of the verse long since impressed me, and gave me much prayerful study; and the result I have now given. There is but *one* other verse which has presented so great a perplexity, and that one is still 'nebulous' yet—cannot upon any 'doctrine of probabilities' be made to outweigh 'the cloud of witnesses' which testify that Jesus knew 'that the Father *had given* all things into his hands, and that he was come *from* God, and went *to* God' (John xiii. 3).

Vicar. To what text do you refer?

Parishioner. To the first verse of the first chapter of John, in connection with the fourteenth verse of the same chapter; for although it is insufficient to sustain the Trinitarian theory—in other words, the Athanasian Creed—yet do these first fourteen verses require the illumination of many others, and of much reflection on the sacred history for their full elucidation. Individually, I do not care to shun the difficulty by asserting with Bretschneider, Schwegler, and Strauss that the Gospel is of late date and has not apostolic authority; for although it is certain that the writer has been influenced by the philosophy of Alexandria and the writings of Plato, yet is he full of the true spirit of Christ; and if his introduction be mystic, yet are his subsequent statements so lucid and plain that to forego them would be a great loss to my argument.

Vicar. Certainly the fourteenth verse with the peculiarly Johannine expression 'sarx egeneto,' is a strong Scriptural basis for the faith, but not more so than the assertion of Paul to Timothy—'Without controversy great is the *mystery* of godliness: God was manifest in the flesh, justified in the Spirit, seen of angels, preached unto the Gentiles, believed on in the world, received up into glory' (1 Timothy iii. 16); or his equally clear statement to the saints and brethren at Colosse, as to how anxious he was that 'their hearts might be comforted, being knit together in love, and unto all riches of the full assurance of understanding, to the acknowledgment of the *mystery of God*, and of *the Father*, and of *Christ*; in whom are hid all the treasures of wisdom and knowledge' (Colossians ii. 1-3).

Parishioner. To those who have seen only their English New Testaments, and are in happy ignorance of *how* their Bibles and Testaments reached them— who to this moment read, with implicit faith in St. John's Epistle, that there are three that bear record in heaven, and that 'these three are one '—the address to Timothy would be very weighty, and approximative to the verse I have referred to. But ἐφανερώθη ἐν σαρκί is a very different expression to σὰρξ ἐγένετο; and, sad to tell, in the verse you have given the word ' God ' is not present in the best texts. Our good Bishop Ellicott, with all his strong Trinitarian faith, after minute personal inspection of the Alexandrian manuscript, declares implicitly for 'who' (ὅς), and no other uncial manuscript pretends to have the word. In no very ancient version can it be found, nor in the quotations by the earliest Fathers of the Church. Mr. Sheldon Green, in his very excellent text and translation, published by Bagster, gives the words ' He that was manifested in the flesh '; and in the ' Revised Version '—which, unfortunately, comes slowly into general use—we read ' He who was manifested in the flesh'; and thus it loses every atom of power for the purpose you have quoted it. Nor has the latter quotation, for the readings of the most ancient manuscripts differ exceedingly; some excluding the word 'Christ, many the word 'Father,' besides arranging the order of the words differently. Mr. Green, to whom I referred just now, gives this passage 'unto acquaintance with the mystery of God; in which are all the treasures of wisdom and knowledge in hidden store'; and the most learned revisers, who have recently finished their labours, omit the word 'Father' from the sentence, and assure us that the ancient authorities vary much in the text of this passage.

Vicar. All these facts show the necessity and the wisdom of the Roman Catholic Church in decreeing that the Church should be the sole interpreter of the Scriptures, and fully justify the warmth with which Pope Pius the Ninth combated the 'Bible Societies' and forbad the reading of the Scriptures by the laity except under the immediate guidance of the priests. I have never felt this so strongly as since our discussion. When it is known that the oldest manuscripts we possess, from which our New Testament *Gospels* have been derived, date nearly or quite four hundred years *after* the Christian era; when we ponder on all the possible—nay, probable—sources of error in the copying of so large a mass of writing; when we reflect on the fact that the oldest, or 'Uncials,' are written wholly in capital letters, without any kind of pause to mark the termination of a word, and remember how strongly religious *feeling* biases the mind, and that this feeling was manifested even in the days of Peter and Paul, and led to their disagreement and separation; when to these facts we add that the first written Gospel did not appear until some fifty years after the death of Christ, and that a message conveyed through many persons for many years does, by default of memory or trick of the imagination, become greatly modified or changed: then must we acknowledge the great need there is that the *Church* should be our guide and teacher in all these matters; nor can we be too thankful for the promise of Christ that he will be with her even unto the end of the world.

Parishioner. The Church of Rome in this, as in many other matters, is sagacious, consistent, and logical; but we are bound as members of the Church of England, if we are loyal to her Protestant origin, to maintain the supremacy of the Scriptures. There is, however, no gainsaying the truth of your statements respecting the many sources of error in the transmission of these documents, and the last few years have shown how countless these errors *have practically been.* As regards the untrustworthiness of oral transmission, there is a 'parlour game' which illustrates this forcibly. A short phrase is *written* on paper and read to the first silently; this person transmits it in a whisper to the second, the second to a third, and so on to a dozen persons; and I have rarely known it to be accurate when given out aloud by the last person. How much more inaccurate would it have been had the message from one to the other extended over months and years instead of as many minutes? Everyone is familiar with the illustrative tale in which 'something as black as a crow' became by transmission '*three black crows.*' As regards the great lapse of time between the appearance of the Synoptic Gospels in a written form and the occurrence of the facts recorded in them, we are relieved very much by the circumstance that St. Paul's Epistles reach us, as it were, cotemporaneously with their issue from his pen, or the pen of his amanuensis.

Vicar. As you attach this importance to the Epistles of St. Paul, permit me to draw your attention to his positive assertion of the Divinity of our Lord in his address to the Philippians—'Let this mind be in you, which was also in Christ Jesus: who, being in the form of God, thought it not robbery to be equal with God' (Philippians ii. 5, 6); and further, to an equally strong expression in his Epistle to the Colossians—'For in him' [Christ] 'dwelleth all the fulness of the Godhead bodily'. (Colossians ii. 9).

Parishioner. We both of us have had occasion to remark that by isolating a 'text' from its context great liability to error is incurred. This is especially the case in your quotation from St. Paul's letter to the Philippians. The very tone of the passage shows that there is some *moral* to be inculcated; and by reading the four verses preceding the two you have given we learn that in this portion of his Epistle the apostle is earnestly imploring the saints and the bishops and deacons of Philippi to live in amity together, to banish strife, to be like-minded, and to cultivate the grace of *humility*, and each to 'esteem others better than themselves'; and to enforce these precepts he brings forward the example of Jesus, who, although he was the 'first-begotten Son of God, in whom HE was well pleased,' yet 'made himself of no reputation taking even the form of a bond-servant' (δοῦλος), nor considering it 'a prize' or 'a thing to be *grasped at*' (as some versions have it) to be on an equality with God. As it pleased the Most High that in Christ should 'all fulness dwell,' and that men should 'honour the Son even as they honour the Father,' there could be no 'robbery' in his claim; and as to being in the form, or shape, or image of God, this statement can hardly be startling, still less confirmatory of any special divinity, to those who 'believe their Bibles' and have learnt therefrom that 'God said, Let us make *man in our image*, after our likeness . . . *so* God created *man* in his own image: in the image of God created he him' (Genesis i. 26, 27). This explains all that is implied in the words being ' in the form of God '; while his words to the Colossians which you have given would be fully understood by them in consequence of what he had *previously* said in the same Epistle; for after having described Jesus as 'the image of the invisible God,' he instantaneously adds 'the first-born of *every creature*,' and proceeds to call him also ' the head of the Church,' as well as 'the first-born from the dead (this last phrase is obscure, because it would seem from it that Paul was ignorant of the many persons who had been raised from the dead prior to the resurrection of Jesus— such as by Elijah, by our Lord himself, and others); 'that in all things he may have the pre-eminence'; '*For*' [mark that word] ' *it pleased* the Father that in him should all fulness dwell.' Thus the Colossians could by no possibility have been impressed with the idea which possessed your mind when you quoted to me the words you have done. Moreover, he earnestly implored them to continue in Christian fellowship, and prayed that their hearts may ' be comforted, being knit together in love, and unto all riches of the full assurance of understanding, to the *acknowledgment* of *the mystery of God*, and of the Father, *and of Christ*; in whom are hid all the treasures of wisdom and knowledge.' Here you cannot fail to notice the pre-eminence and the distinctiveness given to ' God,' and also the *source* from which Christ *obtained* the '*pre-eminence in all things*'; and whatever the '*fulness of the Godhead*' may mean, it was a *virtue* which Paul earnestly hoped might be possessed by '*the saints* and the *faithful* in Christ Jesus' at Ephesus, for in his Epistle to them he said that 'he bowed his knees unto *the Father* of our Lord Jesus Christ,' that they ' might be *filled with all the fulness of God*' (Ephesians iii. 14, 19). Thus in this particular, as I have shown in several others, the believers in, and followers of, Jesus became blessed by God with the same or like privileges with which HE had endowed the 'first-born,' thus realising the pathetic and impassioned prayer of Jesus and consummating his tender utterance,' The glory which *THOU gavest me I have given them*; that *they may be one,* even as *we are one*: I in them and thou in me, that *they* may *be made perfect in one*; and that the world may know that thou *hast sent me*, and *hast loved them, as thou hast loved me*' (John xvii. 22, 23).

Vicar. I have listened with patience and, indeed, with interest to your interpretation of the texts I gave to you, and to the collateral texts by which you strengthened your arguments; and I did so because all your remarks have tended to help me to a decision on a point about which I have for some time been doubtful, namely, the value of the Scriptures as a *final appeal* in matters of doctrine apart from the interpretations and decrees of the Church thereon. Our discussion has convinced me it is a mistake, and the sooner we claim and adopt the principle of the Roman Catholic Church in this particular the better for ourselves, our people, and the common Faith. Your illustration derived from so common or humble a source as a parlour game is demonstrative, in my opinion, of the improbability of oral tradition being quite accurately conveyed through many individuals for long times, and also of any manuscripts being copied faithfully for many years in succession. It is obvious that it would require a *perpetual miracle*—an 'infallibility'—based on a stronger assumption than the Church claims, as the teacher and guide of mankind in spiritual things, to have secured for us an exact and literal transcript of the words and acts of Christ and his apostles, as tens of thousands of Protestants regard the 'Bible' to be. Their opinion rests upon the most profound ignorance; and of those who become enlightened by history, research, and common sense, and learn the true nature of the Bible, too many of them at once fly off into absolute scepticism on all matters of religion; just as the French people, on finding out the fables and mummeries of Papacy, declare at once, 'There is no God!' and become Anarchists in all things. Your arguments have not influenced my judgment in the deep mysteries and verities of the Faith; but they have certainly proved to me that the Queen and Convocation erred when, in drawing up 'The Articles of Religion' for the 'Church of England,' they gave so much supremacy to Scripture as to declare that it should 'not be required of any man to accept as an "article of faith" whatsoever is not read therein, or may be proved thereby,' without having declared more distinctly and sharply *with whom* 'the proof' should finally rest; for at the present moment we have one bishop proclaiming the falsity of the Pentateuch, and another denouncing him as a heretic for his assertions! Can a house be more 'divided against itself'?

Parishioner. Nothing can be more true than that the wild views held respecting 'inspiration' and the idolatrous reverence for the Bible inculcated by the 'Evangelicals' and the founders of 'the Bible Society' upon the rising generation of the first half of the present century, begat a state of religious feeling and opinion, unfavourable to manliness and morality. It diffused a morbid and morose feeling, engendered pharisaism and spiritual pride, banished all æsthetic feeling and appreciation of art, created a dislike to intellectual research of all kinds, gave rise to set phrases in religious discourse which culminated in cant, and caused religion to consist in emotion, sentiment, and a fixed '*doctrine*,' to the discouragement of practical piety and usefulness. Further, it transformed the 'Bible' into something more hallowed and potent than 'the Ark of the Testimony'; a sealed book in its meanings to the myriads, although clear and infallible to 'the children of grace'; and thus it became a kind of 'fetish' to that large class, the lower middle class, which Matthew Arnold calls 'Philistines'; the practical outcome being that the artisans, mechanics, and labourers of our large towns capable of reading and fond of listening to voluble and frothy demagogues have become 'secularists' and scoffers on finding that the idolised 'book' was not, as they had been taught to regard it, 'the immediate, unadulterated, unchanged, and infallible Word of God.' Mischief of the direst kind has befallen our operative classes from this cause. In the past generation the 'plenary inspiration' of the Bible, that is, that every word was divine, was everywhere taught. To demur to the statement excited the greatest indignation among the followers of Simeon, Venn, and Scott. It was to the 'Evangelical' as profane a thing as to doubt the bodily presence of Jesus in a 'consecrated' wafer would be to a devout 'Anglican priest' at the present time! When the spread of education through Board schools and other influences caused men to know that the 'Bible' was an aggregation of books, written some of them hundreds of years apart, containing the history and the poetry of various individuals in various nations; that they had been *translated* from several languages, and, therefore, subject to the same errors as other books which have been written and printed in one language, and after the lapse of years have been translated, and written, and printed in the language of another country, the effect was most sad. The pious error zealously fostered by earnest and ignorant men has (as is always the case with falsehood) culminated in calamity. The scientific errors, the histories of immorality and crime, which are to be found within its pages, have been distorted and exaggerated, and the volume which was once reverenced as a sacred thing is treated with scorn, even as a savage has battered to pieces some 'graven image' to which he had prayed in vain for rain, food, or revenge on his foes. The 'Bibliolatry' of the past, this mistaken fanaticism, has produced such a revulsion of feeling that it has now come to pass that the grandest, the best of books, the book verily containing the words of God, is treated by tens of thousands of persons with neglect, and by hundreds with ridicule or scorn.

Vicar. The picture you have drawn is a sad one,

dark 'as earthquake and eclipse,' but I fear that it is a true one. The literature of the day, whether we look at the daily newspapers, the monthly magazines, or the quarterly reviews, or, sadder still, if we study the essays produced at scientific societies by the greatest *savants*, the Darwins, Spencers, Tyndals, Huxleys, and Cliffords of the age, is marked by a 'scepticism' which would have shocked our forefathers. If we listen to conversation at the clubs by leading politicians, judges, barristers, and physicians of the day, we cannot but observe that the old reverence for, and belief in, many of the statements of Holy Writ have passed away. The vulgar scoff of the early Georgian era may not be heard (the courtesy which high culture creates forbids this), but it would be sheer folly to conceal the fact that many a Biblical record received with reverence by our forefathers is relegated to the chronicle 'of old wives' fables' by the cultured minds of the present generation. No marvel, then, that smatterers in science, whom 'a little knowledge puffeth up,' that designing demagogues and 'agitators' should inflame and intoxicate the minds of the ignorant and discontented with statements and theories calculated to subvert and destroy respect for all order and authority, whether religious or social. The outlook of the future is most gloomy, but may the Great Controller of all events, who can cause 'the wrath of man to praise him,' and 'hath made all things for himself, yea, even the wicked for the day of evil,' direct it to his glory, and the happiness of mankind.

Parishioner. 'Shall not the Judge of all the earth do right?' Doubtless he will. In all our large cities, however, the revulsion is tremendous and widespread. It is, indeed, correspondent with that great law of physics which enforces that the rebound shall be proportionate to the momentum of the original force applied, and the fanaticism in respect to the immediate verbal inspiration, and consequent sacredness of the 'Bible,' was extreme. *Bibliolatry*—for this *it was*—prevailed almost universally. To be engaged reverentially in any manner with the Bible, no matter how mechanically, was deemed a pious act; a work not simply 'well pleasing in the sight of God,' but more so than a faithful performance of the secular duties of life; and consequently they employed themselves in counting its chapters and verses and duly recording them. Nothing in relation thereto was frivolous, but all was 'holy.' Consequently we are gravely informed that the conjunction 'and' occurs thirty-five thousand five hundred and thirty-five times in the pages of the Old Testament, and that in the New Testament it occurs ten thousand six hundred and eighty-four times. Further, we have been told that the twenty-first verse of the seventh chapter of Ezra contains all the letters of the alphabet; and, not contented with numbering the books, chapters, and verses, devotees have assured us that there are seven hundred and seventy-three thousand words; and, further still, that there are three million, five hundred and sixty-six thousand four hundred and eighty letters in the 'Holy Bible.' 'Churchmen' and 'Dissenters' alike smile or pity, according to the depth of their Christianity, when such things are told of Mohammedans in respect to the 'Koran,' wholly unconscious in respect to this kind of idolatry, of 'the beam in their own eye,' while so very cognisant of 'the mote' in the eye of their Mohammedan brother. The revulsion has, as has been already said, however, set in, and the consequences have been most disastrous. Let us hope, however, that the swing of the pendulum will right itself; that the darkness may be the precursor of a purer and greater light; that the widespread infidelity may be of short duration; and that the removal of this vast Biblical error will be like the removal of some huge tumour by a skilful surgeon, which, although painful and bewildering in its immediate action, is followed by vigorous health and lasting vigour. The Great Arbiter doeth all things well. I often think that great poets are true prophets, for even the timid and despondent Cowper, despite his Calvinistic creed, could in his wiser moments write:

> *Heavenward* all things *tend.* For all were once
> Perfect, and all must be at length restored.
> *So God has greatly purposed*; who would else
> In his dishonoured works himself endure
> Dishonour, and be wronged without redress.

These lines seem to convey a sublime truth, however much we may demur to the incidental statement 'for all were once perfect.' The modern teachings of 'biological' science assure us that Tennyson was the more accurate, who, while accepting the theory that heavenward all things tend, tells us—

> They say,
> The solid earth whereon we tread
> In tracts of fluent heat began,
>   And grew to seeming-random forms,
>   The seeming prey of cyclic storms,
> Till at the last arose the man;
> Who throve and branch'd from clime to clime,
>   The *herald of a higher race*,
>   And of himself in higher place,
> If so he type this work of time

Within himself, from more to more;
  Or, crown'd with attributes of woe
  Like glories, move his course, and show
That life is not as idle ore,

But iron dug from central gloom,
  And heated hot with burning fears,
  And dipt in baths of hissing tears,
And *batter'd with the shocks of doom*

To shape and use. Arise and fly
  The reeling faun, the sensual feast;
  Move upward, *working out the beast*,
And let the ape and tiger die.

Vicar. The lines you quote teem with thought and poesy; but I must protest against them as most erroneous and heterodox, warring against the very first principles of our faith, against the teachings of the Bible as to the creation and the prime perfection and fall of man; and as a corollary against the great Atonement as a propitiation for sin, and the redemption of mankind from the consequences of the Fall.

Parishioner. As you have already said, the Bible needs an interpreter. If we sought in its pages for an authentic statement of the creation of man where should we look—to the first chapter of 'Genesis,' or to the second chapter of that book? for the description of the creation differs in each, and has evidently been written by two distinct historians. I will not, however, attempt to disguise from you that I accept neither as accurate literal descriptions of the creation and fall of man. I look upon the story as an imaginative narrative akin to that of 'Paradise Lost,' which Milton has based upon it. No geologist of repute will admit that this world is not six thousand years old, as the chronology of our Bibles would imply. Indeed, most of the 'defenders of the faith' have given this up as a baseless proposition; and to reconcile the statements of the Bible with the known facts of geology various devices have been resorted to. As in aid of the doctrine of the Trinity words and verses have been forged and added to the manuscripts, so to reconcile the first chapter of Genesis with the indisputable facts of science, *word-torture* has been used. 'In the beginning' has been wrested from its context and *made* to mean or signify a pause of æons ages prior to the creation of day and night. The word 'day' has been made to do duty for thousands of years, or any indefinite time; although we are distinctly told that the 'evening and morning were the first day,' and so on through a consecutive series of days and creative acts until we reach the seventh day; and then we learn that 'God blessed the seventh day and sanctified it, because that in it he had rested from all his work which God had created and made' (Genesis ii. 3). This perversion and trifling with words for theological purposes have been sanctioned by the highest dignitaries of the Church, notwithstanding that the same Moses[1] who tells of this procedure of creation *also* tells us after his interview with God on the top of Sinai that the seventh day was to be hallowed for ever, because God had in *six days* created the world and its denizens, and rested on the seventh day. For centuries this commandment has been literally observed by the Hebrews, to whom it was given, in whose *language it was written*, and the word 'day' has been by them regarded as the time between the rising and setting of the

[1] Exodus xix. 20.

sun. A book that needs *such* manipulation cannot be of Divine origin. To 'reconcile' *known facts* with Biblical history, Dean Buckland, in his great 'Bridgewater Treatise,' resorted to this tricksy expedient; and to reconcile the irreconcilable, the scholarship of many divines (good Bishop Ellicott among the number) and the marvellous talents and skilled geological labours of Hugh Miller have been employed in vain. 'The testimony of the rocks' was adverse, and the zealous advocate of a 'pious' theory died overwhelmed with despair. Very recently, I am quite sorry to say, forty bishops, and scores of clergymen, have testified their approval of the book of a pseudo-scientist, who, adopting the pretty theory of Kurst, of a series of panoramic visions passing before the mind of a tranced seer, has daringly stated that the description ascribed to Moses harmonises in every particular with the facts of geology and biological science. By such expedients the tales of Baron Munchausen and the travels of Samuel Gulliver may be made to appear as veritable history.

Vicar. When I said that many a Biblical record accepted as a fact by our forefathers had been relegated to the regions of 'old wives' fables' by scientific persons, I did not anticipate that *you* would throw aside the authority of Revelation, because throughout our discussion you have persistently said to 'the law and the testimony,' and by the Scriptures, and the Scriptures only, you declared that you would justify your non-acceptance of one of the oldest creeds of the Holy Catholic Church. Am I to understand that you have ceased to regard the Book as Divinely inspired—as being, in fact, *the Word of God?*

Parishioner. I think I have already proved—*demonstrated*, in fact, as far as words can demonstrate anything—that the Holy Scriptures give no support to what is called 'The Athanasian Creed'; and I shall further show from its hallowed words—hallowed by age and by the reverence and the love of the highest and purest minds of our race—that the doctrines or ideas contained in that Creed are opposed to the words and the acts of our blessed Lord, to the sayings of the Evangelists, to the teachings of Paul and Peter and James, and to the inspired utterances of the sages and prophets of the Old Testament. As, however, what is called 'the Bible' is not one book, but many: as the writers of some of these books are unknown: as they were written hundreds of years apart: as they vary in moral qualities, and are often contradictory the one to the other: as they have been changed verbally in most important particulars by passing from one language to another, and by the design as well as by the unintentional errors of copyists: as some of the acts applauded therein are revolting to the highest and purest feelings which Christianity inculcates and fosters, I cannot regard the whole Bible as '*the* Word of God,' although I most sincerely believe that in no other book in the world can we find the words of God so frequently and so clearly enforced.

Vicar. St. Paul, in his second Epistle to Timothy, distinctly writes that '*all* scripture is given by inspiration of God, and is profitable for doctrine, for reproof, for correction, and for instruction in righteousness' (iii. 16).

Parishioner. There again is an illustration of the need of an authentic interpreter of the Scriptures, and also an illustration of how fallacious the Bible may, and has, become in the hands of the masses. The text you have given is most misleading through an erroneous translation; it should *not* have been printed '*All scripture is given* by inspiration,' but, as it was written by Paul, '*Every scripture inspired of God is profitable*,' which is a very different matter. I joyfully and most gratefully accept the fact recorded by James, 'that every *good* gift and every perfect gift is from above, and cometh down from the Father of Lights, with whom is no variableness' nor 'shadow of turning.' Not only in the 'old time,' but *in the present*, do I firmly believe that 'holy men of God spake as they were moved by the Holy Ghost' (2 Peter i. 21). God is 'the same to-day, yesterday, and for ever'; and as his wisdom is infinite his power boundless, and his love such that 'his mercy endureth for ever,' *what HE inspires* must ever be in principle *changeless*, harmonious, and consistent with HIS own attributes of justice and truth. His decrees cannot be contingent on circumstances, or change with clime or time. But it seems to me absolutely monstrous that men and women should, as they practically do, bow with slavish fear to every word contained in a bundle of numerous books which, being bound in one cover, is called 'The Bible,' written they know not when or by whom, *and yet* at the same time believe that the operation and teachings of the Most Holy Spirit of God were limited to the land of the Hebrews, and to an epoch which ended with the life of the writer of the mystic book called 'The Revelation of St. John the Divine.' I marvel that it has not aroused hundreds of others besides George Fox into a state of spiritual indignation and frenzy that men should thus limit to place and time the operations of that Divine agency which Jesus told Nicodemus 'bloweth where it listeth.' Moreover, it seems verging on profanity that the external works of God, the eternal laws of justice and morality, the voice of conscience, and the teachings of nature should be tested exclusively by this ancient volume, composite in language and theme, rather than that these great principles should in themselves be the tests of the truthfulness or untruthfulness of a record written by many men at various times and various places. God is revealing himself continuously. Throughout the ages

> An increasing purpose runs;
> And the thoughts of men are widen'd
> By the progress of the suns.

Vicar. My fears are greatly intensified by your remarks. I regret deeply that you do not regard the whole of the *canonical* books as received by the Church of England as directly and exclusively inspired, and not to be contravened by anything whatever. Certainly it would have been better for the avoidance of confusion and the check of schism if the *interpretation* or *meaning* of the Scriptures had been exclusively vested in the Church; but I shall be unable to recognise you as a Christian, still less as a member of the 'holy Catholic Church,' if (as I understand) you do *not* accept *the general sense* of all the canonical books as undoubtedly inspired, and every way indisputable. I hope I may have misunderstood you in this matter.

Parishioner. I must frankly tell you that you have not mistaken me. My intense desire is to be lucid and plain. Truth is dearer to me than life itself. I am battling for no 'idol,' whether of the 'den,' the 'market,' or the 'theatre,' to use Bacon's figures. I have no theory to uphold. The dreams and convictions and superstitions of my earlier time have been wrenched from my soul; a 'new birth' has been realised with sobbing and pain, as all births are. But *this* is past—I have learnt to know that God is ever ready to commune with the spirit of man, to 'send forth his light and his truth' to all who yearn for them. His inspiration is ceaseless; I do not believe that God was more present, more immanent in the grey morning of the world than now. HE speaks to receptive souls even now, as fully as HE did when the young Samuel, from his sleeping cot in the temple, cried, 'Speak, Lord, for thy servant heareth.' But there are delusive voices as there are 'lying spirits,' and it becometh the wise not to believe 'every spirit, but try the spirits whether they are of God: because many false prophets are gone out into the world' (1 John iv. 1); and one infallible test is *consistency*, the never-failing consentient harmony between *all* the words and all the works of God 'in all places of his dominion,' whether in the domain of nature, or the spiritual kingdom, or the heart of man. You speak of 'canonical books' as 'inspired.' Who decreed, out of the numberless 'gospels' which existed in the early centuries of Christianity, which of the many should be 'canonical' and which excluded? Perhaps one of the most august, certainly one of the most influential, of the numerous 'Councils' of the Church was the eighteenth, or General Council of Trent, which assembled in A.D. 1545, and continued (with interruptions) through the pontificates of Pope Paul III., Julius III., and Pius IV., to 1563. This Council decreed what books out of the mass of so-called 'Scriptures' before them should be *canonical*, and pronounced an anathema of eternal condemnation upon all who declined to accept any one of them so decreed. The *Church of England* has *excluded* several of the books *thus authorised* from '*canonical*' rank, and yet, with her accustomed inconsistency in spiritual things, she authorises some of these very 'uncanonical' books (canonical according to the Council of Trent) to be read at her *daily* services, but will not allow them to be read on the Sabbath Day. Do you expect me to accept these books, which are sufficiently good to be read on 'week-days,' but not sufficiently 'holy' to be read on Sundays, as '*inspired*'?

Vicar. Most decidedly not. I distinctly said the whole of the '*canonical books*' as *received by the* '*Church of England*,' and *not* to accept them is, *ipso facto*, to exclude yourself from the ranks of her sons.

Parishioner. The Church of England has deliberately refused to accept into her canon as *inspired* several books which the more ancient Church (from whom she derives all her pretensions to be regarded as a Church having apostolical succession and all that it involves) declares to be 'canonical,' nay, assures us that they 'have been dictated either by Christ's own word of mouth or by the Holy Ghost, and preserved by a continuous succession in the Catholic Church,' and has declared with the same emphasis as the younger Church has of the Athanasian Creed, 'If anyone receive not *as sacred* and canonical these same books entire, with all their parts, let him be anathema!' As an individual, upon 'Protestant' principles, i.e. the right of private judgment, I claim the same privilege of selection as did the 'Reformation' Committee upon the books which the ancient Church had in the most solemn manner declared to have been derived from 'Christ's own word of mouth' or 'by the Holy Ghost.' I do so because, after all, both in the 'Council of Trent' and the 'Reformation' Chamber the reason or judgment of man was the final appeal as to which of the books were 'inspired' and which were not, and most certainly some of the books which the 'Protestant' Church *refused to receive* into her canon are far 'more profitable for doctrine, for reproof, for correction, and for instruction in righteousness' than others which she has accepted, and which you call upon me to receive as directly and wholly the inspired word of God.

Vicar. What can you mean by such a daring statement? Surely you do not presume to say that the 'Books of Maccabees' and the history of 'Bel and the Dragon' are to be compared, for the purposes described by Paul to Timothy, with the writings of Isaiah and David?

Parishioner. No, but I say that the 'Book of Solomon' and 'Ecclesiasticus,' approved by the Council of Trent, are better adapted for such purposes than is 'The Book of Canticles,' which has been preferred before them, which has been retained as 'inspired,' while the other two are denied that distinction. It is an insult to common sense to hold up the Canticles as the direct 'Word of God.' I know what to expect from the credulous, the ignorant, and the fanatical in speaking thus of this book; a book which, by-the-by, used to be an especial favourite among the 'Evangelicals,' and over which I have known more than one young lady go into *hysterical* raptures. The two books I have named abound in sublime thoughts and words full of wisdom, whereas the 'Canticles' read like voluptuous love-songs, and never could have been considered anything otherwise than an amatory poem had not some interpolator introduced parenthetically into a manuscript the words 'Vox Christi,' and some other 'pious' copyist divided the songs into chapters, and put plausible 'headings' to each chapter, by which Christ and the Church are made to take the places of the lover and his beloved. Origen calls it an epithalamium in the form of a drama; he soon, however, clothes it with allegory. Theodore, Bishop of Mopsuestia, the friend and schoolfellow of St. Chrysostom, wisely sets aside the allegory, and regards them as a series of amatory poems written by Solomon to win the affections of an Ethiopian princess; a description which the entire language of the book fully justifies. Be this as it may, when two great Churches like the Western and the Anglican differ as to which books of the Bible *are* inspired, and which books are *not* inspired, a prudent and conscientious man will exercise his own judgment as to which of the decrees he shall accept. In Solomon's Song I recognise strong and passionate love, exquisite poetry, and most voluptuous imagery—imagery not exceeded in lyric sweetness by Anacreon or Moore. What more amatory than, 'Behold, thou art fair, my love; behold, thou art fair; thou hast doves' eyes within thy locks: thy hair is as a flock of goats, that appear from Mount Gilead. Thy teeth are like a flock of sheep that are even shorn, which came up from the washing; whereof every one bear twins, and none is barren among them. Thy lips are like a thread of scarlet, and thy speech is comely : thy temples are like a piece of a pomegranate within thy locks. Thy neck is like the tower of David builded for an armoury, whereon there hang a thousand bucklers, all shields of mighty men. Thy two breasts are like two young roes that are twins, which feed among the lilies. Until the daybreak and the shadows flee away I will get me to the mountain of myrrh, and to the hill of frankincense. Thou art all fair, my love; there is no spot in thee.' Do not these words breathe of 'the clime of the East, the land of the sun'? The metaphor of the 'two young roes that are twins, which feed among the lilies' seems to me unsurpassed for sensuous beauty in the odes of Horace, the poems of Byron, or the songs of Sappho ; but, in the words of St. James, 'this wisdom descendeth, not from above, but is earthly and sensual,' whereas in the thirteenth chapter of 'The Wisdom of Solomon' I read noble words, which, like Adam's morning hymn in Milton's 'Paradise Lost,' appear instinct with 'inspiration' of the highest kind. 'Surely vain are all men by nature who are ignorant of God, and could not out of the good things that are *seen* know him *that is* ; neither by considering the works did they acknowledge the workmaster, but deemed either fire, or wind, or the swift air, or the circle of the stars, or the violent waters, or the lights of heaven *to be the gods* which govern the world ; with whose beauty if they being delighted took them to be gods, let them know *how much better the Lord of them is*, for *the first author of beauty hath created them.* But if they were astonished at their power and virtue, let them understand by them how much *mightier he is that made them. For by the greatness and beauty of the creatures proportionably the Maker of them is seen.*' Here is the philosophy of Paley and Ray, and the best of the Bridgewater Treatises condensed in a passage of poetic prose which clings to the memory for ever.

Vicar. You seem to forget that the 'Canticles,' which you regard as simply a human composition, has been accepted *as 'canonical'* by *both Churches*, and ought therefore to be received by you with reverence and unquestioning faith. Moreover, the one from which you quote with approval has been dismissed as apocryphal by your own Church. It grieves me, however, to observe that you make so little distinction between what is ordinarily called 'genius' and that which Christians of all denominations regard as 'inspiration,' namely, the infusion of ideas into the mind by the holy Spirit of God. Your reference to Milton's poem, for instance, and again the fearlessness with which you bring the most solemn records to the test of some experiment or the facts of physical science.

Parishioner. A *fact is a fact*—nothing *can* gainsay or overthrow it. I *do* say *fearlessly* and *confidently* that if a legend, tradition, or 'historic statement' come down to us, no matter for how long a period or under whatever *authority*, alleging something which is contrary to the evidence of our senses as corrected by experience, by mental analysis, and by all the tests which cumulated science has provided for that end, an honest, God-fearing man cannot do otherwise than *disbelieve it.* No matter how loud may be the cry, 'Touch not, taste not, handle not,' he will not be 'beguiled' by a show of wisdom in will, worship, and humility; for he will be unable to feel that there is *true reverence* in accepting such legends, 'such ordinances,' as St. Paul says, 'after the commandments of men,' or, as Isaiah puts it, 'as is taught by the precepts of men.' A legend, tradition, or command opposed to *such* evidence is *human*, and *not divine*, no matter how clothed with seeming sanctity, hoary antiquity, and priestly authority. The *words* and the WORKS of the Almighty *must be* consistent and harmonious. In the very nature of things—from the absolute perfection which is inseparable from Godhead—they *cannot* contradict each other. The child of God recognises in this great truth the handwriting of *his Father*, and knows therefore the alleged 'inspired' tradition, which is in conflict or contradiction to some known natural fact, to be a human fallacy or a forgery. To accept it would be to dishonour his Father, to place himself in a like position to the Scribes and Pharisees of Jerusalem to whom Jesus said, 'Ye have made the *commandment of God* of none effect by *your tradition*' (Matthew xv. 6). So long as we are ignorant of the facts which do stand in opposition to the alleged inspired tradition, as is the case with thousands of simple believers, *then* is our faith honest and sincere, and cannot be offensive to a just God; but when *the fact* and the *alleged* word *are known* to be irreconcilable, then to accept the latter becomes 'voluntary humility' to a mere human decree; it is 'to bow down his head as a bulrush,' to the mere 'ordinances of men'; it is to *reverse* the noble conduct of Peter and the other apostles who answered and said to the Council and High Priest, 'We ought to obey God rather than men.' Yea, it is as wrongful a thing as to worship 'the circle of the stars, or the violent waters, or the lights of heaven' rather than 'The Author of beauty who has created them.' For a geologist to ignore the *facts* of geology because they war against the legend of Moses is to honour Moses rather than the Great Creator of whom Moses wrote.

Vicar. Am I to understand you that if Charles Lyell or Charles Darwin say one thing, and Moses or Ezekiel state something which is not in accordance with the theories of these philosophers, then the assertions of the Prophets are to be disregarded? This is indeed displacing the Bible from the high place it has held for centuries and clothing it with dishonour.

Parishioner. I took great pains to emphasise the word '*fact*,' because, with the distinguished German scientist Virchow, I affirm that the speculative ideas of philosophers should be kept wholly distinct from scientific *facts*. Their theories do not come within the assured domain of science; they may contain possible truth, but cannot be regarded as *truth* until they have passed the region of speculation, and by accurately tested demonstrative evidence—evidence sifted and tried under every possible condition—are shown to be not ideas only, but *facts*, or *truths*. Joshua and Habakkuk tell us that 'the sun stood still.' The former writes: 'The sun stood still, and the moon stayed, until the people avenged themselves upon their enemies. Is not this written in the book of Jasher? So the sun stood still in the midst of heaven, and hasted not to go down about a whole day. And there was no day like that before it or after it, that the Lord hearkened unto the voice of a man, for the Lord fought for Israel' (Joshua x. 13, 14). Isaiah tells us that the Lord 'will gather together the dispersed of Judah from *the four corners of the earth*' (Isaiah xi. 12); and St. John the Divine assures us that he 'saw four angels standing on the *four corners* of the earth, holding the four winds of the earth, that the wind should not blow on the earth, nor on the sea, nor on any tree' (vii. 1). Now these historic details do not war against a *theory*, or *theories*, of any kind, but taken literally they are misrepresentations of existing things, and could not, therefore, be received by me as the inspired utterances of the Almighty, but merely the figurative expressions or poetic descriptions of the respective writers. It has been established beyond all cavil that the sun does *not* move round the earth in twenty-four hours, and that it is the earth which revolves around the sun. It is only a few monomaniacs who think that the earth is a square plain, having 'four corners,' and therefore I say that the above utterances are the statements of fallible men like unto Herodotus or Livy. Moses describes the coney, or rabbit, and also the hare, as 'unclean . . . because he cheweth the cud, but divideth not the hoof' (Leviticus xi. 5, 6). St. Paul, in one of the most sublime parts of his epistle, writes thus strongly: 'Thou fool, that which thou sowest is not quickened, *except it die*.' Each of these statements is contrary to *fact*: the hare does *not* 'chew the cud'; the seed which a man sows, and which reappears as grain, does *not die*; the outer *wrappers* of the germ die, or undergo physical changes, but the *germ*, the essential *seed*, remains alive, and develops 'first the blade, then the ear, after that the full corn in the ear.' Now, as I *know*, from the evidence of my senses, corrected by my reason, that the sun does *not* sensibly move along the heavens, that the earth is *not* a square plain with 'four corners,' that the hare does *not* 'chew the cud,' and that a corn seed does *not* die before it becomes fruitful, I say that the writers of these statements—Moses, Isaiah, St. John the Divine, and Paul of Tarsus—were not *divinely inspired* to write them, but wrote them simply as truthful men anxious to convey the truth to their hearers or readers, and that they *did* convey a truth, but associated with so much error as to demonstrate that 'plenary inspiration' did not belong to them; their language was truthful so far, as they, fallible men possessing only the knowledge of their age and race, *could* make it; their words were not false words; they were *intended* to convey, and *did* convey, the convictions of the speakers. As good men unaided by *special* Divine power, they could not have done otherwise than they did; they dealt honestly with the semblances of things; for the sun *does appear* to move, the earth *does appear* to have four corners—North, East, West, and South—the hare *does* move his jaws like unto a ruminating animal, and the grain *does appear* to *die*; yet, notwithstanding, and nevertheless, this confusion of appearance and reality proves that for us to reverence the Bible as an organic whole, to receive each and every statement of every writer therein as the immediate *inspired* Word of God, is to commit the same error in respect to the words of these men—to the *words* of Paul, for instance—as did the men of Lycaonia in respect to the *persons* of Paul and Barnabas when they 'lifted up their voices, and said, The gods are come down to us in the likeness of men' (Acts xiv. 11). Individually, I cannot perceive the necessity of a man being 'inspired' to narrate truthfully a fact within his own cognisance. On the other hand, I have no desire to withdraw my former statement as to the 'inspiration' of all men who have clothed noble thoughts in noble language, or who have been prompted to self-sacrificing and noble deeds—as Paul before Felix, Festus, and Agrippa on Mars Hill, and in the dungeon at Rome; Servetus at Geneva; Huss at Constance; Luther at Erfurt, and before the Diet at Worms; Howard in the prison dens of England and Europe, and the plague-smitten regions of Tartary; Clarkson as he sat on a stone-heap on the road-side in Cambridgeshire, and vowing a vow to grapple to the death with slavery; Latimer in the Star Chamber, and on the burning pile at Oxford; Ambrose as he confronted the bloodthirsty Emperor Theodosius; John Wesley among the miners in Cornwall; Henry Martyn translating the Scriptures into Oriental languages under the burning sun of Persia; John Williams at Rarotonga and Erromanga; and Moffat and Livingstone in the far-off barbarous regions of Southern Africa.

Vicar. Really these are bold statements from one who so positively stated his great reverence for Scripture and was so emphatic in his appeals 'to the law and the testimony' in support of his arguments. Therefore I must remind you that the *prophets* could not have been otherwise than Divinely inspired; the future which they portrayed was hidden from mere mortal vision or mental foresight. Moreover, we have the direct authority of Scripture itself on this point, for Peter tells us: 'The prophecy came not in the old time by the will of man: but holy men of God spake as they were moved by the Holy Ghost' (2 Peter i. 21); and so all-important to the sustenance of the faith is this word of prophecy, that St. Peter calls it 'a more sure word' even than his own personal testimony as to the voice of recognition, which from heaven proclaimed Jesus as God's beloved Son, in whom he was well pleased, and which he and his companions, James and John, 'heard when we were with him in the Holy Mount.' This very statement shows that the words of prophets, inspired thus, transcend all *human* testimony; for assuredly no higher human testimony could hardly be asked for—or if asked for, obtained—than that of three men of moral worth testifying to a fact seen and heard by all three of them simultaneously.

Parishioner. This is the second or third time you have been somewhat satirical as to my varying estimate of the Scriptures; but I fail to recognise any inconsistency on my part. As I have already said, I rely wholly on their teaching as to the Nicene and Athanasian Creeds, and shall yet revert to them in connection with these; although to do so *further* seems superfluous iteration, for the texts already quoted render my position Scripturally unassailable. To quote more texts certainly entitles me to the satire, 'And thrice he routed all his foes, and *thrice he slew the slain.*' Yet, to show to you what a wealth of evidence sustains my conclusions, more Scriptural proofs shall be forthcoming. I have no desire (for it is no part of my present purpose) to controvert the powerful passage you have given as to the 'sure word of prophecy,' although it is taken from an Epistle which has been more discussed, perhaps, than any other in the Canon, and that Eusebius, Didymus of Alexandria, and St. Jerome regarded it with more than distrust. Whether Peter, at the time of stating the words, if he did state them, began to feel that his experience in the Mount may have been illusory, I cannot say; but of all the stupendous illustrations of human weakness I have ever heard, none approaches this alleged fact in the life of Peter: that he, who had seen with his bodily eyes Jesus transfigured before him, so that 'his face did shine as the sun and his raiment was white as the light'—saw and heard Moses and Elias (who had been dead for centuries) talking with Jesus—that this very Peter who so appreciated the celestial manifestation as to exclaim to Jesus, 'LORD, it is good for us to be here!' and to propose the building of three tabernacles, 'one for thee, one for Moses, and one for Elias'; and heard, moreover, 'a voice out of a bright cloud, which said, 'This is my beloved Son, in whom I am well pleased; *hear ye him*' (Matt. xvii. 1-4)—that alone, of all the disciples of Jesus, this very Peter, *after this* august experience and *celestial demonstration*, should 'curse and swear, saying, I know not this man of whom ye speak,' is the most marvellous fact recorded in the annals of history. Your narration of the circumstance, however, is hardly accurate, for we have not *three men* testifying to a fact which *they saw simultaneously*; for it is most astonishing that neither John in his Gospel nor James in his Epistle alludes to this miraculous manifestation of Divine power, this stupendous attestation of the relation in which Christ stood to the SUPREME.

Vicar. It is painfully evident to me that, however much, for the end you have in view, you may quote the Bible, there is a large portion of the 'Canonical' Scriptures which you have ceased to accept as authentic. You state that you have no desire to controvert the powerful passage I gave as 'to the sure word of prophecy'; but you immediately hinted that it was obtained from a doubtful source, or a source more doubtful than other portions of the Scripture. But even if it came from a solely secular source, it recites *a fact* which is historically true, for most assuredly men in 'the old time' *did* prophesy; and that they *were* 'moved by the Holy Ghost is *proved* by the circumstance that their 'prophecies' forestalled history by many centuries, and yet were they verbally accurate and true. Thus, Jacob, in his dying moments, more than sixteen hundred years before the coming of Christ as the Messiah, distinctly assured his sons that 'the *sceptre* shall not depart from Judah . . . until Shiloh come' (Genesis xlix. 10); and as respects the history of the Transfiguration, if neither James or John refer to this sublime incident, it is most fully recorded by *all* of the synoptic writers— Matthew, Mark, and Luke; so that the event has three historians, beside that of one of those immediately at the scene.

Parishioner. My views on inspiration have been expressed already; and if the Church had adopted centuries ago the opinions which are *now* published by some of her most advanced theologians, the unbelief which now pervades the minds of the vast majority of the intellectual classes and the mechanics and artisans of Europe would never have sprung up. If irrational and absurd theories, and equally absurd facts, had not been pressed upon them by authority; the 'Bible' had not been represented to them as the 'Koran' is to myriads of Mohammedans—as divine and sacred to its *minutest syllable*—they would never have turned upon it with the disdain and contempt they now do. If its *true character* had been taught them they would have accepted the good and rejected the evil; but as *all* is proclaimed as the infallible 'Word of God,' they turn with disdain from the 'Word,' and, alas! even dispute the existence of its alleged Author. But to revert to your statement as to the literal fulfilment of Jacob's prophecy after the lapse of so many centuries, even this prophecy, which has for ages been quoted by divines as a most illustrative proof of 'the sure word of prophecy,' is melting away under the advanced and advancing knowledge of the present day. It happened to me individually that nearly thirty years ago I was acquainted with a most intelligent Jew, and I asked him whether he had ever read the 'Old Testament' in the English language, and in the version generally accepted by the Protestants of this country. He said he had read it most carefully. I then asked him whether it accorded with the *Hebrew* Scriptures as he read them. He replied, 'For the most part, but there *is one most momentous misstatement* as to what Jacob said respecting the coming of Shiloh. If our Hebrew records contained it we could *not be* as now, hoping that a Messiah would yet come to the redemption of the Jews from their long wanderings, and their restoration to power, prosperity, and greatness in Palestine; for most assuredly hath " the sceptre departed from Judah," and there is no " gathering of the people," and they are now as much as ever scattered and dispersed over every nation of Europe and Asia, although not now treated as they once were, except perhaps in the

M

dominions of Russia. Many individual Jews are very wealthy and most influential in various countries; but as a *nation* we are kingless and without a sceptre, and yet the Messiah has *not* come to us.' Since this conversation I have been informed by good Hebrew scholars that the verse, properly translated from the Hebrew into English, would give to 'Shiloh' the meaning of a *place*, and not a person. The very oldest version of the Old Testament, the Septuagint, gives the verse as follows: 'A prince shall not fail from Judah, nor a captain out of his loins, until the things come that are laid up for him.' This is by no means so definite a prophecy of the realised Messiah. But on this subject, as on several others, I am waiting patiently for the revision of the 'Old Testament' by those learned Hebrew scholars and critics who are now engaged upon this most important and most serious labour.[1]

Vicar. Looking at the ripe scholars and sound divines who have been so long labouring at this important task, there is not the slightest probability of the general text being so altered as to harmonise with your statements.

Parishioner. It may not be so altered in its general statements, but I shall certainly be surprised if the individual text to which I have referred be not altered

[1] Eighteen months have passed since the above was written, and the new revision of the Old Testament has since appeared, and the words 'until Shiloh come' remain as in the old, but in a marginal note the following words are given : ' till he come to Shiloh'; and for the sentence ' Unto him shall the *gathering* of the people be,' the revised Bible gives ' Unto him shall the *obedience* of the people be,' while a marginal note reads ' having the obedience of the peoples.' Moreover, as a matter of historical fact, the 'sceptre' *had* departed from Judah many years before the birth of Jesus of Nazareth.

in the manner I have indicated. The days of 'bibliolatry' are, however, numbered. The manner in which even clergymen abstain from reading in their families the *whole* Bible : the fact that, instead of being as formerly the *chief book read in schools*, it is now, by statute, made exceptionable in Board schools, and indeed optional with each individual scholar : the dread which many intelligent mothers have of their daughters reading many of the chapters of the Old Testament : the fact that dignitaries of the Church, such as a prebend of a cathedral and a chaplain in ordinary to the Queen, have felt it prudent to publish 'A School and Children's *Bible*,' '*shorter*, and at the same time better adapted for the use of children or *young persons*' : all show that the superstitious reverence of the past is fading away, and that the most thoughtful and pious Christians are recognising the truth written by Professor Jowett, the Regius Professor of Greek in Oxford University, more than twenty years ago (which *then* roused indignation), namely, that 'the Bible *should be interpreted like any other book.*' Because it has not been so, it has, to use the words of that profound scholar, come to pass that 'the Book in which we believe all religious truth to be contained is the most uncertain of all books, because interpreted by arbitrary and uncertain methods.' I am firmly convinced, from the observations and reflections of forty years, that the unbelief, the 'agnosticism' which now pervades the intellectual professions, and the 'upper' and 'lower' classes of society, is due almost exclusively to the teaching and practice of the 'Evangelical' or 'Low' Church parties during the first half of the present century. Their superstitious exaltation of 'the Word,' and their wild and fanatical perversion of St. Paul's teachings: the scorn they expressed for all deeds of beneficence and moral excellences through their dogma 'that works done by unregenerate men, although they *may be things which God commends, and of good use to themselves and others*, yet because they proceed not from a heart *purified by faith* (i.e. by the acceptance of their theory) *they are therefore sinful*, and cannot please God, *or* make a man meet to receive grace from God': *this* conduct coupled with the more audaciously presumptive statements that 'they who, having *never heard* the Gospel, know not Jesus Christ, *cannot be saved*, be they never so diligent to frame their lives according to the light of nature or the laws of that religion they profess,' and not being saved they are cast out 'from the comfortable presence of God,' to endure 'most grievous torments in soul and body, without intermission, in hell-fire *for ever.*' For ever! as a popular preacher of this School in our day has said, 'When the doomed jingle the burning irons of their torment, they shall say, " For ever!" While they howl, echo cries, " For ever "—

> '" For ever " is written on their racks,
>   " For ever " on their chains :
> " For ever " burneth in the fire,
>   " For ever " ever reigns.'

Such horrible dogmas as these, I say, are the parents of the present unbelief in God. It was this kind of teaching which made the intelligent *Mill* (according to his own statement) an Atheist. And I doubt not that it was through such perverse teaching that one so gifted, so amiable, and so philosophic as the late Professor Clifford, could have been induced deliberately to describe Christianity as 'that awful plague which has destroyed two civilisations and but barely failed to slay such promise of good as is now struggling to live amongst men.'

Vicar. I have long mourned over the fact that the teachings of the 'Low Church' party well-nigh deprived the Church of England of her highest gifts—the apostolic succession, and the sacramental graces involved therein; the regeneration by baptism; absolution of sins; and the blessed efficacy of the Holy Eucharist—but I have not credited them with the fearful consequences to which you refer. I know their doctrine was exclusive and selfish, and their worship cold and negative, preaching being considered of more importance than prayers or praise. But where do you obtain the dogmas you ascribe to them?

Parishioner. They are to be found in the writings of all their leading men of forty or fifty years ago. I have been familiar with them from my childhood, as I have already told you; I was nurtured in that creed; and just as the animal taste for some special kind of food in early childhood rarely, if ever, forsakes the adult, however changed his circumstances may be, so in early manhood, and long after, I advocated them by pen and word, in the page, and on the platform. Such things cleave to you with almost the tenacity of your bodily skin. These national and hereditary beliefs are seldom set aside; never, I believe, after the age of fifty years. The changes which do ensue are the results of a general intelligence acting on the minds of a rising generation. Harvey said no physiologist over the age of forty years accepted his theory of the circulation of the blood, demonstrated as it was to the very senses of men; and the testimony of our fathers and our own experience have shown that the universal belief in witches was not overthrown by the arguments of any individual, but has disappeared (except in remote villages among the very ignorant) as the minds of men have become enlightened on the general laws of nature and of life. It is in this manner that 'Evangelicalism' and many other 'isms' are fading from the minds of men; it is by the operation of this law that Paul is receding before Christ, or rather, I ought to say, that the teachings *imputed* to Paul are fast disappearing and the true meanings of that brave and ardent apostle are becoming understood and accepted. The great and eternal truths which Paul in common with his Lord and Master taught—namely, that 'God is not mocked,' and that 'whatsoever a *man soweth*, that he shall also *reap*'; that 'love is the fulfilling of the law'; that 'blessed are the merciful, for they shall obtain mercy'; that 'now abideth *faith*, hope, love, *these three, but the greatest of these is love*'—are rapidly becoming the simple creed of the intelligent and good in all nations.

Vicar. What do you mean by Paul receding before Christ?

Parishioner. I have already told my meaning. If I must be more explicit, I say that in all the more powerful or popular pulpits of the time to which I have referred, the *life and teachings* of Christ were seldom referred to, although his name was constantly on the lips, yea, uttered with a frequency—I had almost said flippancy—which deprived it of all reverence; his words, his teachings were ignored, and the theory of 'justification by faith' was interminably dwelt upon, and carried to such an excess that deeds, acts, services, were practically despised, nay, regarded as *hindrances* to salvation, and the reprobate and openly profane were pronounced to be in a safer position than the known moral man or philanthropist. *Doctrine* was placed first in the category of requirements, instead of in the second ; as Jesus said, ' If ye *do my will* ye shall *know of the doctrine.*' Clergymen regarded *preaching* as their first and highest duty. In truth their views were precisely those expressed by the Presbyterians in their ' Catechism ' to the following question, ' What are the outward means whereby Christ communicates to us the benefits of his meditation ?— The outward and ordinary means are all Christ's ordinances, especially the Word, sacraments, and prayer ; all which are made effectual *to the elect* for their salvation. The spirit of God maketh the reading, but *especially the preaching of the Word* an *effectual means of enlightening.*' The keeping of the ' Lord's day' in a super-Jewish manner, and especially by listening to long gloomy sermons, and by introducing into ordinary speech a number of set phrases linked to the holy name of ' Jesus,' were considered the chief characteristics of ' a child of God,' the mark of ' one of the elect ' who had been ' saved by grace.' To expatiate on the parables of the Samaritan and the Good Shepherd ; to tell 'of ninety and nine just persons which need no repentance,' and of those in the Judgment hour who professed ignorance of Jesus and yet were rewarded for their ' good deeds,' while those who had cried ' Lord, Lord,' who had prophesied ' in his name,' and in his ' name had cast out devils,' and ' in his name done many wonderful works,' were *not accepted*—was to be reproached by the popular clergy of that day as ' unsound,' ' self-righteous,' and 'without the pale of the covenanted mercies of God.'

Vicar. You have given me a very gloomy picture, but as a young priest I am glad to hear of the experience of one who felt an interest in religious things before the great 'Tractarian' movement in Oxford, to which the Church and the nation owe so much. Will you tell me something further of the broad distinctions which marked the conduct of the parochial clergy and the more serious or religious members of the Church of England prior to that event?

Parishioner. The change is so great, the distinctions are so vast and so numerous, that I seem to be living in another age or in another country. From 1830 to 1845, for instance, the sermons that I heard occupied from forty minutes to an hour in their delivery, instead of, as now, from fifteen to thirty minutes. Although I rarely missed a morning service I never once heard any allusion to passing events or national incidents, except occasionally to the death scene of some parishioner. I never once heard the love of money denounced, or the importance of any special social virtue, except the support of 'Missions to the Heathen' may be considered such. The utter depravity of man, the glorious privileges of the elect, the all-sufficiency of faith, and the eternity and torments of hell for the 'unregenerate,' were the staple and almost unvarying themes. Sunday after Sunday these subjects were given in long dull discourses, seldom varied even in their sentences, and never in their illustrations. Then the *name* of Jesus formed a portion of every third or fourth paragraph; *now* I frequently hear sermons in which the name is not uttered, although the *spirit* of his teaching is *always apparent*: *then* a greater portion of the hour's essay consisted in the quotation of isolated texts of Scripture; *now* I seldom hear these profusely introduced, except by some young and timid curate preaching soon after his ordination: *then* the Devil as a personality and the physical torments of hell were preached with 'much unction'; whereas for the past five years I have not heard one or the other minutely and specifically described: *then* the *eternity* and *never-ending torments of the* 'damned' was a frequent theme; *now* it is seldom or only incidentally referred to, and not once during five years have I known it used as an *inducement* to repentance and newness of life: *then* the 'fierce anger' and the 'wrath of God' were continuously preached; *now* the 'love of God' and the 'mercy which endureth for ever' are the most frequent themes from the pulpit: *then*, as I have already said, the national, political, and social incidents of life were not used to inculcate lessons of warning or encouragement; *now* they are frequently brought forward, and efforts are made to convince the hearers that the spirit of Christianity should pervade and influence all the transactions of the senate, the mart, the counting-house, and the family life: *then* the terrors of Sinai were brought forward and enforced with all the passionate rhetoric the preacher could command; *now* the Beatitudes of the Mount are dwelt upon with all the tenderness and persuasive eloquence which a loving father might employ in addressing his own children: *then* the hymns were seldom exultant and grateful, often simply doctrinal, and frequently painful and ghastly in their rhythmical descriptions and contrasts of God's wrath and Christ's love, of the Judgment-day and the torments of the damned ; *now*, happily, they are often sweetly prayerful and loving, like unto Newman's 'Lead, kindly light,' Mrs. Adam's 'Nearer, my God, to Thee,' and Bishop Heber's 'Thou art gone to the grave,' and Mr. Lyte's 'Abide with me.' The three first-named hymns, moreover, imply and *predicate* the *coming* of *even a better time*, inasmuch *as they are used in all Churches*, although they are written respectively by a 'Roman Catholic,' a 'Unitarian,' and a bishop of the 'Church of England.' The hope—the dream, perhaps you will call it—of my life has been to see a *National Church*, in which all could pray and worship in a spirit of catholic unity ; that some form or system could be adopted which all God-fearing men could accept as readily as they now accept the same hymns for praise—notably, 'Lead, kindly light' and 'Nearer, my God, to Thee,' whose authors are separated as 'far as the poles asunder' by their respective Churches at the present moment.

Vicar. This is what our Church continually prays for in accordance with the teachings and prayers of her Divine Head ; her litany breathes it, as I have already pointed out to you ; and if I may use such a phrase, she pours out a very diapason of prayer for this result in her noble Collect on Good Friday, where she says, 'Have mercy upon all Jews, Turks, infidels, and hereticks, and take from them all ignorance, hardness of heart, and contempt of thy Word ; and so fetch them home, blessed Lord, to thy flock, that they may be saved among the remnants of the true Israelites, and be made one fold under one Shepherd, Jesus Christ our Lord.'

Parishioner. Yes, the Church prays for this desirable

result, or I ought to have said the *Churches,* for each one of the seventy or eighty offer to the Great Eternal some such prayer; but in each case it is meant that the 'one fold' is their *own special sect, Church,* or *conventicle,* and the condition of entrance is the adoption of their especial 'shibboleth' or creed. The '*great* Western Church' will exclude the '*great* Eastern Church' so long as it refuses to add the words 'Filioque' to its elaborate creed; the 'Church of England' and the 'Independent Church' stand aloof on the question of 'elder,' 'presbyter,' or 'bishop'; and the 'Baptist' shudders with horror at the idea of 'suffering little children' to be baptised; and so on through the whole series of sects and churches. The Roman soldiers cast lots as to which of them should possess the seamless robe of Christ, rather than tear it into parts and each take a share; but modern 'Christians,' less respectful of Christ's 'seamless' doctrine than the Pagans of his seamless robe, have torn it into many fragments, each taking a part, and then holding up its little fragment as the *whole garment,* or the most essential part of it; and '*to put on Christ*' *is* to accept *this scrap of theirs* as the whole garment of truth, wholly regardless of the other fragments which are to be found elsewhere, and which are cherished with equal fanaticism by *their* possessors. I have heard of sailors who are fearless in every storm because they possess a 'bit of the true Cross,' and 'that never goes down in the most troublous ocean.' And so it is with the sects: each one has 'a bit of the truth' (many who have only a fragment look at it through so magnifying an illusion as to consider it the whole), which they regard as so potent as to enable them above all others to sail in safety amid all the storms and tempests of life to the Land of Eternal Peace.

Vicar. These are painful delusions. There can be but *one* faith, *one* hope, *one* baptism; there can be but one Church of Christ. It may admit possibly of some controversy as to whether the Anglican or the Roman be the Church; but the question is limited to that postulate. But I have no desire to discuss this matter now, as I so much wish to hear of your past experiences in the practice and teachings of our Church. I especially wish you to give me some illustration of what you have yourself heard from a pulpit in the Church of England as to 'original sin' and the 'eternity of torment.'

Parishioner. Of the first I have heard nothing inconsistent with the ninth Article of your Church; and all that now appears to me erroneous, viewed in the light of Christ's teaching, was in *perfect accord* with the ninth, tenth, and thirteenth Articles of your Church. In truth, preachers were *consistent* in their theories; and although I believe the effects of their sermons were ultimately mischievous, as, being opposed to the great principles of justice and mercy, and the innate sense of these qualities in the rightly cultured mind, *they have led* to the present widespread apostacy throughout Europe, yet were they most logically consistent with the '*Articles of Religion*' to which they had pledged themselves, with, perhaps, the exception of the manner in which they dealt with the punishment of the unconverted and unregenerate, for neither the 'Articles' nor the 'Catechism' of the Church of England pronounce on this awful subject except *inferentially*. It is unfortunately true that such preachers *could* quote the eighth Article of their Church as authorising them to pronounce an eternity of punishment to the misbelieving, for it asserts that the Athanasian Creed 'ought thoroughly to be received and believed,' and this Creed affirms that those who do not believe it ' shall *without doubt* perish everlastingly.'

Vicar. 'To *perish* everlastingly' does not necessarily include an *eternity of torment* ; and the sacrament of baptism is the antidote to the consequences of original sin. But I should like you to avoid discussion and to give me an *illustration* from your own experience of the manner in which the awful subject of a never-ending personal torment was treated in the pulpit of the Church of England more than a quarter of a century ago.

Parishioner. 'To perish everlastingly' may admit of two interpretations, but I question whether *you* would accept the doctrine of personal annihilation. I feel assured that the Church meant by these words those horrible and never-ending tortures so graphically described by Tertullian, and depicted with such force by the pencil and brush of Orcagna on the walls of Santa Maria Novella in Florence. As for the merciful qualification you suggest for many, through the sacrament of baptism, the clergymen under 'whose ministry I sat' did not admit of the sacramental grace of baptism as applicable to *all* who were baptised : one of them published a book on the subject, from which I have already quoted. He was a sincere and earnest man. He declared 'all my prejudices both by nature and education were in favour of baptismal regeneration; and I used earnestly to contend for that which I now believe *to be* a *theory of man's inventing*.' In few things is there a greater revulsion of opinion in the Church than on the subject of '*sacramental*' grace. In my humble judgment it is a retrograde action. Materialism appears to be gaining an ascendency over the spiritual life—a reaction like unto that which Paul feared in the Church at Galatia when he wrote, 'After that ye have known God, or rather are known of God, how turn ye again to the weak and beggarly elements, whereunto ye desire again to be in bondage?' (Gal. iv. 9). However, we are not dealing with this now, or, I must declare, that there was more of *personal piety*, more of the *deep sense of spiritual things*, a more *vivid* realisation of the *presence and power of the Most Holy Spirit*, than is *now* recognisable in many of the so-called 'priests' of the Church of England, with whom forms and ceremonies and 'beggarly elements' seem to be the aim and the end. To return to your question, and to be a faithful chronicler of my experience, I must say that although the clergy of my earlier days shrank with horror from calling themselves 'priests,' yet was the term 'a preacher of the Gospel' a misnomer. It was no *euangelion*, no 'good tidings of great joy which shall be to *all people*,' that they preached. 'Does he *preach the Gospel*?' became a cant question. A 'sound man' and a 'Gospel minister' became cant phrases to describe the clergymen who preached in all their bold unmitigated form 'original sin,' 'entire depravity,' 'predestination,' 'election,' 'sovereign grace,' and, to the many, 'reprobation' and an 'eternal hell.' The

Gospel (*euangelion*, the good message), the 'good tidings of great joy which shall be to *all people*,' as proclaimed by angel voices over the fields of Bethlehem, was seldom preached in its integrity and fulness. As I have already said, 'gospel' became a cant word, and signified the very opposite of its original meaning, as completely as in common parlance the word 'prevent' now differs and has become degraded from its primitive meaning of 'going before'—to aid, assist, and further. That beautiful word 'gospel' had ceased to mean 'good news' or 'tidings of *great joy to all people*.' 'Preaching the Gospel' meant, in the 'vernacular' of the 'Evangelical' party, the 'Clapham Sect' (which became for some years the most influential 'section' of the Church of England), the preaching of all those 'horrors' which I have already described, and which may be epitomised by stating that it implied that the Great Creator of all men had created many millions of souls which would 'without doubt perish everlastingly'—no, not '*perish*,' but suffer, and shriek, and writhe with the most excruciating agonies for ever and for ever—while he had also created a comparative few (of whom the preacher was invariably one) whom he had 'predestined' and 'elected' 'to be saved' 'through the precious Blood of Christ'; further, that the more heinous and criminal the lives of the 'elect,' the 'greater glory to God'; further, that the bulk of mankind had not, and could not have, the *will* or the *power* to turn to God. But I cannot trust myself to speak on this subject; but happily I have here the exact answer given categorically on this question by a great 'Evangelic' authority: 'What is effectual calling? Effectual calling is the work of God's almighty power and grace, whereby (out of his free and special love to his elect, and from *nothing in them* moving him thereunto) he *doth* in his accepted time invite and draw them to Jesus Christ, by his word and spirit savingly enlightening their minds, renewing and *powerfully determining their wills*, so as they (although in themselves dead in sin) are hereby *made willing and able* freely to answer his call, and to accept and embrace the grace offered and conveyed therein. *All the elect*, AND THEY ONLY, are *effectually* called, although others may be, and often are, outwardly called by the ministry of the Word.' As I have already said, there is really nothing in this fearful statement which is not embodied in the seventeenth and eighteenth Articles of the Church of England. The 'Articles' in the present day are *practically buried* in the pages of the Prayer Book; but these men made them a living power. I heard a lady— a most diligent attendant at her parish church—say, the other day, that she had *never seen* or *heard of* 'the Articles'! I am glad that this is so. In my early manhood it was far otherwise. Yet still the *fact remains* that these 'Articles,' and these Articles only, are the *legal tests* of orthodoxy in our law courts whenever the question of doctrine becomes the subject of judicial inquiry. It is one of the many logical inconsistencies of practical life that hundreds—nay, thousands—call themselves, or are called by others without contradiction, 'members' of a Church of whose doctrines they are in absolute ignorance. This *fact* leads me to hope that as thousands thus 'worship' in 'the Church,' without any knowledge of 'the Articles,' and with little conception of the meanings of the words of the 'Creeds,' the time may come when neither creeds nor articles will be demanded of priest or people beyond the simple confession, 'I believe that Jesus Christ is the Son of God,' upon which Philip the Apostle, when under the special guidance of 'the Spirit,' baptised the treasurer of Candace, the Queen of the Ethiopians.

Vicar. You have spoken at great length, but have hardly complied with my request. I wished you to tell me how the subject of eternal torment was dealt with by Anglican preachers of your earlier day, and you have dwelt long upon subjects which the more influential and, I may add, the more cultured of our priesthood have agreed as far as possible to ignore and never refer to. I think the doctrine on which you have spoken a very fearful one when separated from the sacramentarian system, which is the antidote of the many evils which afflicted the Church during the later parts of the Georgian period. I have not read the 'Articles' since my ordination, and *then* only for 'pass' purposes; but I cannot think they state in any distinctive form the doctrines which you quoted as a categorical reply to the questions of 'election' and 'predestination'; but as they belong to the misnamed 'Reformation' period of our Church they never attracted and rivetted my attention as did our glorious liturgy, and thus I have largely forgotten them. But do you seriously mean that the doctrines which you have delineated can be fairly drawn from them?

Parishioner. Yes, and no others. The 'Prayer Book,' if its appendix, the Articles (and, as I have said, these are the *title deeds* of your office and its rights), is a part of it, is as twofold and as antagonistic the one to the other as are the 'High' and 'Low' Church clergy whose duty it is to read it. The Church is nobly consistent in her catechism, her liturgy, and all her formularies. The priest who accepts her 'catechism' can perform all her rites and ceremonies with heartiness and probity, without the 'mental reservation' and word-torture which others resort to to justify their inconsistency. From the moment he takes the infant in his arms to bless it with the holy rite of baptism and thereby make it 'a member of Christ, a child of God, and an inheritor of the kingdom of heaven,' to the day when he in his official capacity proclaims that 'it hath pleased Almighty God of his great mercy to take unto himself the soul of our dear brother here departed,' and gives 'hearty thanks' that it *hath* thus pleased HIM to deliver this our brother out of the miseries of this sinful world,' all his acts are consistent and harmonious. The liturgical offices of the Church are a beauteous unity, full of brightness, of hope, of calm contentment and peace. But her 'Articles of Religion,' so dear to the 'Evangelists' as being 'according to the Word of God,' are not so tranquillising by reason of their espousing in all its fierceness the doctrines of 'predestination,' 'election,' and 'grace' to which I have referred. The eighteenth Article, for instance, embodies the spirit of every phrase which I quoted, and which seems to be so very repulsive to your feelings. All the myriads of human beings who follow Brahma, Buddha, Confucius, and Mahomet, all the tens of thousands in Africa and elsewhere who have never heard the name of Jesus, are left in a hopeless condition; nay, further, the Article hurls its anathema against those who, remembering the words of Paul, should presume to say that 'there is no respect of persons with God'; that those 'who have sinned without law shall also perish without law'; that 'when the Gentiles, which have not the law, *do by nature* the things contained in the law, these, having not the law, are a law unto themselves.' This 'Article,' like to the 'Westminster Confession,' pours contempt on such a notion. It has, however, the great merit of clearness and plain speech; it is not 'jesuitic,' equivocal, or beset with that vile philosophy which gives to words a 'non-natural' sense and an 'inner meaning.' Moreover, it has this merit: it is not written 'in a tongue not understanded of the people,' but all is clear, terse, and forcible—as follows: 'They also are *to be had accursed* that *presume* to say that every man shall be saved by the law or sect which he professeth, so that he be diligent to frame his life according to that law and the light of nature.'

Vicar. Really this appears very repellent. I am glad that I have never from the pulpit—or, indeed, anywhere else—enunciated such views. I think they are calculated, as you say, to cause people to distrust and to disbelieve, when opinions so at variance with the natural sense of justice (to say nothing of mercy) are taught by persons in authority.

Parishioner. Alas! my dear friend, we can all of us see the minute mote in our brother's eye more readily than we can behold the beam which is in our own eye. Candour compels me to say, in the words of your favourite classic, Horace,

              Mutato nomine de te
  Fabula narratur.

As I have already said, the doctrines of predestination, and election, and 'sovereign grace' have led to fearful statements. For instance, I have known an 'Evangelical' preacher say that 'there were infants in hell not a span long.' But *your* doctrine on the all-importance of *baptism* has produced exactly the *same* results. The emphatic statement of the Nicene Creed which thousands of 'Church people' utter every Sunday, 'I believe in *one baptism* for the *remission of sins*,' and which faith has been the faith of centuries, has produced results as tragic as any which have arisen *practically* from the theory which has excited your displeasure. The 'Evangelical' theory has never in England been aided in its tyranny by the civil power, and all its preachings have had reference solely to the *spiritual* or *eternal* state; whereas this creed respecting baptism to this hour inflicts on the unbaptised babe the same ignominy which falls to the lot of the murderer or the suicide, namely, to be interred without any religious rites, and, in fact, to be buried, to say the least, as a pet dog. In fact, the history of infant baptism teems with ridiculous as well as tragic stories. I know few things which so blend the laughable and the horrible as the teachings of 'the Fathers' in this matter; and it has, as I have said, exerted its influence for ages. As a student I once had to read Wall's 'History of Infant Baptism,' in which he states that with the exception of Vincentius, who speedily retracted his 'heresy,' he was unable to discover any *orthodox* divine during the first eight centuries of the Christian faith who *believed otherwise* than that unbaptised infants never entered heaven. Indeed, *Saint* Fulgentius (happily his work is in Latin), in his treatise

'De Fide,' preceded by many centuries my Evangelical friend in his notions of the baby habitants of the infernal world, for he says, 'Be assured, and doubt not, that not only men who have obtained the use of their reason, but also little children who have *begun* to live in their mother's womb, and *have there died*, or who, having just been born, have passed away from the world without the sacrament of holy baptism, *must be punished by the eternal torture of undying fire.*' Can it be wondered at that the Hindoos and Mohammedans shrink aghast from a 'religion' which teaches such things? or that English philosophers like Mill and Clifford turn from it with disdain? I said that some ridiculous results ensued from this 'dogma,' and assuredly they did; but the *horror* which springs up in my own soul from this theory of 'baptism' prevents my enumerating them. The mental anguish which a mother nurtured in such a faith must have felt when 'her hour was come' (more especially if it had come prematurely), and she far away from priests, passes the power of words to describe. No, my dear Mr. Hierous, you are not in a position to cast a stone at your 'Evangelical' brother on the cruel consequences of your respective beliefs. But I cheerfully admit that it has not occurred *to you*, as it did not occur *to them*, to realise in full the absolute horror which such theories inspire in unsophisticated minds. They ask you to believe the respective doctrines to be the teachings of Holy Writ—believe that they are the ordinances of the Most High God—and teach them accordingly; the *result* being that intellectual men whose plastic childhood has not been moulded into such dogmas, and also hundreds of other *reflecting* minds who *have been reared* under such theories, but who have by natural, intellectual, and moral force emerged from the thraldom of hereditary ideas, turn alike from the Church and from the Book which inculcate, or are supposed to inculcate, such ideas. They *know* them to be at variance with the intuitions of a sound mind and a sound heart, and with the courage that appertains to rectitude they denounce them as false, and say with emphasis, 'Fiat justitia, ruat cœlum.'

Vicar. Your notions are very painful to me, and I ought not to listen to such implied heresy. The creeds which have come down to us through so many centuries, hallowed as they have been by the acceptance of some of the most wise and most holy of men, cannot be otherwise than true, from that very circumstance. Had they been false and untrue they would long since have come to an end. Are you aware that Dr. Pusey, one of the most pious and most learned theologians of the present day, has written a profound and elaborate volume sustaining and enforcing those very views which you say have produced such dangerous results? and, further, that the saintly poet of 'The Christian Year' recognised the transforming power of the most holy rite of baptism? I can never forget his expressive lines—

> A few calm words of faith and prayer,
> A *few bright drops of holy dew*,
> Shall *work a wonder there*
> Earth's charmers never knew.
>
> What sparkles in that lucid flood
> Is water, *by gross mortals ey'd;*
> But, seen by *Faith, 'tis blood*
> Out of a dear Friend's side.

And then, as if he were well-nigh transported with the transforming and transfiguring influence of this rite upon the babe visible before him, he sings—

> O tender gem, and full of Heaven !
> Not in the twilight stars on high,
> Not in moist flowers at even,
> *See we our God so nigh.*

Parishioner. The writings of these men are not unknown to me, nor the men themselves. Neither possessed a *judicial* mind. Each was incapable of weighing evidence—nay, would not listen to, much less accept, evidence which seemed to militate against their preconceived notions. Although kindly in their family and social relations, both would have persecuted as bravely as Bonner himself had the civil laws permitted them. Witness their conduct towards Hampden, the late Bishop of Hereford, and towards others. As I have already said, I lived in the same town as Keble, and *know* that he avoided, as he would avoid a poisonous snake, some of the clergymen in the district who held views on baptism and 'sacramental grace' different from his own. I *know* that it would be 'as a voice crying in the wilderness' to say anything which implied that the 'saintly Keble' could be sullen and morose, and it would serve no useful purpose to proclaim it. In truth, I rejoice in the great results which his widespread fame produced after his death, and that tens of thousands of pounds were lavishly poured in by *partisans* and others to found and sustain a memorial college to his perpetual honour. He possessed great qualities of mind and heart, but certainly not so great as the reverence felt towards him by Cardinal Newman and others would seem to indicate.

But he was peculiarly deficient in the cool mental qualities which would have fitted him for the judicial bench or have enabled him to attain rank as a 'scientist.' By living a life of seclusion from his earliest childhood, under the constant hourly supervision of an affectionate and learned father, by incessant application and study under the same father's guidance, through natural reserve and shyness shunning the companionship of boys of his own age and the sports of boys, he gave himself wholly up to reading. I rarely saw him without a book in his hand, whether riding on horseback or walking; and by these unusual circumstances he attained, as might have been expected, a large amount of learning of a special kind at a very early age; he had, in fact, been 'coached' from his infancy for that particular 'scholarship' which he gained before he had quite completed his fifteenth year. His father had himself been a successful competitor for the same 'scholarship' in his own youth; and, moreover, to arrive at a strictly accurate conclusion as to the precise merit of the attainment, it must not be forgotten that 'Corpus' was a small college; that in awarding the 'scholarship' there was always a strong bias on the part of the examiners in favour of *youth* in the candidates; that these circumstances, together with the special studies and special conduct likely to attain success, were known thoroughly to the youthful Keble's preceptor, his own father, who had always kept up his intimacy with 'Corpus' and its 'heads.' The father personally accompanied his highly-trained son to Oxford when he went up for the examination. So excellent a 'coach' was Mr. Keble for this particular 'scholarship,' that both John Keble and his brother Thomas were successful competitors for it. These exceptional and peculiar advantages do not, of course, deprive the 'boy-Fellow' of a great honour, but they go far to intimate that there was no 'prodigious' marvel about it, requiring an intellect of exceptional power or genius to achieve it. His great attainments afterwards, such as winning 'double first class' in his university, were such as few men reach; and few there are who have been so early, so exclusively, and so persistently trained for a given end. However, to have achieved in his university the same distinction which shed honour on the illustrious statesman Sir Robert Peel entitles Keble to a high niche in the temple of Fame, and will 'keep his memory green' in the hearts of English 'Churchmen.' His friendly biographer, Sir J. T. Coleridge, writes that Keble's fame 'must rest upon his sacred poetry.' This is probably true; yet any impartial critic must admit that the 'sacred poetry' owes much of its popularity, and its writer his extensive influence, to the same causes which made the hymns of John Wesley so popular, and John Wesley the power he was, and is, among teeming thousands of his countrymen—namely, the poetry of Keble and of the Wesleys was popular because it ministered to the feelings, the desires, and opinions of large 'religious' bodies holding special religious theories, which they rejoiced to see championed in melodious verse. In poetic power, *per se*, 'The Christian Year' is not equal to *many* poems which have not attained the half of its popularity, and even as '*sacred poetry*,' were it not linked to a large and enthusiastic section of the Church of England, it would not be regarded as superior to the poems of James Montgomery, the modest poet of Sheffield.

Vicar. Really your views of poetry are as heretical as your opinions on other subjects. Surely you do not mean seriously to state that John Keble was not distinguished for his extreme humility and modesty? And may I ask you to take an early opportunity to read his beautiful hymn for 'St. Mark's Day' (which, by-the-by, was his own birthday), and you will then see what a fine spirit of Christian sympathy and catholic tolerance he possessed. Moreover, when you allege that his was not a judicial mind I think you ought to have given some fact or facts in illustration of this; and as you yourself claim to be liberal and tolerant, may I be allowed to remind you of the just sentiment, 'De mortuis nil nisi bonum'?

Parishioner. I have great admiration for the life and some of the writings of the author of 'The Christian Year.' What I wished to convey is, that he was no Colossus either in intellectual power, moral attainments, or administrative capacity, as the lavish honours which have been paid to his memory would imply. His fame is the fame of a party chieftain, and will wane as the opinions of the party recede before the advancing intelligence of the age. As for his humility, I have no desire to question it. He was, constitutionally, the most shy man I have ever known—so shy that it was embarrassing to him even to write in the presence of strangers—so much so that he has been known to say, 'I hate any one to see how I hold my pen'; and this congenital shyness, timidity, or diffidence—by whatever name you call it—helped to swell the chorus of praise which was bestowed upon him for his 'Christian humility' and modesty. Moreover, all persons—princes, potentates, or pigmies—

gain immeasurably in renown by privacy and seclusion. The Latins inculcate this in the proverb 'Omne ignotum pro magnifico,' as the English do by saying of its opposite, 'Familiarity breeds contempt.' We learn from various biographies that John Keble was less frequently in the 'common room' at Oriel than was any of the very distinguished Fellows of his time, and a Fellow of the same college, in his charming 'Reminiscences,' has pertinently observed that 'the slightest word he dropped was all the more remembered from there being *so little of it*, and from it seeming to come from a different and holier sphere.' This retiring habit enabled him to sustain unimpaired the great reputation which his 'youthful Fellowship' had procured. Fortune favoured him. The 'Tractarian movement' at Oxford welded a chain which linked him to the esteem of a powerful party. 'The Christian Year' and the 'Prayer Book' speedily became twin companions in the esteem and reverence of hundreds, both in the sanctuary and the home. The two books became as symbolic of the 'Puseyite' and 'High Church' parties as the unctuous phrases of the 'Blessed Gospel,' 'sovereign grace,' 'the Lord's Day,' and the like were of the Evangelical, or 'Low Church,' party. At a time when the 'Evangelical' party excluded everything ornamental—music, painting, and sculpture —and held the material 'cross' in special dislike as symbolic of popery, excluding it from their churches, and when possible from the graveyards, the covers of 'The Christian Year' became ornamented with a gilt cross, or with some other symbolic monogram device, and its pages were duly adorned with 'church red lines, and the like ; thus enhancing its sale by thus becoming more expressive of party zeal and purpose. Such ornaments are common to religious books now, but it was very different fifty years ago. The white surplice in the pulpit and the 'cross' on the altar-cloth or book-cover were as '*war-paint*' to an Indian savage, exciting the warmest emotions, and thus enhanced the sale of 'The Christian Year' and the popularity of its author. As party zeal toned down, the book, from its attractive appearance, and the tranquil nature of its themes, came to be adopted as a 'gift book' among 'Church people' generally, who, without strong 'views' of any kind, were still desirous that such books as they *did* give to their young friends should be religious and 'proper,' and consistent with their own position as 'Church-going people.' In addition to these circumstances, the 'Christian renaissance,' so to speak, which has diffused itself among all classes of society in reference to symbolic ornament, has had its influence in inducing *such* purchasers to select a 'religious' book which at the same time had the 'nicest-looking covers.' From all these causes 'The Christian Year' attained a circulation which is unparalleled in the annals of poetry; but, I repeat, it is not its 'poetry,' but its character as a '*Church book*' and a party-poem, that has kept it alive and maintained its sale.

Vicar. You deal with the beautiful poem of 'The Christian Year' in the same daring manner, and explain its popularity and its answer on the same principles, as Gibbon had the audacity to do in reference to the spread of Christianity itself; that is, you explain it by secondary causes rather than from its own inherent excellence and diffusive power. This must be prejudice on your part. You have not, however, ventured to dispute the Christian, catholic, tender, and tolerant spirit of Keble for which I reverence him, and which breathes so holy a fragrance from every line of his beautiful hymn on St. Mark's Day. I observe also that you have evaded my remonstrance in respect to the opinion you have given as to Keble's not possessing that honest and robust mind which would enable him to be strictly judicial in his conclusions. For my own part, I believe him to have been so God-fearing a man as to prefer truth before all things, and that, like unto his beloved Master, his 'zeal' for his Father's house made him wish to purge the Church of 'all them that sold and bought in the temple,' and of all other polluting things ; that self-advancement and 'love of money' were things which *he* never coveted after ; that he fled 'these things and followed after righteousness, godliness, *faith, love, patience*, and meekness.'

Parishioner. You have formed no inaccurate opinion of Keble as to his zeal for his Father's house, and of his desire to purge his beloved Church from all polluting things. He was ordinarily as meek as was becoming in a man ; he was tender as a child in all his family relations ; he was very benevolent to his parishioners at Coln St. Aldwin's. Although his father was *legally* 'vicar,' yet, for all practical purposes, the poet was the vicar and pastor of the place all the time that I knew him. His family means enabled him to be a liberal almoner of blankets and coals at Christmas, and he was therefore held in great reverence and esteem by the humble villagers in that place ; yet his excessive shyness often caused him to be awkward, distant, and reserved in his *personal* intercourse with them, and many even of his charities were performed by deputy. He had real sympathy for the suffering and respect for the lowly, but the great seclusion in which he had been nurtured from earliest childhood, his practical inexperience of 'life' in its various phases, his ignorance of its necessities and business requirements often made him confused and embarrassed in conversation and in his private ministerial addresses. He was frequently glad under such circumstances to fall back upon the Book of Common Prayer and to 'read the Offices.' This excessive shyness—and it was almost morbid—even so late as 1833 caused him to be very little at Oxford, where his distinction as the 'boy-Fellow' and 'Professor of Poetry' had been deservedly gained. He preferred the seclusion of his most secluded home at Fairford, and when compelled by duty to be in Oxford he sought, not rooms in far-famed Oriel, but in a private house in the city. I am quite sure that this excessive 'nervousness,' as it is miscalled, served to heighten his reputed humility and modesty, humble and modest as he certainly was. In respect to my seeking for secondary causes to explain many of Keble's qualities, I avow at once my full belief in the formative influences of a man's environments. No nunnery was more secluded from observation or more shut off from the power of observing incidents external to itself than was John Keble's birth-place and home at Fairford. I knew it well, having lived in it for several years, and spent many hours of reading in the little room in which a great portion of 'The Christian Year' was written. The house was shut in by a lofty wall from the high road which passed in front of it. At the outer side of the western boundary of the patrimonial property there were four or five cottages, but these were scarcely visible from the grounds, and their occupants could not, even from the upper windows, catch a glimpse of the garden opposite, because of the lofty wall, high elms, and other trees. In other directions were fields and gardens only, and Mr. Keble's 'paddock,' which joined his garden, was rendered quite 'private' by walls and lofty trees, which formed an oblong embowered parade very dear to the musing poet. The approach to the residence was at one end of it, and from its own grounds, and no one approaching the house could see its inmates, except by the rarest chance, as only one window at the corner of the dining-room was visible in this direction. The town itself afforded few, if any, visitors, for the Vicar of Fairford and his parishioner Mr. Keble were not on cordial terms of friendship. There were very few young men of his own status in society in the neighbourhood with whom he desired to associate ; hence the shyness, reserve, and love of solitude which marked his after career. When this shyness was surmounted by personal intimacy, he became genial, pleasant, and, as is frequently the case with shy people, even demonstratively exuberant with fun. In the family of a dear friend of my own, I am told that, when he was young and frequently visited them, after the reserve of the few first hours had been melted away by their geniality, welcome, and kindness, he could, and did, become very merry and exultant ; that before he was ' ordained ' he enjoyed a dance with their daughters very much ; and afterwards he often displayed much merriment, was fond of giving them grotesque riddles to solve, and was otherwise very diverting. His letters at that period—about 1820-21, I think—were much appreciated by them, as they abounded in humour, quaint descriptions, and scraps of poetry; while over all was diffused, as it were, a spirit of purity; and the peroration of each letter, if one may so describe it, almost invariably referred to high and holy matters. His pathetic nature and reserve were, I think, intensified very much after the death of his father, although he had reached his ninetieth year; and among the other influences which helped to mould his character were the frequent illnesses of his sisters, to whom he was warmly attached: one, Sarah, he lost early from consumption; Mary Ann, his favourite sister, the most cheerful, bright, and sparkling of the three sisters, died in 1826. So fond, indeed, was he both of Mary Ann and Elizabeth that in writing to my friend Mrs. P. purposing to introduce Mary Ann to her, he said, 'Not my *wife* Elizabeth, but my *sweetheart* Mary Ann.' It was with her that he walked and rode most, and she was (to use his playful words) his 'sweetheart'; but in Elizabeth also he had a 'wife who sympathised with him in all reverence of holy things, and in loving care of the humble, the sick, and the needy.' She lived long—yea, even to three score years and ten. Although in comparatively early life she had to undergo the amputation of a leg, and was in other respects an invalid, yet was she habitually cheerful and serene, ever reflecting the purity and goodness of her Divine Lord. She passed away in peace—so peacefully that her loving brother, who was, in his hoary age, reading to her a psalm, was unconscious that her spirit had fled until the attendant nurse informed him that Miss Keble had been dead some minutes. He buried her at his dear village of Horsely. Sarah and Mary Ann sleep beneath the shadow of the beautiful church at Fairford, whose 'storied windows' are a pictorial illustration of the life of Jesus whom they loved so well. Not the house of Bethany, when Mary and Martha and Lazarus lovingly ministered to their gracious benefactor, was the home of purer and more Christian affection than was the home of Keble, at Fairford, when in 1823 he gave up the office of tutor in Oxford and returned flushed with honours to his aged father and beloved sisters—'his sweetheart and his wife,' as he so happily and affectionately described them.

Vicar. You have interested me intensely in your later remarks, as they seem to me an apologetic recantation of your previous depreciatory remarks on 'The Christian Year,' and of its sainted author. Your tone then was such as to suggest that you must have been smarting under some personal feeling which excited prejudice and caused you to take a harsh, and therefore an unjust, view of the poetry, as also a very exaggerated view of the spiritual defects of the writer. Your reference to the home of Bethany and its inmates whom Jesus loved prompts the thought that, after all, you regarded the Keble family as peculiarly and especially Christ-like, with an abiding, steadfast, even joyous sense of the immediate presence of their Lord.

Parishioner. I repeat I have no bias. I strive to hold the balance steadily and uprightly. If it did oscillate it would be in the direction of undue praise. A man would be indeed crass, stupid, and unjust were he to deny merit to a book which has found hundreds of thousands of purchasers, and which continues to be in demand in the households of pious Churchmen. As to the writer, I personally know that he was kind, pious, generous, and sympathetic ; and further, zealous in the extreme for the honour and the power of the Church of which he was a priest ; but I *know, also*, that the very ardour of his piety and the positiveness of his convictions made him harsh, morose, nay, severely unjust towards those who held other views and were, like himself, positive in their convictions and eager to impress them upon others. I have never heard, and have never read of, more than one man who *could be just* and *tender* and *true* under *all* circumstances of conflict of opinion and personal wrong, and, alas !

> Now he is dead ! Far hence he lies
>   In the lorn Syrian town ;
> And on his grave, with shining eyes,
>   The Syrian stars look down.

Vicar. You should give some facts illustrative of Keble's aversion to others, more especially of the priesthood, which you think at variance with my opinion of his very large-hearted, Christian catholicity—that spirit of love which is greater than faith and hope—the spirit which prompted and gave utterance to these beautiful lines in his poem on ' St. Mark's Day ' :

> And sometimes e'en beneath the moon
> The Saviour gives a gracious boon,
>   When reconciléd Christians meet,
> And face to face, and heart to heart,
> High thoughts of holy love impart
>   In silence meek or converse sweet.
>
> O then the glory and the bliss,
> When all that pain'd or seem'd amiss
>   Shall melt with earth and sin away !

> When saints beneath their Saviour's eye,
> Fill'd with each other's company,
> Shall spend in love th' eternal day!

Here, as it seems to me, is the true spirit of Christian love and of catholic unity, the foretaste and joyful recognition of the 'communion of saints,' far removed from that jealous and invidious spirit to which you have so often referred. What can be further apart in spirit than these lines and the conduct of John, who forbad one from casting out devils in Jesus's name 'because he followeth not with us,' and what more in harmony with HIM who said, ' Forbid him not: for he that is not against us is for us'? I wish also to remind you that you have not given me any fact corroborative of your idea that Keble was too timid—in other words, not robust enough—honestly and judicially to investigate *facts*, and to *accept the consequences*, whatever they may be, as 'scientists' or the great investigators into natural phenomena claim to do.

Parishioner. I could give some which have fallen under my own immediate observation, and which would prove that in 1835 it was not only the fault of the then Vicar of Fairford that there was no realisation of the beautiful lines you have quoted—the

> gracious boon,
> When reconcilèd Christians meet,
> And face to face, and heart to heart,
> High thoughts of holy love impart
> In silence meek or converse sweet.

The said Vicar believed and published that the views on baptism promulgated by Dr. Pusey and espoused by Keble were unscriptural; and this proceeding excited in the latter an 'aversion' or repulsion of the kind which I have stated. Sir J. T. Coleridge, in his biography of Keble, refers to it as a 'discomfort which would have decided him now, *of itself*, against choosing Fairford as his residence when his choice was free.' The 'discomfort' must have been considerable, when it is remembered that Fairford was his 'birthplace,' and the 'burial-place' of his family, and the 'home' his own personal property or that of his brother. But you seem to forget that I *have* instanced his conduct towards Hampden, and also to Arnold, with whom he was at one time friendly; from both of these men he became estranged because they chose to think differently on 'Church matters.' But, as bearing on this particular, I might quote Newman, who in his 'Apologia,' writing of John Keble, for whom he once had a reverence almost idolatrous, says, 'He was shy of me *for years* in consequence of the marks which I bore upon me of the *Evangelical* and Liberal schools; at least so I have ever thought' (p. 18). In fact, like too many saints of whom history tells, Keble was too apt to associate intellectual difficulties, and the conscientious scruples and inquiries springing out of them, with a sinful heart and 'the pride of reason,' and was by no means so quick to perceive that 'intolerance' and a lack of charity *sometimes* spring from 'spiritual pride.' In fact, as even his all too partial biographer states, 'those with *whom he lived* and of *whom he saw most* had such a reverence for him, that his opinions were seldom canvassed *with that freedom in conversation with himself which is good for the wisest of men*'; and again the writer thinks that the *querulous* and *severe* spirit which he sometimes manifested would have been kept in abeyance, and that it would 'have conduced to the *holding of opinions with more charity*, if honours had been offered to and accepted by him.' In short, what I may have said which appears to you unfair to the reputation of Keble, and which I *know* to be the shade necessary to make the picture *lifelike* and *true*, can be substantiated by two or three little incidents: for simple circumstances occur sometimes which lift the veil and reveal the true character of a man. In a letter to a friend he writes, 'I don't care to read "Ecce Homo," but it will be a very agreeable disappointment if the writer turns out *a Christian* at last, and I will pull off my hat to him and beg his pardon.' Here is an illustration of a conclusion, not altogether charitable, drawn of a man (however right it may accidentally have proved) because of the writing of a book he deemed heretical, although he had not *cared to read it*. Again, here is a statement, written by the son of Keble's most friendly biographer, of an interview he had enjoyed with the poet and divine: 'I was telling him how much I had been impressed with the difficulties as to the inspiration of Holy Scripture, which were growing stronger and spreading more widely day by day; and that it seemed to me this would shortly become (this was in the year 1851) the great religious question of the time. I added that there was not, as far as I knew, any theory or statement on the subject which even attempted to be philosophical, except Coleridge's, in his "Confessions of an Inquiring Spirit," and that I wished Mr. Keble, or some one as competent as he, would take up the subject and deal with it intellectually and thoroughly. He shewed great dislike to the discussion and put it aside several times, and on my pressing it upon him, he answered shortly *that most of the men who had difficulties on this subject were too wicked to be reasoned with.*' Surely, here was the spirit of Torquemada ; here the idea and the principle upon which the Spanish Inquisition was founded, through which the auto-da-fe was lighted up, and by which the Massacres of Bartholomew were perpetrated and justified. One sees not in this speech the Christian love which ' hopeth all things,' but rather the mischievous zeal and sectarian discipleship which prompted James and John to go to their Divine Master and to implore from HIM permission to 'command fire to come down from heaven and consume' those who did not further their wishes, and which called forth from the Holy One the severe rebuke, ' Ye know not what manner of spirit ye are of.'

Vicar. You have, indeed, come to startling conclusions respecting the holy man whom the Church, at least a large section of it, has honoured for these twenty years as pre-eminently distinguished for tenderness and humility. It would excite the indignation of tens of thousands had they heard, as I have been pained to hear, the name of the sainted Keble associated with the blood-stained name of Torquemada. I must ask you to withdraw the comparison for your own sake, if you desire to be thought truthful and just, and to escape the strong censure of the religious world.

Parishioner. There is one Tribunal before which I am anxious to appear truthful and just, because before *that* Tribunal appearances and realities are one and the same thing. Other tribunals are influenced almost exclusively by appearances, and they may misjudge me, and they *would do so* if they thought, as you appear to do, that I placed the popular poet of 'The Christian Year' on the same plane of moral worth as the notorious Torquemada. As to the indignant 'censure of the religious world,' this is one of the inflictions which the truth-seeker and the truth-lover must expect. For example, were he to say in Cairo, or Constantinople, or within the precincts of the Grand Mosque of the Omar, or even in Jerusalem itself, that 'Mahomet was an impostor,' he would possibly be stoned to death or trampled under foot by 'the religious world.' 'The chief priests and the scribes' of every religion have been, in every country and in every age, prone to the cry of 'Crucify him' against all 'who have difficulties on the subject' of their dogmas. 'They are too wicked to be reasoned with' is their general feeling ; and if these 'too wicked' ones cannot now be beheaded or burnt in London, Oxford, or Gloucester, as were More, Latimer, and Hooper, and scores of others in other places, yet are they 'ostracised' by such 'priests,' and 'boycotted' from all social intercourse with 'the religious world.' Yea, even now in the nineteenth century such truth-seekers 'are too *wicked to be reasoned with*' by the 'unco' gude' of all sects ; and hence their doctrines spread among the majority of the laity ; and thence it has come to pass that in this country that which in 1851 was as 'a little cloud out of the sea like unto a man's hand' has now spread far and wide, and pervades the highest literary reviews and journals of the time, and dominates powerfully the minds of some of the highest officials in the State. It is very sad, but it *is the fact*, that some of the kindest and most tender men in their family circles have from religious zeal become great persecutors ; yea, in persecuting the lowly followers of the Prince of Peace they have thought ' they were doing God service.' Some of the most benevolent men I have known in private life have been the most strenuous upholders of the doctrine of eternal torment ; yea, Keble himself was one of these ; and I have heard the gentle Wriothesley Baptist Noel dilate upon this theme with a zeal which has sent a thrill of anguish through my soul. These are the men who unconsciously spread ' agnosticism ' and atheism over our land. Dr. Pusey even, tender as he was in his domestic relations, *did, by* this very idea—by mistaking ' difficulties ' for ' wickedness ' (like his friend Keble)—exercise a priestly sternness and reproof which hurried one agitated soul into the public avowal of atheism. As Polonius said of Hamlet's madness, so say I of this priestly intolerance—

'Tis true ; 'tis true 'tis pity ;
And pity 'tis 'tis true.

Vicar. As followers of Him who said it was ' better to pluck out an offending eye or to cut off an offending hand rather than the whole body should be cast into hell,' they could not do otherwise than thus speak and act towards those who disturb faith and are given to change, and with whom you sympathise too much. Your reference to Dr. Pusey seems to me pointedly precise. Are you at liberty to name the special instance of a person who was led to the public avowal of atheism, or, to use your words, was ' hurried ' on to its 'avowal' through want of tender sympathy and Christ-like love on the part of that venerable and venerated man you named?

Parishioner. It has not very much astonished me that even you, habitually kind as you are, should so readily acquiesce in, and even espouse, this stern and cruel conduct; although I did not quite expect that your thoughts would so quickly rush to the extreme of 'casting into hell' those who, having 'difficulties' on the subject of the 'inspiration of Holy Scripture,' and who, consequently, 'were too wicked to be reasoned with.' It would seem as if there were something special in the studies and training for the priesthood which disposes men to become intolerant and punitive in respect to speculative thought; and further, to associate and link together sin and punishment, to regard all suffering as the direct penal result of sin in a punitive sense, as did the early disciples of Jesus when they asked him 'who did sin, this man, or his parents, that he was born blind?' Jesus answered, 'Neither hath this man sinned, nor his parents: but that the works of God should be made manifest in him' (John ix. 2, 3). The feelings of 'Caiaphas' seem to be indigenous to the priestly mind: as a class, they are quick to discern when a man 'hath spoken blasphemy,' to become intensely excited—if not, as Caiaphas, so as to 'rend their clothes,' yet, like him, to be disposed to say to those who resort to advice and persuasive argument, 'Ye know nothing at all, nor consider that it *is expedient for us, that one man should die* for the people, and that the whole nation perish not.' General experience has shown that neither in the cruelty and shame of slavery, nor in the harsh penal code of our forefathers, nor in the severity and unwholesomeness of our prisons, nor in the ignorant barbarities of our lunatic asylums, did the clerical mind so quickly and clearly recognise iniquity as it did in a speculative 'dogma'; nor did they protest against them until Clarkson, and Romilly, and Howard, and Conolly raised their voices and wielded their pens, and devoted their lives to their removal or reform. Indeed, that distinguished philanthropist Dr. Conolly, who stripped every strap, manacle, and chain off every lunatic in 'Hanwell,' and never once permitted one to be placed on the many hundreds who were under his care, has again and again told me that he never knew a clergyman who, when in official capacity, did not uphold the idea of physical force and punishment. He had known many who in their private capacities were kind and beneficent, but never one who as member of a committee, or in any administrative capacity, did not advocate 'restraint' in all its material forms and 'chastisement' as the most efficient corrective of evil. My own experience, which has not been slight, confirms his so far as it relates to the treatment of the insane. The idea that 'this man had sinned'—that the malady differed in essence from other diseases, and was moral rather than physical—seemed generally present to them when going through the wards of a lunatic hospital. Consequently they always favoured the repressive system in all its varied forms. 'Demoniac possession' seemed to be present to their minds, and they appeared unable to detach the demonised from the 'demon.' Often have clergymen reminded me by their inquiries and by their conduct of the vigorous monk Luther, who is reported to have said, 'Idiots are men in whom devils have established themselves; and all the physicians who heal those infirmities as though they proceeded from natural causes are ignorant blockheads, who know nothing about the power of the demon. Eight years ago, I myself saw, and touched, at Dessau a child of this sort which had no human parents, but had preceeded from the Devil. He was twelve years old, and in outward form exactly resembled ordinary children. He did nothing but eat, consuming as much every day as four hearty labourers or threshers could. In most external respects he was, as I mentioned, just like other children; but if anyone touched him he yelled out like a mad creature, and with a peculiar sort of scream. I said to the Princes of Anhalt, with whom I was at the time, "If I had the ordering of things here I would have that child thrown into the Moldau at the risk of being held its murderer." But the Elector of Saxony and the Princes were not of my opinion in the matter.' Fortunately for the poor child, the 'lay' Elector of Saxony and the Princes of Anhalt had not had their minds and their hearts hardened by 'dogmatic' training in their childhood, and were therefore unwilling, I presume, to believe that the child 'had no human parents,' or that it could claim direct descent from his Satanic Majesty. My experience has probably been 'unfortunate' in respect to the clergymen and the Dissenting ministers I have known; but certainly the greater proportion of them were very intolerant of opinions adverse to their own, and, like Keble, were prone to regard their opponents 'as too wicked to be reasoned with.' While ready to 'compass heaven and earth' to retain or 'make proselytes,' they were comparatively indifferent to conduct, so long as their friends were 'sound in their faith' and strict observers of the forms, ceremonies, and sacraments of their respective Churches. They were always ready to *believe* good of those who were 'of the household of faith,' but not so ready to believe in the good motives and pure conduct of those 'of the contrary part,' and to accept the teaching of the Great Master—'A good tree cannot bring forth evil fruit, neither can a *corrupt* tree bring forth *good fruit*. . . . Wherefore, by their *fruits shall ye know them.*'

Vicar. There is a covert satire in your remarks which I shall not endeavour to imitate. Neither lay nor clerical finds it easy to act up to the sublime doctrine which you have quoted from the Gospel of St. Matthew, and I will admit that it is the highest attainment in the Christian life. But just now I am wishful to hear of the incident you referred to in the conduct of that holy man Pusey, whose teachings and whose conduct I reverence only short of the teachings and conduct of our blessed Lord and his immediate apostles.

Parishioner. It is no secret now; it has been published to the world. Mrs. Besant, the wife of a clergyman, was beset with difficulties in respect to the deity of Christ. She had in past years great reverence for Pusey, who had wielded a great influence over her, and whose writings had taught and guided her for many years. She corresponded with him, receiving many letters, and subsequently received a kindly invitation to a personal interview, which she joyfully accepted. I need not recite all the details, but will give the closing part of the interview in her own words, as given in the journal she now edits, entitled 'Our Corner.' 'He had no conception of the feelings of the sceptical spirit ; his own faith was solid as a rock, firm, satisfied, unshakable ; he would as soon have committed suicide as have doubted of the infallibility of the " Universal Church." " It is not your duty to *ascertain the truth*," he told me sternly. " It is your duty to accept and to believe the truth as laid down by the Church ; at your peril you reject it : the responsibility is not yours so long as you dutifully accept that which the Church has laid down for your acceptance. Did not the Lord promise that the presence of the Spirit should be ever with his Church to guide her into all truth ?" " But *the fact* of the *promise*, and its value, are *the very points* on which I am doubtful," I answered. He shuddered. " Pray, pray," he said ; " Father forgive her, for she knows not what she says." It was in vain I urged that I had everything to gain and nothing to lose by following his directions, but that it *seemed to me that fidelity to truth forbade a pretended acceptance of that which was not believed*. " Everything to lose ? Yes, indeed. You will be lost for time and lost for eternity." " Lost or not," I rejoined, "I must, and *will, try to find out what is true*, and I will not believe until I am sure." " You have no right to make terms with God," he answered, " as to what you will believe and what you will not believe. You are full of intellectual pride." I sighed hopelessly. Little feeling of pride was there in me just then, and I felt that in this rigid unyielding dogmatism there was no *comprehension* of my difficulties, no *help for me in my strugglings*. I rose, and, thanking him for his courtesy, said that I would not waste his time further, that I must go home and just face the difficulties out, openly leaving the Church and taking the consequences. Then for the first time his serenity was ruffled. "I forbid you to *speak* of your *disbelief*," he cried, "I forbid you to lead into your own lost state the souls for whom Christ died." *Slowly and sadly I* took my way back to the station, *knowing that my last chance of escape had failed me.*'

The emphases are my own. To me this scene appears like to some poor creature sinking into the wave and clinging to a person on the shore, who, failing to wring from her a specific promise, shakes her off from him with horror and leaves her to perish. Well might Mrs. Besant add, 'I recognised in this famous divine the spirit of the priest which could be tender and pitiful to the sinner repentant, humble, submissive, craving only for pardon and guidance, but which was *iron to the doubter*, to the heretic, and *would crush out all questionings* of "revealed truth," *silencing by force, not* by argument, all *challenge of the traditions* of the Church.' That opinion of Mrs. Besant respecting the character of Dr. Pusey is precisely the opinion which personal knowledge, information derived from friends who knew him intimately, and the perusal of his writings have compelled me to form of the author of 'The Christian Year,' and which I have endeavoured to convey in our long and rambling 'parley' respecting him.

Vicar. I recognise nothing in the conduct of the saintly Pusey towards Mrs. Besant as described by you which derogates from his high character. As a priest of the Most High God, pledged by solemn vows to be ready with all faithful diligence *to banish and drive away all erroneous and strange doctrines* contrary to

God's Word, he could not have acted otherwise than he did. You seem to forget that the divine Paul, when he ordained Timothy to the priesthood, commanded him to *reprove* and to *rebuke*, and to Titus also he emphatically said, 'Speak, and exhort, and *rebuke with all authority. Let no man despise thee.*'

Parishioner. You do well to quote Paul; he is a fair type of the Puseys, the Kebles, and other good men ' who seemed to be pillars of their Church.' The man who ' made havoc of the church, entering into every house, and taking men and women, committed them to prison ' : the man who, ' breathing out threatenings and slaughter against the disciples of the Lord, went ' [most wisely for his purpose] ' unto the *high priest*, and desired of him letters to Damascus to the synagogues, that if he found any of *this way, whether* they were men or *women*, he might bring them *bound* unto Jerusalem ' : the man who, after being struck to the earth as a '*persecutor*,' rose again with *new ideas*, but with the *old, ardent*, zealous, persecuting, self-confident *spirit*, so that he could as confidently and as heartily ' breathe out ' threatenings against the co-believers of his former ' faith ' as heretofore against the Christians, and exclaim, ' If an *angel from heaven*, or if *any man* preach any other gospel than that which *we have preached, let him be accursed*' : is a fair representative of the divine who was ' iron to the doubter,' and would crush out all questioning of revealed truth, '*silencing by force, not* by argument,' all who opposed him. Paul should have remembered his own sincerity and honesty of purpose when he ' profited in the Jew's religion,' and was ' exceedingly zealous of the traditions of his fathers,' and not have been so ready to pour out anathemas on others; should have remembered that his divine Master looked upon and loved the young ruler who had sought of him the way to inherit eternal life, although he was unable or unwilling to obey Jesus and to sell all he had and give to the poor, 'and come, take up the cross, and follow me.' I have said in my haste that Paul should have remembered the conduct of his Lord; but Paul was human, and in him, as in others, Christianity is a principle of growth, and has its stages of perfection, which no man has more fully described than himself. I had in my warmth forgotten for the moment that a time did come when Paul nobly recognised the rights of the individual conscience, and placed on record rules and principles which will ultimately crush all religious intolerance and establish the reign of equity and love. All I have said is apposite and true, but for the moment his great after-growth in holiness and spiritual insight had been forgotten, and I sketched his defects and errors as one might have spoken of Peter only in his hour of cowardice, falsehood, and denial, instead of remembering him in later years when penning his noble epistles. Paul's persecuting zeal was fiery and wrong, but it belonged to those weaker moments when 'the law in his members warring against the law of his mind' was temporarily triumphant. Never may it be forgotten of him that 'although he *knew* and was *persuaded* by the Lord Jesus that there is *nothing unclean* of itself,' yet could he bear with the weaker brother who *did* regard a thing as unclean (Rom. xiv. 14). Here was an inspired man, inspired as to this very subject, bearing with an erring and ignorant brother. It is an unparalleled example among Christian teachers. Even the 'Pilgrim Fathers' who left our shores to find a land where they could escape tyranny, and, like Paul, 'worship the God of their fathers' after the way which they call heresy, became in their turn intolerant, despotic, and cruel, exceeding in their bitterness—towards the 'Quakers,' for instance—all the 'persecutions for Christ's sake' which they themselves had received at the hands either of Queen Elizabeth, King James, or Charles the First. Irrational zeal too often blinds the intellect and hardens the heart, and causes a poor purblind mortal to usurp the authority of the Most High and *practically* to say to HIM, Be it mine

> thy *bolts* to throw
> And deal damnation round the land
> On each I deem thy foe.

Vicar. I fear that the latitudinarianism of your views has destroyed in you that reverence and zeal for *God's law* which are necessarily entertained by all good men. The awfulness of violating any law of God is with them so intense that they feel that the wrong-doer must be punished for his sin, otherwise the sovereignty of God is impugned, the distinction between sin and holiness is dimmed, and the kingdom of Satan is made to throw its pernicious shadow over the kingdom of God. All demarcations are confused, and right and wrong become interchangeable words. You seem wholly to forget that there never was a time in the whole range of Bible history when the disobedience and infraction of any Divine law went *uncensured* and *unpunished*. Each sin had its penalty: the Sabbath-breaker was stoned to death, nor less so those—whether son, daughter, brother, 'or the wife of thy bosom, or thy friend, which is as thine

P

own soul'—who endeavoured *to entice others to a worship* other than that which had been prescribed to them by Moses. To spare, to conceal, to pity such an one became a sin of the deepest dye. The language of the Divine command is clear, explicit, and stern as to how the faithful Israelites are to act under such circumstances : 'Thou shalt surely kill him ; *thine hand shall be first upon him* to put him to death, and afterwards the hand of all the people. And thou shalt stone him with stones, that he die ; because he hath sought to thrust thee away from the Lord thy God, which brought thee out of Egypt, from the house of bondage.' And the explicit reason for this condign punishment is fully and distinctly given, namely, that '*all Israel shall hear, and fear,* and *shall do no more any such wickedness as this is among you*' (Deut. xiii. 9-11). 'Moses was very meek, above all the men which were upon the face of the earth,' yet he displayed a holy zeal in carrying out these commands ; and Pusey was following in his footsteps by the conduct which has called forth your condemnation. It is good not to be wise above that which is written. Strict and literal obedience to God's command is the best sacrifice that man can offer, as Saul had to learn when he spared the best of the sheep and of the oxen of the Amalekites, even though they were reserved 'to sacrifice unto the Lord God' (1 Sam. xv. 15). To crush one's own feelings, even though they appear to be right and tender and just, as did Abraham when he climbed the mountain of Moriah in obedience to the command, 'Take now thy *son, thine only son Isaac, whom thou lovest,* and get thee into the land of Moriah ; and offer him there for a burnt-offering upon one of the mountains which I will tell thee of' (Genesis xxii. 2), is the becoming conduct of man. Abraham did not stop to inquire of the proud reason whether it was right to be cruel, nay, whether it might not be *murder* which he was about to commit. The acts and words you have censured in Keble and Pusey became them as saints of God, and the impulse which swayed their souls was precisely the same feeling which prompted David, the 'man after God's own heart,' to sing, 'Do not I hate them, O Lord, that hate thee? and am not I grieved with those that rise up against thee? I hate them with perfect hatred: I count them mine enemies' (Ps. cxxxix. 21, 22). You seem to have forgotten that the humble and the meek can be heroic and judicially severe, and who it was that made 'a scourge of cords,' 'overthrew the tables,' 'poured out the changers' money,' and drove the 'money-changers' out of the temple pell-mell with 'sheep, and oxen, and those that sold doves.' And remember that, paradoxical as it may seem, it was not from the wrath of the lion, but from the *wrath of the Lamb*, that 'the *kings* of the earth and the great men, and the *rich* men, and the *chief captains*, and *the mighty* men' hid themselves in dens and in the rocks of the mountains, when the prophetic seer described the awful vision of the opening of the sixth seal. It was because of 'the wrath *of the Lamb*' that the 'chief captains' and the 'mighty men' implored the mountains and the rocks to fall upon and hide them, 'for the great day of his wrath is come; and who shall be able to stand?' (Rev. vi. 15–17.)

Parishioner. I have listened patiently to your justificatory plea for persecution; although, notwithstanding your somewhat bitter remark on my latitudinarianism, there was nothing new in it, and very little from which I should dissent, *provided* the *conditions*, or rather the circumstances, were always as clear and indisputable as in the cases to which you have referred. The 'good' and 'gentle' persecutors to whom you have alluded, wished to persecute because of the *opinions* held by certain individuals; whereas nearly every Scriptural incident that you have brought forward in support of your theory had to do with *deeds*, not *ideas*, with facts and overt deeds, and is thus altogether in another category from the cases condemned by me. The Sabbath-breaker, the picker-up of wood, violated the *law* of his tribe by an overt act, and thus became amenable to the punishment which the special law prescribed. The case might have been approximatively parallel to the cases of uncharitable judgment to which I have alluded if the wood-gatherer had been punished—*not* for *gathering* up the wood, but for disputing with his tribe whether such a Sabbath law had *ever been* promulgated by *Jehovah*. The 'enticing' to a strange worship approaches somewhat nearer, but is still removed or separated by an immense distance, and by the huge contrast in value, *as evidence*, between the testimony of a man who is an *eye- or ear-witness of a fact* and the man who receives something as an alleged fact centuries after its occurrence, and after it has been transmitted through two or three distinct and separate languages. The enticer and enticed were contemporaneous with the miraculous events by which they were brought 'out of Egypt and from the house of bondage'; and certainly, if not contemporaneous, they were the offspring of those who were so, and their great leader Moses was still with them. Gratitude, reverence, and parental obedience all indicated and urged obedience, and the 'enticer' was committing *treason* against God, their immediate ruler, and despite also to his human parents and to the appointed ruler of the people. Of course in the long ages this condition of things would have changed; but, in any way, all my reasoning has been to the effect that full, absolute, immediate obedience to a command of God *is* the imperative *duty* of all mankind. The subject respecting which we are at issue *is*, What *has* been, what *is*, the *conduct* demanded of us *by the Most High*? We are at one in all that you have said respecting Abraham and the conduct of Saul. I do not see what bearing they have on our discussion. I have not consciously once argued *against* persons making *justice* precede mercy, or that any *feeling*, however benevolent in itself, should cause us to forego a clear and unequivocal command of our Maker. I battle for freedom of thought and opinion as to *what constitutes* such a command. The command being known—*known* to have emanated from the source of all wisdom in the *form* which it is presented *now* to the individual—*then* obedience—absolute, unconditional obedience—becomes us, and this only. If you will do me the favour to recall my earlier statements you will perceive how sincerely I have upheld this principle: that it is the very basis on which I have proceeded, and for which I contend; it is not only the foundation-stone, but the foundation itself, upon which all my arguments have rested.

Vicar. Your tone in reference to the sainted

champions of our Church, Dr. Pusey and the gentle Keble, justified me in my remarks, because you certainly more than implied that they were wrong in their deportment towards unbelievers, and it was needful for me, in justice to their memories, to show that they were acting as holy men of old had acted under similar circumstances. I was jealous of their reputation. I was unwilling that they should be charged with imperfections so gross as those which you implied, and I found it easy to show that *kind* and *tender*-hearted men could keep those feelings in check under their high sense of duty to God. I wished to assert, and most emphatically to assert, that both were truly Christian men, thoroughly anxious to know the truth, and to value it above all things.

Parishioner. And I was equally anxious to show that, good in a sense as each of them was, they fell far short of that high standard of Christian excellence to which you thought they had attained. Both were self-confident. Each of them partook somewhat of the spirit of the Pharisee who thanked God that he was not as other men, or even as *that publican.* In their priestly arrogance they could treat others who took intellectually a different view of the requirements of the Christian life with harshness and personal dislike. Under such circumstances they became too quickly indignant; too ready, if need be, to 'rend their robes' in furious protest against 'the blasphemy' which their imaginations had conjured up; and in other respects to show an unmistakable 'sacerdotal succession' from the high priest Caiaphas to whom I have referred. As I have said, and cannot refrain from repeating, it is the sense of 'expediency'—the 'necessity' to destroy the individual to 'save the nation,' to 'put out of the synagogues' those that bow not to their authority, to kill 'heretics' and 'think that he doeth God's service'— which cause vain men who 'have a zeal for God, but not according to knowledge,' to become 'persecutors of the Church of God.' Hence the feeling towards the Huguenots, which made Alva exclaim, 'Kill them all : God will know his own,' and induced Pope Gregory the Thirteenth, in his confidence, self-glorification, and blind zeal, to have a medal cast as a triumphant commemoration of the 'Massacre of St. Bartholomew'—that 'glorious victory' when at least 70,000 persons were murdered in the name of Jesus. But to revert again to our immediate subject, to return to our estimate of the character of John Keble. I am compelled to say that he had not the courage to grapple personally with arguments adverse to his own creed. He loved the placid calm which comes from an unquestioning faith ; it was so even in secular matters. He was once travelling with the brother of an acquaintance of my own. When they came in sight of Lichfield Cathedral Keble was charmed with the west front of that beautiful structure, and expatiated on its excellence, on the devotion and skill which it indicated on the part of the designers and builders of churches and cathedrals in the past ; and then, as if mourning over the degeneracy of the present time, and exulting in the 'ages of faith,' he exclaimed, ' They do nothing like that in these days.' When his companion assured him that he *had seen the entire front chopped away* and ' sheets of copper laid on the rough wall, big nails driven in, tarred cords stretched from nail to nail, and all the niches, saints, and angels of the old work *reproduced* in Roman cement upon this artificial banking,' so far from being grateful for the information, as a man 'thoroughly anxious *to know the truth*' and 'to value it above all things' would have been, and as you say Keble was, he became annoyed, and rebuked his companion sharply 'for not letting him *remain under an illusion.*' 'What good could it do to him *to know* how the thing was done?' 'Ex uno disce omnes.' This incident reveals fully, entirely, completely the *innate* character of the man. In that fact any observer and reflecting psychologist would find the key to all his conduct as a 'Churchman,' and a rational exposition of his theological tenets.

Vicar. Are you quite sure that the incident is authentic? I may, perhaps, have to take your own line of argument and be exceedingly desirous for clear *proof* for every statement. Still it is not improbable that the poet of 'The Christian Year' would form a very different estimate of the inquisitive spirit than you do. He knew well that it was the craving for the '*knowledge* of good and evil'—the desire to 'be as gods, knowing good and evil'—that led to

> man's first disobedience, and the fruit
> Of that forbidden tree, whose mortal taste
> Brought death into the world, and all our woe.

Every poem he wrote breathes of faith, of humility, of trust, and reverence. I regard him with love and honour because of this dislike of questioning, and the child-like spirit of acceptance of the teachings of the Church which he everywhere, at least indirectly, inculcates. 'In quietness and confidence shall be your strength' was the 'motto' of his banner—was the special 'sword of the spirit' which he loved to wield in moments of distrust or difficulty. He would, I am sure, have asked in the words of Job, 'Canst thou by searching find out God? canst thou find out the Almighty unto perfection? It is as high as heaven; what canst thou do? deeper than hell; what canst thou know?' (Job xi. 7, 8). Yes, Keble had heard and obeyed the voice of Him who said, 'Come unto me ... for I am meek and lowly in heart, and ye shall find rest unto your souls.' Thrice happy in this well-founded faith himself, he wished others to find it also. Like Andrew of old, he was anxious to tell all, 'We have found the Christ' and 'to bring them to Jesus.' From his own spiritual experience he could write, as in his exquisite poem for Christmas Day—

>   Thee, on the bosom laid
>   Of a pure virgin mind,
>   In quiet ever and in shade
>   Shepherd and sage may find—
> They who have bowed untaught to Nature's sway,
> And they who follow truth along her star-paved way.
>
>   The *pastoral* spirits first
>   Approach thee, Babe divine,
>   For *they in lowly thoughts are nurs'd*
>   *Meet for thy lowly shrine*:
> Sooner than they should miss where Thou dost dwell,
> Angels from heaven will stoop to guide them to thy cell.

His was the spirit of those blessed ones who 'have not seen and yet have believed,' and his dislike, if he had it, to ratiocination was from *the consequences it led to* by disquieting the minds and hearts of many.

Parishioner. I admit and admire all that you say respecting the actual *desires* of Keble. Doubtless he wished that all should possess his own serene belief and his own theological theories. His intentions were pure, and the spirit inculcated in the sweet poem you quoted is Christ-like and captivating. What I deplored, and deplore, was the bitter, narrow, persecuting feeling which sprung up when others were unable to see *mentally* as he saw, or to accept the doctrines which he believed to be essential to salvation. He could not rise to that philosophic spirit which breathes in the fourteenth chapter of St. Paul's Epistle to the Romans; he was too apt to forget that each individual soul had its own perceptions of right and wrong, and that 'to his own master,' and to his 'own master' alone, 'he standeth or falleth'; 'yea, he shall be holden up, for God is able to make him stand.' Perhaps all may have been different— I need not say perhaps, for his conduct *would have* been different—had he been trained under scientific rather than ecclesiastic influences; for, as I have before intimated, with the first *doubt* is a stimulus to inquiry, with the latter it is regarded as a 'sin.' The first accepts no 'authority' as final apart from facts; and as for 'reverence of the past,' he thinks with Lord Verulam that 'we have a mistaken apprehension of antiquity, calling that so which in truth is the world's nonage— "Antiquitas sæculi est juventus mundi."' Ecclesiastical training, as I have already said, is the opposite of all this; obedience to authority is here a virtue, and the ironical sarcasm of Juvenal—'Marcus dixit. Ita est'— reads to them like a truism. Some of Keble's earlier college associates had not this slavish respect for 'authority' and disdain of 'rationalism'—notably Arnold of Rugby; and, singularly, the 'judicious Hooker,' whose works Keble so lovingly edited, could write, 'For men to be tied and led by authority, as it were with a kind of captivity of judgment, and though there be reason to the contrary not to listen unto it, that to follow like beasts the first in the herd—they know not, nor care not, *whither*—this were brutish.' Again : 'That authority of men should prevail with men either against or above reason is no part of our belief'; and further: ' Companies of learned men, be they ever so great or reverend, are to yield unto reason.' Moreover, with all his powerful pleadings for the authority of the Church, Hooker can yet write, ' Be it in matter of the one kind or the other ' [doctrine or order], 'what Scripture doth plainly deliver, to that the first place both of credit and obedience is due ; the next whereunto is whatsoever any man can necessarily conclude by force of reason ; after these the voice of the Church succeedeth ' (vol. i. p. 446). In these sentences are to be found the 'potentiality and the power' of developing all I wish in respect to the rights of the individual ' Churchman ' as in opposition to the practical conduct of Keble towards the doubting and inquiring minds around him. Keble should have edited ' Jewel ' rather than the 'judicious Hooker.'

Vicar. You somewhat surprise me by these quotations ; but still, no honest man can read Hooker carefully without being impressed with the power, the lucidity, and the earnestness with which he upheld the ' ecclesiastical policy ' of our Church, and defended that policy as against the Papacy on the one hand and Puritanism on the other. And, as you yourself have said more than once, anything can be proved by separating isolated passages from their context; and although Jewel in his ' Apology ' may appear to you more in harmony with Keble's conduct than were the writings of Hooker, yet no one will, I think, agree with you who reads both books carefully; for while Jewel wrote '*apologetically*' for his Church, Hooker established a basis on the broad principles of universal law, which showed that the Church of England needed no apology inasmuch as she was 'built upon the foundation of the apostles and prophets, Jesus Christ himself being the chief corner-stone.'

Parishioner. Perhaps so. I do not feel that I am in a position to discuss the point further than to reiterate my belief that the quotations I have given would not have been endorsed by your hero. In those phrases of Hooker are the germs of that 'freedom of faith' for which I contend. It is possible that, like other men of profound wisdom before him, Hooker uttered truths of which he himself was not fully conscious of the greatness and ultimate fruition. Men of thoughtful and philosophic minds have, indeed, often done so. They have been the unconscious prophets of the science of the future. Long before the now-accepted facts of psychology were known, Parmenides said the 'highest degree of *organisation* gives the highest degree of thought'—a fact which has since widened the whole domain of scientific research, and which at this moment is the basis of the philosophy of Darwin, Spencer, Huxley and others. Parmenides' statement was like gold hidden in a mass of ore, which concealed it, and thus a long age of bewildering metaphysics occupied the study and thoughts of mankind. It has been so even in the regions of physics and material things. Centuries before Watt utilised the powers of steam, its power had been indicated by Hero of Alexandria (200 years B.C.); and in our own country the Marquess of Worcester, in the seventeenth century, had detailed experiments which are now seen to contain the elements of all that has since been achieved by Papin, Savory, Newcomen, and Watt. The progress of knowledge is slow although sure, and even the greatest minds cannot wholly emerge from their 'environments.' Even Newton thought and wrote foolishly on some topics; and Sir Thomas Browne, perhaps the most learned physician of his age, Sir Matthew Hale, and even William Shakspere, thought, spoke, and acted on the subject of *witches* in a manner which would now create a smile on the face of a boy in the 'sixth standard' of a charity school. Thus

> All throughout the ages an increasing purpose runs,
> And the thoughts of men are widened by progress of the suns.

Vicar. And what has been the practical result of this wide-spread knowledge of material things? An increase of irreverence, self-confidence, and irreligion; a willingness to rest wholly in a knowledge of secondary causes; a substitution of nature for God, of a blind, impelling, impersonal force in lieu of a creative and upholding will. Even in its least repellent form—I mean that which one of her Majesty's inspectors of schools (who is the distinguished son of an illustrious divine) calls 'the eternal power, not ourselves, that makes for righteousness'—it is a frightful dream, of which one might almost say, as of Ezekiel's roll, that it is replete 'with mourning, lamentation and woe.' A frightful dream, because the 'eternal power' which this literary athlete has so misnamed is described by himself as a power which does not 'think, or will, or love,' and essentially, therefore, is the same blind 'necessity' of which Lucretius wrote some nineteen hundred years ago—

> Since too of its own nature the vast mass
> Sprang forth spontaneous, rousing every power
> To every mode of motion, rashly oft,
> Oft vain and fruitless, till at length it formed
> Th' unchanging rudiments of things sublime,
> And heaven and earth, and main and mortals rose.
>
> . . . .
>
> These truths avowed, all Nature shines at once,
> Free in her acts, no tyrant to control,
> *Self-potent*, and *uninfluenced* by the gods.
>
> Book 2.

The cold blighting materialism, the godless universe, which seem generally to be the offshoot 'of science, falsely so called,' were an ample apology for Keble's dislike to it. I think more is lost than gained when the rainbow, for instance, is simply looked upon as the necessary prismatic result of light shining through water, and nothing more. I sympathise from my soul with Campbell in the lines:

> 'Triumphal Arch, that fillest the sky
>   When storms prepare to part,
> I ask not proud Philosophy
>   To teach me what thou art.
>
> . . . . .
>
> *When Science from Creation's face*
>   *Enchantment's veil withdraws,*
> *What lovely visions yield their place*
>   *To cold material laws!*
>
> And yet, fair bow, no fabling dreams,
>   But words of the Most High,
> Have told why first thy robe of beams
>   Was woven in the sky.

> When o'er the green undeluged earth,
>   Heaven's covenant, thou didst shine,
> How came the world's grey fathers forth
>   To watch thy sacred sign !
>
> . . . . .
>
> How glorious is thy girdle, cast
>   O'er mountain, tower, and town ;
> Or mirror'd in the ocean vast,
>   A thousand fathoms down !
>
> . . . . .
>
> As fresh in yon horizon dark,
>   As young thy beauties seem,
> As when the eagle from the ark
>   First sported in thy beam :
>
> For, faithful to its sacred page,
>   Heaven still rebuilds thy span,
> *Nor lets the type grow pale with age*
>   *That first spoke peace to man.*

Parishioner. I sympathise no less than yourself with those exquisite lines. They are very beautiful even if not true in all their details. They were true to the writer, and poetry does not cease to be poetry in every case, even

> When Science from Creation's face
>   Enchantment's veil withdraws.

For my part, I consider Shakspere's lines on adversity, in the play of 'As you like it,' very poetical, although I know that the simile he uses is no longer accepted by naturalists. When Shakspere wrote it was fully believed ; and if 'Science' has withdrawn the veil of enchantment,' and the alleged fact is fact no longer, yet has Shakspere wedded it to a moral in such consummate language that the wand of his genius restores the glamour of 'enchantment'—

> Sweet are the uses of adversity;
> Which, *like the toad, ugly and venomous,*
> *Wears yet a precious jewel in his head.*

And so with the image in that exquisite comfort-giving Psalm of David's, in which he sings, 'Who redeemeth thy life from destruction; who crowneth thee with lovingkindness and tender mercies; who satisfieth thy mouth with good things; so that *thy youth is renewed like the eagle's.*' We feel the illustrative force of the simile, although a scientific experience may tell us that the youth of the eagle is simply like the youth of other creatures—a 'golden age' of sunshine, happiness, and power; an *evanescent* season of love and joy; *never* to 'be renewed,' although in a subdued form it may, when past, linger for a while in the memory as a sweet remembrance, as the after-glow of an autumn eve may brighten the horizon for a time with the gorgeous hues and reflections of a sun that has set with a golden glory, to be followed speedily by the darkness of a night of *never-more*. Science may tell us all this, but Hope will whisper of a 'life' saved from destruction,' and the soul will cling to the image 'of a youth renewed like the eagle's,' to the fond dream of a Psyche emerging from the chrysalis of death, clothed with immortal youth, and dowered with every capacity for rapture and love.

Vicar. I have listened with a pleasant surprise to this outburst of emotion on your part, so far removed from all your previous pleadings for knowledge, so different from your strong wish that the clear cool light of science should be thrown upon the mists of theology to dispel their 'mirage' and to open up the realities of life and experience. The 'increasing purpose' and the 'widening thoughts' which come 'with the progress of the suns' do not, then, it appears, meet every want of the human soul : *there are* requirements and needs which neither the scales and the tests of the chemist, the scalpel of the anatomist, the microscope and researches and experiments of the biologist, nor the batteries, the cells, and the coils of the physicist can supply! I hope, even yet, that increased and increasing reflection, joined with that honesty of purpose which you claim, may show you that divines have not been wrong in resisting in every possible way the assumptions of science and the 'dogmatism' (for *dogmatism* is not *confined* to clerical circles) of too many of its professors. I believe that not only has the teaching of the modern school of biologists and physicists tended to dry up the sources of poetry, but that it is also, as I have said before, the main cause of the irreverence and irreligion which characterise alike the 'club circles' and the workshops and factories of our large and flourishing towns at the present moment.

Parishioner. That oratory and poetry alike flourish best in the earlier stages of civilisation, as do the singing of birds and the fragrance of flowers in the springtime and early summer, I will not dispute. Knowledge has certainly a tendency to diminish wonder and to check the exuberance of fancy ; and the songs of the syrens and the dances of Pan and the dryads and nereids disappear from our shores and our forests when the geologists and the botanists explore their recesses. Still, poetry is not likely to leave the earth so long as the human heart beats with the emotions of passion, of hope, of fear, and of ambition ; and the very discoveries and expositions of science will furnish their own marvels and their own attractions and beauties. One of our very greatest poets has, in sooth, sung of philosophy itself in the following lines:

> How charming is divine philosophy !
> Not harsh and crabbed as dull fools suppose,
> But musical as is Apollo's lute,
> And a perpetual feast of nectar'd sweets,
> Where no crude surfeit reigns.

It becomes, therefore, a man of prose to be silent on this topic after so poetic a defence from such a source; but I demur wholly to your statement as to the advance of scientific knowledge being the *primary* cause of the irreverence and irreligion to which you refer. We have already spoken on these topics, and I shall not open them up further than to state that advancing knowledge, and the rigid, impartial, and fearless research which science enjoins, did cause thoughtful and reflecting minds to *question* some of the dogmatic statements of divines; and these statements, having been fiercely defended and upheld by theologians as all-important, and among the very essential truths of revelation, led to an investigation which caused their overthrow and abandonment.

In brief, the injustice and general wrongfulness of some of the leading tenets of what is accepted as *orthodox* Christianity, and a belief in which is 'necessary to salvation,' have led to a very considerable revolt from the ranks of popular Christianity; but I do not consider that the progress of science is to be blamed for this disturbance. Ahab, in his mental blindness and self-complacency, could say to Elijah, 'Art thou he that troubleth

Israel?' overlooking that the true and primary source of the trouble was the conduct of his father and himself; as Elijah said, 'in that ye have forsaken the commandments of the Lord, and hast followed Baalim' (1 Kings xviii. 17, 18). So advancing science has tried, as by fire, every dogmatic tenet: 'of what sort it is,' and the wood, and the hay, and the stubble' *have* 'suffered loss.' *Their* disappearance has caused too many to think that other constituents of the foundation will disappear, overlooking the fact that the 'gold and the silver' admit of purification 'by fire,' and are made more resplendent by the very agency which has destroyed the 'hay and the stubble.' We are living in a state of transition, of doubt, and of agitation; but good men should remember *Who is* the refiner, Who it is that, in the language of Malachi, 'sits as a refiner and purifier of silver,' who shall purge even the gold and silver from dross, and thus restore a condition of things when 'the offering of Judah and Jerusalem shall be pleasant unto the Lord,' as in the days of old, and as in former years.

Vicar. Apart from the Athanasian and Nicene Creeds, which, to my grief, you hold in so little reverence, what are the special tenets to which you refer as having contributed to the wide-spread distrust in religion, and to the irreverence in respect to holy men and holy things of which I complain, and which is so very antagonistic to that reverential, humble, obedient, and childlike spirit displayed by Keble, by Newman, by Pusey, and other distinguished sons of our venerable Church?

Parishioner. I am not aware that I said much about 'holy men' and 'holy things,' or 'reverence' and 'irreverence,' for it grieves me to observe that our noble language is, as it were, being defaced, if not degraded, by fashionable slang on the one hand and the cant terms of religious sects on the other. Words of the gravest import are foolishly travestied, and effeminate men and masculine women toss them about incessantly in their glib and jejune utterances. The young school-girl thinks it indicates womanly wisdom and *haut ton* to talk to her brothers and others of being 'awfully jolly,' of an 'awful swell,' or a 'jolly boss,' and the like; and in your own ranks the words 'holy' and 'reverence' in various combinations have become well-nigh as marked a *shibboleth* of your party as were the words 'the Gospel,' 'the Lord's day,' 'the grace of God,' and 'the blessed Jesus'—pronounced with a special nasal unction—the characteristics of the Evangelical section when, some thirty or forty years ago, it was a power in the State. I wish that all this mischief to our literature and language could be prevented; for sublime words lose their sublimity and their meaning when so long made the vehicle of brainless folly, and their place can never be filled up. The linguistic cant I have named repelled many persons of culture and taste from the Evangelical party who had no special dislike to their theory of salvation; and the fine adjective 'holy' is becoming tarnished by its too frequent use among the 'guilds' and 'fraternities' of your section or regiment of the Church militant.

Vicar. Without discussing this matter, it is everywhere felt that the reverential spirit is fading from our midst; it is perceptible even in the family circle, and, as in other spheres, a mischievous slang is its exponent, and, as I believe, often its instigation. We are in accord as to the infinite importance of words. The solemn utterance of our Divine Master on this topic seems to be wholly forgotten by society. In presence of the universal flippancy of speech, it is a fearful thought to remember that 'for every idle word that men shall speak, they shall give an account thereof in the day of judgment.' Habit or custom may, perhaps, mitigate its irreverence; but it is difficult to believe that a son who habitually speaks of *his father* as 'the governor' or 'the boss' possesses that filial piety or reverence which he ought to have; or think otherwise than that the fifth commandment is forgotten, and therefore disregarded and violated. As I have said, you may see this want of reverence even in families; it is still more conspicuous in the deportment of children towards their seniors; still more so in the deportment of labourers, mechanics, and others towards their superiors who are not their immediate employers. The Catechism, learnt and acted upon by a past generation, is shamefully forgotten in the present day. Keble, when at Horsley, was indefatigable in instructing the rising generation in this the Church's noble epitome of religion; and as he was himself pre-eminently distinguished for his reverence and humility, I should hope that in *that* district the peasantry are exceptions to the denizens of our large towns, who seem never to have known what is their duty to their neighbour. How few, if asked the question, would individually and cheerfully say, 'To love, honour, and succour my father and mother; to honour and obey the Queen, and all that are put in authority under her; to *submit* myself to all my governors, teachers, *spiritual pastors* and masters; to order myself *lowly and reverently* to all my betters.' Irreverence and a disregard of 'authority' (which, by-the-by, you seem to regard as a virtue) are the earlier outcomes of that teaching (not immediately by our schools) in our papers and reviews to which I have so frequently referred; the ultimate fruit of which will be agnosticism, atheism, and anarchy.

Parishioner. The outlook *is* most serious. We are likely to suffer from the consequences of the past. Erroneous teachings, the love of mammon, the wealth and luxury which that love has created, the huge and hideous contrasts which exist among us of enormous wealth and extreme indigence, of voluptuous magnificence and unutterable squalor and wretchedness, grovelling superstitions and brazen-faced atheism, make up a condition of things at which the stoutest heart might tremble. I cannot, and I do not, wish to disguise from my view the facts of irreverence and insubordination to which you have referred. But the case is far from hopeless. Each individual (or rather, I might have said, you and I) may rest in the assurance that God is supreme; and though 'the earth may be removed, and the mountains be carried into the midst of the sea,' all humble and trusting souls may safely say, 'The Lord of Hosts is with us; the God of Jacob is our refuge.' But apart from these personal considerations, there is a line of conduct to be pursued which may avert the national calamity which seems impending. There *is* such a thing as a *grovelling* reverence and a blind submission to authority, which is a stupendous evil; and these two evils have, I repeat, been largely contributory to the calamity which now threatens us. I maintain that your views are too constricted, and, if I may say so without offence, too clerical or priestly. There is no reason why we should dash against Scylla merely to avoid Charybdis, for our duty is to steer between them. Their position is well known. Virgil tells us:

> Dextrum Scylla latus, lævum implacata Charybdis
> Obsidet ;

and, as Ovid properly says:

> In medio tutissimus ibis.

One divine at least in our own day has clearly and wisely described the limits of that 'reverence' on which you so fondly expatiate. Arnold of Rugby, in his 'Lectures on Modern History,' said: 'Reverence shown for that which does not deserve it is no virtue; no, nor even an amiable weakness, but a plain folly and sin. But if it be meant that he is wanting in proper reverence, not respecting what is really to be respected, *that* is assuming the whole question at issue; *because what we call divine* he calls an idol; and, as, supposing that we are in the right, we are bound to fall down and worship, so, supposing him to be in the right, *he is no less bound* to pull it to the ground and destroy it' ('Modern History,' pp. 210, 211). That is the sentence of a wise man and of a just man. The blind reverence, or rather the slavish reverence, 'to authority' inculcated by the Church of Rome, and by her admirers and secret disciples in the Church of England, will never be accepted by the present generation; and our prospects would now be brighter if it had never been accepted in the past. There are some minds prone to reverence, and it is a beautiful quality when under the control of the intelligence; otherwise it degenerates rapidly into slavish and abject awe. Gall, Spurzheim, and Combe have all published 'casts' and portraits of men distinguished for this feeling; they called the 'organ' 'veneration,' and placed it high up on the head. The portrait of John Frederic Oberlin, the good and benevolent pastor of the Ban de la Roche, was, I well remember, selected as a 'fine example' of this configuration; and the handsome head of Cardinal Newman meets all the requirements of the *late* phrenologists in this particular. If Spurzheim were now living he would like a cast of it, and he would tell his followers to observe how large was the organ of 'veneration,' and would then ask them to listen to the following facts in the Cardinal's autobiography as demonstrative that the material configuration and the mental attribute associated with it were in accord: 'The first time that I was in a room with him' [Keble] 'was on the occasion of my election to a Fellowship in Oriel, when I was sent for into the Tower, to shake hands with the Provost and Fellows. How is that hour fixed on my memory after the changes of forty-two years—forty-two this very day on which I write! I have lately had a letter in my hands, which I sent at the time to my great friend John William Bowden, with whom I passed almost exclusively my undergraduate years. "I had to hasten to the Tower," I say to him, "to receive the congratulations of all the Fellows. I bore it till Keble took my hand, and then felt so abashed and unworthy of the honour done to me, that I seemed *desirous* of *quite sinking into the ground.*" . . . When one day I was walking in High Street with my dear earliest friend just mentioned, with what eagerness did he cry out "There's Keble!" and with *what awe did I look at him!*' ('Apologia pro Vitâ'). These incidents reveal the essential character of the man as clearly and as truly as a chemical test, or tests, reveal the constituents of a fluid. This anecdote is as expository of Newman's character as was the Lichfield incident that of Keble's. Newman was profoundly reverential, and, as I have already said, his *feelings* are the *same* now as heretofore; *differently directed*, but in themselves unchanged, as the zeal of 'Saul of Tarsus' differed only in direction from the zeal of 'Paul called to be an apostle of Jesus Christ.'

Vicar. I have been waiting for you to describe the tenets which you think have conduced or contributed to the wide-spread infidelity of the present time, and my incidental praise of the reverential spirit has caused you unduly to expatiate upon it, and has ultimately brought you round again to your too favourite theory of the interdependence of cerebral organisation and mental attributes—a theory which I have censured as destroying free will and being otherwise most mischievous to the spiritual interests of mankind.

Parishioner. As to the matter of 'free will,' I must leave you to discuss it when you have occasion to deal with the ninth of the Articles of your religion; or if you are desirous of combating it, I can refer you to a combatant worthy of your steel in Martin Luther, and his commentary on St. Paul's Epistle to the Galatians. And speaking of Martin Luther, it may be an interesting exercise to you some day to compare an authentic portrait of that pugnacious polemic with one of Melancthon. As a preliminary study, I would suggest that you look also at the portrait of some prominent pugilist, like to Sayers, or, as a true transcript from nature, at the head of Charles the Wrestler in Maclise's fine picture from Shakspere's play of 'As you like it,' and then, recalling the life, the 'table talk,' and general conduct of Luther to your mind, contrast the *form* of *his* head with the large, full-fronted, well-domed, lofty head of Melancthon, and see whether there is not *something in that contrast of form* and *contrast of character* which will justify a further research on your part as to the relation between 'matter and spirit,' between 'mind and organisation.' I shall feel personally very grateful to you whenever you will show to me a person distinguished for his religious toleration, his benevolence, his great intelligence and reverent spirit—men, I mean, like unto Melancthon, Oberlin, Heber, Dean Stanley, and the late Frederick Robertson of Brighton—in whom the anterior and superior portion of the head is not large, handsome, and smoothly arched; in whom, that is, a perpendicular line, carried upwards from the opening of the ear to the top of the head, and an horizontal line taken from the same spot to a point corresponding with the anterior termination of the forehead, would, by having a third annexing-line drawn from a level with the second at the middle of the anterior base of the forehead, form a smooth convex outline, thus, ⌂; or—what would be an equivalent fact—show me a person possessing a like character to Melancthon, to Stanley, or to Robertson, having a *low* and *narrow* forehead—low and narrow as compared with the large and protuberant mass of skull behind a line drawn vertically from the apex of the head to the opening of the ear; and I will abandon immediately my present firm conviction 'that the highest degree of organisation gives the highest degree of thought'; yes, will abandon it for ever as a mischievous heresy, and will endeavour to believe that when Paul wrote to the Romans respecting the potter having the 'power *over the clay, of the same lump* to make one vessel *unto honour*, and another to dishonour'; and again to Timothy, concerning the vessels in a great house 'of gold and silver, but, *also* of wood and of earth, and some to honour, and some to dishonour,' he did not mean to imply any material or physical distinction, or any insuperable obstacle to the formed lump making itself into some other vessel, or that the 'wood and the earth,' the 'gold and the silver' were permanent forms having fixed and unchangeable qualities; but, *until then*—until you, or someone else has shown me an individual in whom very high qualities have been associated with the low configuration I have described—I shall continue to accept the lessons which nature and observation have hitherto taught me; viz. that there are men, as there are vessels, of whom some *are made* 'unto honour,' and others 'unto dishonour.' Perhaps I ought to apologise for having dwelt so much upon this theory, because *in it*, and in it alone, I find a solution for what is otherwise a deep and insoluble mystery, namely, the different conclusions to which men come from the *same facts*. We find it so in all matters, whether they relate to conduct, to sermons, books, speeches, works of art, or any other thing to which their attention is drawn. This difference of opinion has existed through all time. In the classic ages, Terence tells us, 'Quot homines tot sententiæ'; and Horace, in the second book of his Epistles, writes:

> Denique non omnes eadem mirantur amantque :
> Carmine tu gaudes ; hic delectatur iambis ;
> Ille Bioneis sermonibus et sale nigro.

And only a few days ago a most striking illustration—perhaps the most instructive that could be possibly given—occurred in the great judicial Court of Appeal (where, alas! it was no rare thing), where men of the highest attainments, and with minds perfectly unbiassed and of the most honourable purpose, were in *absolute agreement* as *to the facts*, but came to *opposite* conclusions respecting them. A daily paper states as follows : 'Lord Coleridge, in giving judgment on Saturday in the case of Regina *versus* Powell, said the case exhibited a very serious instance of the different conclusions which educated minds could come to on *one state of facts*. The question to be decided was whether on the facts of the case, there was a false pretence. He and his brothers Huddleston and Mathew were strongly of opinion that *there was*, while his brothers Grove and Manisty *were as strongly of opinion* that there was not. *Neither party could understand the decision arrived at by the other.*' These Judges are differently organised, and hence the above condition of things. This being so with contemporaneous *facts*, with facts which *all accepted as facts*, does it not become us to be absolutely tolerant one of another in respect to conclusions on religious matters? Does it not become a crime—yea, a murder—to destroy a fellow-creature because he draws 'conclusions' from *ancient history* which we choose to brand as 'heresy'? If two judges, equally able, equally just, draw different conclusions and give a different decision on the facts (the *same facts respecting which all are agreed*) from the decision of three other judges, and 'neither party *could understand the decision of the other*,' how absurd, how mad is it to expect uniformity of opinion on the conflicting facts and conflicting statements of a history transacted centuries ago! If the constitution of human nature precludes unanimity on earthly matters, how can it be in perfect accord on 'heavenly things'? Well might the great 'teacher come from God' say, 'If I have told you earthly things, and ye believe not, how shall you believe if I tell you of heavenly things?' A generous toleration of religious opinion ought to be—yea, I will venture to say, even to atheism—the most universal of sentiments, instead of being the most rare. It is sad to think that even John Locke, in writing his noble work on 'Toleration,' could not 'rise to the height of his great argument,' but must needs except the Papist for political, and the Atheist for moral reasons.

Vicar. Such a universal toleration can only coexist with a universal indifference to religion and an utter disregard of the glory and honour of God. Very different was the spirit of Hezekiah, and Josiah, and Jehoshaphat, who broke down the altars, burnt the groves, and destroyed the sepulchres of those who had held in honour the 'gods of the heathen.' Moreover, it is directly antagonistic to the commands of the Most High as given in 'Exodus' and 'Deuteronomy,' where the command to the Israelites is imperative to 'destroy their altars, break their images, and cut down their groves: for thou shalt worship no other god: for the Lord, whose name is Jealous, is a jealous God' (Exodus xxxiv. 14).

Parishioner. If we were now under a theocracy as

the Israelites were at that time, I should not have said anything respecting toleration ; but all the circumstances are altered—so changed that the true worshippers of God are not always distinguishable ; so changed, indeed, that centuries ago the very high priest of the temple of God could charge Jesus himself with blasphemy, while the common people shouted, 'We found this fellow perverting the nation ... Away with him ... Crucify him, crucify him'; while later on priests and people alike, under the same frenzy, shouted against the holiest man of the time, Stephen, 'Away with such a fellow from the earth ; for it is not fit that he should live.' From that unhappy hour, through long ages, the blind infatuated zeal of theologians has caused them to act on a like principle and to shout the same cry. The ascendency of the secular power has during the past century controlled this zeal, and rendered it civilly impotent as regards inflicting penalties on life or property ; yet many pious men and thousands of pious women still regard themselves as exclusively right, and others who differ from them as *wickedly* wrong. There are few lives known to me so religious, so holy in its general career, as that of Cardinal Newman, and yet how painful it is to read some of his addresses and essays, and to observe how an ecclesiastical system and theory have steeled a heart naturally susceptible and kind. In his essay on 'Anglican Difficulties' he gives us most touching details of the sayings of many good men in their dying hours—sayings which would have demonstrated to any impartial observer how great was their faith, their trust in and love for God. The dying words of such men as Bunyan, Harvey, Whitefield, Walker, Arnold, and Scott have been gleaned from their respective biographies to show their futility. There is scarcely a word of sympathy; they are given to show how delusive such expressions and feelings are apart from the belief in a special ecclesiastical system of 'sacramental grace.' He depicts the end of one well known to him—one who was beloved by such men as Whately and Max Müller—one whose whole life was a life of self-sacrifice to what *he believed* to be the truth (and Newman has done no more)—one who breathed thoroughly and truly in all his actions the prayerful spirit of the hymn composed by Newman himself—

> Lead, kindly light, amid the encircling gloom,
>   Lead thou me on;
> The night is dark, and I am far from home,
>   Lead thou me on.
> Keep thou my feet; I do not ask to see
> The distant scene; one step enough for me.
>
>   .   .   .   .   .   .
>
> So long thy power hath blest me, sure it still
>   Will lead me on
> O'er *moor* and *fen*, o'er crag and torrent, till
>   The night is gone,
> And with the morn those angel-faces smile
> Which I have loved long since, and lost awhile.

Yes, of the good Blanco White, whose bodily sufferings were most intense and prolonged, the Cardinal wrote thus: 'Alas! there was another, who for three months "lingered," as he said, "in the face of death." "O my God," he cried, "I know thou dost not overlook any of thy creatures. Thou dost not overlook me. So much torture. . . . to kill a worm! Have mercy on me! I cry to thee, knowing I cannot alter thy ways. I cannot if I would, and I would not if I could. If a word would remove these sufferings I would not utter it." "Just life enough to suffer," he continued, "but I submit, and not only submit, but rejoice." One morning he woke up, and, with firm voice and great sobriety of manner, spoke only these words: "Now I die!" He *sat as one in the attitude of expectation*, and about *two hours* afterwards *it was as he had said*. And he was a professed infidel, and *worse than an infidel, an apostate priest*' ('Anglican Difficulties'). Such is the point of callousness to which ecclesiastical training can reach! It can so operate on the mind and the heart of a naturally kind man as to enable him to pen such sentences as those I have related, and 'to think that he is doing God service.' It certainly wrung from his instinctive natural conscience the words, ' Of course we think as tenderly of them as we can ' [but, alas! then came the awful ' but '], '*but* the claim in their behalf is unreasonable and exorbitant if it is to the effect that their state of mind is to be taken in evidence, not only of promise in the individual, but of truth in his creed. . . . The *Catholic*, and HE ALONE, has *within him* that union of external with internal notes of God's favour which sheds the light of conviction over his soul, and makes him both fearless in his faith and calm and thankful in his hope' ('Anglican Difficulties,' p. 70). Newman would be startled and pained, grievously pained, if he were charged with falsehood; and yet, practically, the most wilful fictionist could not more falsify truth than the Cardinal has done in the above passages of his essay. His casuistry may, perhaps, enable him to defend himself successfully in a conclave of cardinals or in a 'convocation ' of York or Canterbury, but certainly not before a jury of twelve men trained to weigh and balance evidence and to sift the alleged facts upon which the evidence is based. His own narrated facts, given for a different purpose, *prove* to the extreme point of demonstration that others beside 'the Catholic' possess every grace which 'can shed the *light* of *conviction* over his soul, and make him *fearless* in his faith and *calm* and *thankful* in his *hope.*' He records of Bunyan that his *last* words to his friends sorrowing around him were, 'Weep not for me' [as if he had been a saint!], 'but for yourselves. I go to the Father of our Lord Jesus Christ, who, doubtless, through the mediation of his Son, will receive me, though a sinner, when we shall ere long meet, to sing the new song and be happy for ever.' 'Mr. Whitefield rose at four o'clock on the Sabbath day, went to his closet, and was unusually long in private; laid himself on his bed for about ten minutes, then went on his knees, and prayed most fervently he might that day finish his Master's work.' Then he sent for a clergyman, 'and, before he could reach him, closed his eyes on this world without a sigh or a groan, and commenced a Sabbath of everlasting rest' (Sidney's 'Life of Hill'). What 'notes,' internal or external, are wanting in the above instances? Where did the '*light of conviction*' shine brighter on the soul, where was ever a more 'fearless faith,' where a more 'calm and thankful hope,' than the conviction, than the faith and the hope displayed by Bunyan and Whitefield? My soul writhes with the mingled feelings of pain and indignation as I reflect on the cold scathing words of Newman over the memory of Blanco White—'*worse than an* infidel, an apostate priest!' Terrible words to be uttered of one who had displayed such sublime submission to the will of his Father and his God'—a submission reminding one again of the tender words of Job : 'Though he slay me, yet will I trust in him!' More terrible still that they should have been written by one who, if not 'an apostate priest' himself, *had* 'apostatised' from the Church to which he had bound himself by sacred vows; who had 'apostatised' from the 'order and ministry of priesthood of the Church of England'—by the man and priest who, to use the words of the historian Carlyle, had 'apostatised from *his old faith in facts, and took to believing in semblances.*' All this is most sad and most mischievous, provokes a bitter spirit, and urges to an unchristian-like retaliation. When I read these cold and cruel words of Newman over Blanco White, whose spirit had undergone like conflicts with the soul of Newman, although they led to a more manly issue, the words of Hamlet came rushing to my lips, and I could have said to him :

> I tell thee, churlish priest,
> A minist'ring angel shall (this man) be
> When thou liest howling.

Vicar. It certainly seems a sad thing thus to speak, more especially of one who, like himself, had foregone the most solemn vows in obedience to strong convictions and the irresistible voice of conscience. Still, as the Cardinal maintains, there *is a standard of truth* wholly apart from the convictions and the feelings of individuals ; and it would be a most dangerous principle to accept what you imply—that so long as a man is in earnest and personally truthful, it would matter little what his creed may be. Such a system would abolish order and lead directly to anarchy and chaos. You should not forget that tender, and loving, and charitable as was our Divine Lord, his utterances towards the Pharisees were scathing and terrible, and exceeded in their condemnation all the phrases that you have reported as bitter and wrong in the pious Cardinal.

Parishioner. I accept your statements as regards the procedure of our Divine Lord. They are veritable history, and if the Cardinal possessed the same power of reading the heart, and the same Divine intuition of knowing what *was* truth, as did Jesus of Nazareth, I should recall my statements. Moreover, could it be shown that in drifting from 'Evangelicalism' to 'Anglicanism,' and from 'Anglicanism' to the most gross tenets of Popery, he had sought guidance with greater humility and with a more intense desire to reach the truth than did Blanco White under corresponding conditions of spiritual perplexity : or could it be proved that Blanco White sought guidance from any other source than from the great God who made him : I should at once acknowledge that your defence is just and irrefutable ; but as the case stands, I reiterate my statement that the Cardinal's remarks are severe, yea, presumptuous. The sentences which he has given us as proceeding from Blanco White in his bodily anguish indicate a sublime submission and a noble faith. They remind one of the grand utterance of Job in his affliction : ' Though HE slay me, yet will I trust in him.' The same pious thought—that seeming loss may prove great gain, that the withholding or withdrawal of light may lead to still higher revelations of God's love—breathes in one of

White's sonnets—as grand a sonnet as human poet ever penned, called

Night and Death.

> Mysterious night ! when our first parent knew
> Thee from report divine, and heard thy name,
> Did he not tremble for this lovely frame,
> This glorious canopy of light and blue !
> Yet, 'neath a curtain of translucent dew,
> Bathed in the rays of the great setting flame,
> Hesperus with the host of heaven came,
> And lo ! creation widened in man's view.
> Who could have thought such darkness lay concealed
> Within thy beams, O sun ! or who could find
> Whilst *fly*, and *leaf*, and *insect* stood revealed,
> That to such countless orbs thou mad'st us blind !
> Why do we then shun death with anxious strife ?
> If light can thus deceive, wherefore not life ?

Vicar. Certainly that is a highly poetic sonnet, full of philosophic thought ; and, with the author's unsettled yet conscientious mental history, and his great and long-continued bodily suffering, can hardly fail to make all kindly hearts sympathise with him—that is, so far as to compassionate and to be sorry for him. To use Newman's words, ' Of course we think of him as tenderly as we can ' ; but there remains the excruciating thought that he died without the pale of the Church, with no direct acknowledgment of the sole ransom for guilt which has been provided against the consequences of the primæval sin, and no sacramental grace for the blotting out of the numerous sins which he had committed subsequent to his baptismal regeneration. But this sad episode is carrying us somewhat beyond our subject ; and moreover, I am anxious again to enter my solemn protest against your materialistic theory, which links mind inseparably with matter, and intrudes into the spiritual kingdom by limiting the capacities of individuals for spiritual attainments in this life, and thus inferentially their enjoyment of celestial happiness and bliss.

Parishioner. Pardon me, for my warmth compels me to say that it matters little with what measure of 'tenderness' you and the Cardinal 'can think' of that struggling, heroic, yet submissive man of whom we have been speaking: his spirit has gone up to the Tribunal of 'his Father, and your Father; of his God, and your God,' and, even in this life, not Paul himself could say more heartily than he, 'With me it is a very small thing that I should be judged of you, or of man's judgment: yea, I judge not mine own self'; and had he made direct verbal prayers to the Great Ransom you refer to, it would not have 'lightened' his darkness in the estimation of the Cardinal, who places in the same category of doubtful conditions some who died uttering tones of triumphal trust in the 'Redeemer.' The authority of 'the Church,' with all the attributes annexed to it, has no firmer basis than the 'faith of those men, whose testimony to their creed is so worthless in the estimation of a priesthood claiming, like you and the Cardinal, apostolic descent. The enlightened *reason* of men must necessarily be the final test of any 'religious tenet,' whether it be discussed in Councils, in the closet of the Pope, the Westminster Assembly, or the Privy Council of her Majesty. Butler and Hooker are, I think, in accord on this matter. My 'materialistic theory,' as you are pleased to define it, has no further limitations to the spiritual capacities of individuals, or to their celestial enjoyments, than have the metaphors of Paul to which I have referred, and finds it prototype in these words of Jeremiah: 'Then I went down to the potter's house, and, behold, he wrought a work on the wheels. And the vessel that he made of clay was marred in the hand of the potter: so he made it again another vessel, as seemed good to the potter to make it. Then the word of the Lord came to me, saying, O house of Israel, cannot I do with you as this potter? saith the Lord. Behold, as *the clay is in the potter's hand*, so are ye in mine hand, O house of Israel' (chap. xviii.). It is because each individual has been thus especially moulded—some 'marred' in the moulding, some re-moulded 'again into another vessel,' 'some to honour and some to dishonour,' while another shall be 'a vessel unto honour, sanctified and meet for the Master's use'—that the *same facts* and the *same arguments* from the *same facts* produce such *different convictions* on *different minds*, and lead to all the varieties in the forms and tenets of religion which are scattered through Christendom. This has already been sufficiently dwelt upon; but I must remind you, in passing, that the 'vessels of wood and of earth' have their respective uses in the 'great house'; that they are under the same roof and the same guardian or ownership as are the 'vessels of gold and silver.' And as to limitation of 'celestial happiness,' I cannot think of a more apt illustration of the joys of heaven in relation to individuals than one used by Samuel Johnson: 'People of varying capacity reach heaven, where *all* will be *full* of happiness, but, like great and little bottles, some will contain much more than others. Surely, to be full is all-sufficing; as 'limitless' as heart could wish so far as measure or quantity is concerned. 'Materialist' and 'materialism' have been made to signify opprobrious terms; but there is nothing inherently base in matter, and its indestructibility is complete, inasmuch as it takes the same Almighty Power to destroy as it did to create it. No reverential mind need shrink from it as a base or unworthy thing, for the Almighty Being can clothe it with whatever attributes it may please HIM. It was an act of *reverential faith*, entailing salvation from suffering *and death*, in the time of Moses to look upon a *brazen* serpent; seven hundred years later, in the days of Hezekiah, it became an act of righteousness well pleasing in the sight of God to break it into pieces, inasmuch as in 'those days the children of Israel did burn incense to it.' Legend, tradition, credulity, superstition, had in the course of ages, then as now, perverted what was once a proper and religious act into gross idolatry. The image had for centuries ceased to fulfil a good purpose; it had become what King Hezekiah called 'Nehushtan,' a piece of brass; and 'he did right in the sight of the Lord' 'to break it into pieces,' although it *was once* 'the brazen serpent *that Moses* had made.' 'Relics' like unto this, and like unto those which the Cardinal extols— the nails of the Cross, the crib at Bethlehem, the winding-sheet at Turin, and 'pieces of our Lady's habit to be seen at the Escurial,' near to which the poor dupes see 'incense burnt,' and of which they are told 'each particle of each has in it at least a dormant, perhaps an energetic, virtue of supernatural operation'—should always be broken to pieces when they have become simply 'Nehushtan,' for who other than a 'materialist' in its worst sense could now attach 'a supernatural operation' to 'relics' so legendary, so wide-spread, and so numerous as those which the priestly imagination of the Cardinal has described with such glowing eloquence as among the 'paraphernalia' of the Church he has so warmly espoused—paraphernalia none the less precious that they are despised by the 'Spouse' to whom he (the Cardinal) pledged his earliest love and his earliest vows, from whom he has been divorced in order to espouse another of whom he once deliberately said, and *swore*, that she ought not to have any 'authority, ecclesiastical or spiritual, within this realm. *So help me, God.*' When the mighty thus fall, how tolerant ought we to be one to another, how slow to brand 'as worse than an infidel, an apostate priest,' a fellow-priest or layman who has seceded from our creed. How ready ought we to be to deal with 'such an one in the spirit of meekness, considering thyself, lest thou also be tempted.' I have nothing further to say as to the efficiency of direct spiritual guidance to each inquiring soul: 'the quietness and the confidence' which come down upon a soul so blessed; the 'doctrine' and the 'speech,' 'which drop as the rain and distil as the dew'— 'as the small rain upon the tender herb, and as the showers upon the grass'—upon the heart and intelligence of one in whom the Spirit of Christ dwells.

Vicar. You appear to me, my dear friend, quite unconscious of the heresy you have imbibed. It seems to me that you are in ignorance of the sole scheme of religion which God has provided for the redemption of mankind. You are in the same condition spiritually as were bodily the countless persons who were struggling in the primæval flood around the floating ark, after 'Noah had entered, and the Lord shut him in.' There *is*, there *can be*, no safety external to the Church ; she is the depository of God's truth, the exponent of his word, the preserver and distributor of his sacraments, and must ever be so, else would God be without trustworthy witnesses in this world. It is by virtue of the grace of apostolical succession that a due order of ministers has been preserved throughout the Christian ages, and without such qualified and authorised ministers the sacraments could not be administered, which sacraments, as the Church has diligently taught you, are 'generally necessary to salvation—that is to say, baptism and the supper of the Lord '—by the first of which you were ' made a member of Christ, a child of God, and an inheritor of the kingdom of heaven,' and the second is that in which ' the Body and Blood of Christ are verily and indeed taken by the faithful, and by which their souls are strengthened and refreshed,' as are our bodies by the bread and wine. It is by accepting these propositions as absolute facts, without cavil or dispute, that you can ever attain peace. Dark bewilderment, confusion, chaos, anxiety, mental distress, *must* ever follow all attempts to decide by 'private judgment.' Intellect, however great ; purity of intention, however sincere, even when combined, are fallacious guides. Uncertainty, discrepancy, schism, are the results. Ponder on the conclusions of the men for whom and for whose writings you have so high an esteem. How different, how discrepant are their opinions on holy things ! Observe the honest philosopher Faraday joining himself to a small obscure sect calling themselves 'Sandemanians' (the latter part of the name very suggestive), while on the very opposite pole of thought and feeling we see Darwin and Tyndall, almost deifying *matter*, and the marvellous mathematician Clifford pouring scorn and censure on 'Christianity' as the destroyer of 'civilisations.' Even the greatest of all great scientists, Sir Isaac Newton, forewent the creed of his fathers, and accepted, as I fear you do, the negations of a cold and sterile Arianism; and almost sadder still, the pure-minded Matthew Arnold, one of the great leaders of 'Oxford thought,' the eloquent advocate of 'sweetness and light,' denies the existence of any God who 'thinks and loves,' and has in elegiac strains thus described the hopes and aspirations of the followers of Jesus (as, indeed, you have before related):

> That thorn-crowned Man!
> He lived *while we believed*.
>
> While *we believed*, on earth He went,
> And open stood his grave.
> Men called from chamber, church, and tent
> And Christ was by to save.
>
> *Now* he is *dead*! far hence he lies
> In the lorn Syrian town,
> And on his grave with shining eyes
> The Syrian stars look down.
>
> . . . . .
>
> Ah, o'er that silent sacred land
> Of sun, and arid stone,
> And crumbling wall, and earthy sand,
> Sounds now one word alone!
>
> From David's lips that word did roll,
> 'Tis true, and living yet:
> *No man can save his brother's soul,*
> *Nor pay his brother's debt.*

> Alone, self-pois'd, henceforward man
> Must labour, must resign
> His all too human creeds, and scan
> Simply the way divine.

Such, yea, such are the sad results of 'private judgment.' I have referred to these men (although scores may have been taken from other departments of human science) because they belong to a class whose special training and pursuits you yourself honour, to show that there is no logical resting-place between scepticism and an implicit adoption of all the dogmatic teachings of the Catholic and Apostolic Church. The scores of wild sectarians demonstrate this to be a truth. Out of consideration to your views, I have named men accustomed to investigate facts, and to weigh evidence—Faraday, Darwin, Clifford, Tyndall, Newton, and Arnold—and have shown to what different conclusions they have come in religious opinions or convictions. I selected these men of science as being less prone to be swayed by the feelings, less disposed to be credulous, or what, perhaps, you might term fanatical, than others; had I looked for ordinary individuals anxious respecting their spiritual state and their future life, the divisions would have been almost endless. There are more than two hundred places of meeting for religious worship in England and Wales certified to the Registrar-General on behalf of persons calling themselves by different names, such as 'Believers in the Divine Visitation of Joanna Southcote,' 'Sandemanians,' 'Inghamites,' 'Old Baptists,' 'Strict Baptists,' 'King Jesus' Army,' 'Ranters,' 'Humanitarians,' 'Recreative Religionists,' and the like. To avoid all this awful confusion, there is but one resource to cleave to, and implicitly to follow—the 'one Catholic and Apostolic Church' appointed by Christ when he said unto Peter, 'Blessed art thou, Simon Bar-jona: for flesh and blood hath not revealed it unto thee, but my Father which is in heaven. And I say also unto thee, That thou art Peter, and upon this rock I will build my church; and the gates of hell shall not prevail against it. And I will give unto thee the keys of the kingdom of heaven: and whatsoever thou shalt bind on earth shall be bound in heaven: and whatsoever thou shalt loose on earth shall be loosed in heaven.' Into that Church you have been baptised, and from which you have not openly seceded, although you have been culpably negligent of some of her most important rites; and to her I now invite you to come penitentially. As a faithful although unworthy servant of that Church; as a priest to whom the Holy Ghost has been given by the imposition of apostolic hands, for the special purpose that I should thereby become a faithful dispenser of the Word of God and of his holy sacraments, and to be enabled to forgive or to retain sins, I implore you to lead a new life, and henceforth to walk in holy ways by partaking *habitually of that Holy Sacrament which has been specially ordained* ' *to preserve thy body and soul unto everlasting life.*' This is my last, my most urgent appeal to you as your pastor and priest. 'Liberavi animam meam.' And may the merciful God, to whom the Church ever prays to have mercy upon all Jews, Turks, infidels, and heretics, take from you all ignorance, hardness of heart, and contempt of his Word, and bring you fully home to his fold, the Church, so that you may be saved among the remnant of the true Israelites, and not be among those unhappy ones who, not 'holding the Catholic Faith whole and undefiled, shall without doubt perish everlastingly.'

Parishioner. I thank you very much. Your arguments and your words, touched with such deep emotion, would have operated powerfully upon me some years ago—as, indeed, they now would upon hundreds who are willing to accept of an external authority rather than have to think, and study, and pray for themselves. But your pleadings, kindly meant as they are, *necessarily* fail to produce a like sudden effect upon a mind which, possessing the Berean spirit, inquires 'whether these things *were so*,' and more especially on any one who had accepted the teachings of the Divine One who, instructing his disciples on teachers and 'rabbis' and 'masters,' said, 'Call no man your father upon the earth.' Were I, my dear Vicar, to adopt your arguments, I could not seek the 'fold' you represent, but should forthwith repair to the older, more consistent, and more logical Church from which 'the Church of England' has seceded. To the 'Berean'-like mind, under such appeals as you have made to me, there comes the inevitable inquiry, *Whence is* this 'authority' derived? Such an anxious soul, if in any degree cultured or educated, at once seeks information from the *earliest* records of the Christian life—the sayings ('*logia*') of Christ and the 'Acts of the Apostles'—and in these he cannot find an 'atom' of 'authority' for the dogmas you inculcate and the 'creed' you enforce with such appalling conditions. Moreover, he from thence learns the gratifying fact that there *is* a Power, a Spirit, promised, which 'will guide you into all truth.' I have already shown that even such profound divines as Butler and Hooker admit that the 'private judgment' of the individual—that is, the reason of the enlightened conscience—must be the deciding power in the ultimate appeal of the course to be pursued. It was so even with Cardinal Newman. Although he has since crushed into abject slavishness the highest attribute of humanity, and his reason now lies prostrate under the Papal toe, yet was it by this very faculty that he detected (assumed he detected) and adopted the Romish Church as the infallible guide and source of all 'authority' in spiritual things. Having abandoned his own prerogative of inquiry, the Cardinal (as the foxes in Æsop's Fables, when deprived of their tails, expatiated on their inconvenience and uselessness, and urged upon all other foxes to deprive themselves of their distinguishing appendages) now denounces all inquiry in matters of faith as impious, and, in reference to his adopted Church, writes, 'Let a man cease to inquire, or cease to call himself her child.' But let this pass. In 'my mind's eye,' as Hamlet said, the opinions of even Butler and Hooker, still more the abject utterances of Newman on this point, pale and fade away before these words of the great Nazarene, 'When he, the Spirit of truth, is come, he will *guide you into all truth*'; 'The Comforter, which is the Holy Spirit, whom the Father will send in my name, *he shall teach you all things*'; and all these sublime statements are confirmed by the apostle who spoke latest in this world of all the immediate disciples of Christ—even the 'disciple whom Jesus loved'—who told his Christian followers, 'Ye have an unction from the Holy One, and ye *know all things.*' '*Know* all things' —these are his words; not *think, opine, speculate, infer,* but '*know.*' Such Christians need not, therefore, the councils of 'pope,' 'priest,' 'monk,' 'father,' or 'confessor' to guide them through the labyrinths of paradoxical creeds—creeds by which monk and priest alike err in *teaching for doctrines* the commandments of men ' (Matt. xv. 9). ' Know all things ' necessary to salvation. Blessed, thrice blessed, is this revealed truth. The ' Holy Spirit ' is indeed the '*Comforter*' also to weary and anxious souls ; yea, the Comforter as well as the *one* sole, safe, and steadfast Light which, amid the mists of doubt and the waves of perplexity and trial, shines with unclouded ray to guide them safely to their home of everlasting rest. The words of the beloved disciple, my dear Vicar, will still sustain me, because they tell of '*the Comforter*,' and declare that 'the anointing which ye have received of him *abideth in you*, and ye need not that *any man* teach you : but as the same *anointing* teacheth you of all things, and *is truth*, and *is no lie*, and even as it hath taught you, ye shall abide in him ' (1 John ii. 27). Under *such* teachings, forms, ceremonies, 'vain oblations,' ' incense,' ' appointed feasts,' ' beggarly elements,' ' new moons,' ' the calling of assemblies,' ' even the solemn meeting,' take a subordinate position. The spirit-illumined soul is ' made a priest to God ' by an '*anointing*' more sacred than the ' laying-on of hands ' of any pontiff, prelate, or pope, and may therefore fearlessly cast aside the metaphysical jargon of an alleged Athanasius, or any mere human ' dogmas,' and disregard the threats of all who in sacerdotal garb are, to use the words of Jesus, '*teaching for doctrines the commandments of men*'; accepting in all their tenderness, their beauty, and their holiness the teachings of its Divine Master, clasping the sacred and sublime truth that 'this is life eternal, that they might know thee THE ONLY TRUE GOD, and Jesus Christ, whom THOU HAST SENT' (John xvii. 3). It may well smile at the anathemas of those who declare that unless it accept their paradoxical and irrational creed 'whole and undefiled, it shall without doubt perish everlastingly.' It *knows*, yea, verily *knows*, '*the Lord our God is one Lord*' (Deut. vi. 4); it has read, 'Unto thee it was shewed, that thou mightest *know* that the Lord *he is God*; there *is none else beside HIM*' (Deut. iv. 35). It still listens with reverence to the tender words, and accepts the Divine teachings of its Master as given to the woman of Samaria, '*Believe me*, the *hour cometh*, when ye shall neither in this mountain, nor yet at Jerusalem, worship the Father . . . the hour cometh, and now is, when the *true worshippers* shall worship the Father in spirit and in truth : for the Father seeketh such to worship him. God is a Spirit, and they that worship him must worship him in spirit and in truth' (John iv. 21-24). Enough. 'Sic itur ad astra.' Farewell.

A LIST OF
KEGAN PAUL, TRENCH & CO.'S PUBLICATIONS.

8. 86

1, Paternoster Square,
London.

A LIST OF KEGAN PAUL, TRENCH & CO.'S PUBLICATIONS.

CONTENTS.

	PAGE		PAGE
GENERAL LITERATURE .	2	MILITARY WORKS .	35
PARCHMENT LIBRARY .	20	POETRY .	36
PULPIT COMMENTARY .	23	NOVELS AND TALES .	42
INTERNATIONAL SCIENTIFIC SERIES .	32	BOOKS FOR THE YOUNG .	44

GENERAL LITERATURE.

A. K. H. B.—**From a Quiet Place.** A Volume of Sermons. Crown 8vo, 5s.

ALEXANDER, William, D.D., Bishop of Derry.—**The Great Question, and other Sermons.** Crown 8vo, 6s.

ALLEN, Rev. R., M.A.—**Abraham : his Life, Times, and Travels,** 3800 years ago. Second Edition. Post 8vo, 6s.

ALLIES, T. W., M.A.—**Per Crucem ad Lucem.** The Result of a Life. 2 vols. Demy 8vo, 25s.

   A Life's Decision. Crown 8vo, 7s. 6d.

AMHERST, Rev. W. J.—**The History of Catholic Emancipation and the Progress of the Catholic Church in the British Isles (chiefly in England) from 1771-1820.** 2 vols. Demy 8vo, 24s.

AMOS, Professor Sheldon.—**The History and Principles of the Civil Law of Rome.** An aid to the Study of Scientific and Comparative Jurisprudence. Demy 8vo. 16s.

Ancient and Modern Britons. A Retrospect. 2 vols. Demy 8vo, 24s.

ANDERDON, Rev. W. H.—**Evenings with the Saints.** Crown 8vo, 5s.

ANDERSON, David.—**"Scenes" in the Commons.** Crown 8vo, 5s.

ARISTOTLE.—**The Nicomachean Ethics of Aristotle.** Translated by F. H. Peters, M.A. Second Edition. Crown 8vo, 6s.

ARMSTRONG, Richard A., B.A.—**Latter-Day Teachers.** Six Lectures. Small crown 8vo, 2s. 6d.

AUBERTIN, J. J.—**A Flight to Mexico.** With Seven full-page Illustrations and a Railway Map of Mexico. Crown 8vo, 7s. 6d.

Six Months in Cape Colony and Natal. With Illustrations and Map. Crown 8vo, 6s.

BADGER, George Percy, D.C.L.—**An English-Arabic Lexicon.** In which the equivalent for English Words and Idiomatic Sentences are rendered into literary and colloquial Arabic. Royal 4to, 80s.

BAGEHOT, Walter.—**The English Constitution.** New and Revised Edition. Crown 8vo, 7s. 6d.

Lombard Street. A Description of the Money Market. Eighth Edition. Crown 8vo, 7s. 6d.

Essays on Parliamentary Reform. Crown 8vo, 5s.

Some Articles on the Depreciation of Silver, and Topics connected with it. Demy 8vo, 5s.

BAGOT, Alan, C.E.—**Accidents in Mines:** their Causes and Prevention. Crown 8vo, 6s.

The Principles of Colliery Ventilation. Second Edition, greatly enlarged. Crown 8vo, 5s.

The Principles of Civil Engineering as applied to Agriculture and Estate Management. Crown 8vo, 7s. 6d.

BAKER, Sir Sherston, Bart.—**The Laws relating to Quarantine.** Crown 8vo, 12s. 6d.

BAKER, Thomas.—**A Battling Life;** chiefly in the Civil Service. An Autobiography, with Fugitive Papers on Subjects of Public Importance. Crown 8vo, 7s. 6d.

BALDWIN, Capt. J. H.—**The Large and Small Game of Bengal and the North-Western Provinces of India.** With 20 Illustrations. New and Cheaper Edition. Small 4to, 10s. 6d.

BALLIN, Ada S. and F. L.—**A Hebrew Grammar.** With Exercises selected from the Bible. Crown 8vo, 7s. 6d.

BARCLAY, Edgar.—**Mountain Life in Algeria.** With numerous Illustrations by Photogravure. Crown 4to, 16s.

BARLOW, James W.—**The Ultimatum of Pessimism.** An Ethical Study. Demy 8vo, 6s.

Short History of the Normans in South Europe. Demy 8vo, 7s. 6d.

BAUR, Ferdinand, Dr. Ph.—**A Philological Introduction to Greek and Latin for Students.** Translated and adapted from the German, by C. KEGAN PAUL, M.A., and E. D. STONE, M.A. Third Edition. Crown 8vo, 6s.

BAYLY, Capt. George.—**Sea Life Sixty Years Ago.** A Record of Adventures which led up to the Discovery of the Relics of the long-missing Expedition commanded by the Comte de la Perouse. Crown 8vo, 3s. 6d.

BELLASIS, Edward.—**The Money Jar of Plautus at the Oratory School.** An Account of the Recent Representation. With Appendix and 16 Illustrations. Small 4to, sewed, 2s.

The New Terence at Edgbaston. Being Notices of the Performances in 1880 and 1881. With Preface, Notes, and Appendix. Third Issue. Small 4to, 1s. 6d.

BENN, Alfred W.—**The Greek Philosophers.** 2 vols. Demy 8vo, 28s.

Bible Folk-Lore. A Study in Comparative Mythology. Crown 8vo, 10s. 6d.

BIRD, Charles, F.G.S.—**Higher Education in Germany and England.** Being a brief Practical Account of the Organization and Curriculum of the German Higher Schools. With critical Remarks and Suggestions with reference to those of England. Small crown 8vo, 2s. 6d.

BLECKLY, Henry.—**Socrates and the Athenians:** An Apology. Crown 8vo, 2s. 6d.

BLOOMFIELD, The Lady.—**Reminiscences of Court and Diplomatic Life.** New and Cheaper Edition. With Frontispiece. Crown 8vo, 6s.

BLUNT, The Ven. Archdeacon.—**The Divine Patriot, and other Sermons.** Preached in Scarborough and in Cannes. New and Cheaper Edition. Crown 8vo, 4s. 6d.

BLUNT, Wilfrid S.—**The Future of Islam.** Crown 8vo, 6s.

Ideas about India. Crown 8vo. Cloth, 6s.

BODDY, Alexander A.—**To Kairwân the Holy.** Scenes in Muhammedan Africa. With Route Map, and Eight Illustrations by A. F. JACASSEY. Crown 8vo, 6s.

BOSANQUET, Bernard.—**Knowledge and Reality.** A Criticism of Mr. F. H. Bradley's "Principles of Logic." Crown 8vo, 9s.

BOUVERIE-PUSEY, S. E. B.—**Permanence and Evolution.** An Inquiry into the Supposed Mutability of Animal Types. Crown 8vo, 5s.

BOWEN, H. C., M.A.—**Studies in English.** For the use of Modern Schools. Eighth Thousand. Small crown 8vo, 1s. 6d.

English Grammar for Beginners. Fcap. 8vo, 1s.

Simple English Poems. English Literature for Junior Classes. In four parts. Parts I., II., and III., 6d. each. Part IV., 1s. Complete, 3s.

BRADLEY, F. H.—The Principles of Logic. Demy 8vo, 16s.

BRIDGETT, Rev. T. E.—History of the Holy Eucharist in Great Britain. 2 vols. Demy 8vo, 18s.

BROOKE, Rev. S. A.—Life and Letters of the Late Rev. F. W. Robertson, M.A. Edited by.

    I. Uniform with Robertson's Sermons. 2 vols. With Steel Portrait. 7s. 6d.
    II. Library Edition. With Portrait. 8vo, 12s.
    III. A Popular Edition. In 1 vol., 8vo, 6s.

The Fight of Faith. Sermons preached on various occasions. Fifth Edition. Crown 8vo, 7s. 6d.

The Spirit of the Christian Life. Third Edition. Crown 8vo, 5s.

Theology in the English Poets.—Cowper, Coleridge, Wordsworth, and Burns. Fifth Edition. Post 8vo, 5s.

Christ in Modern Life. Sixteenth Edition. Crown 8vo, 5s.

Sermons. First Series. Thirteenth Edition. Crown 8vo, 5s.

Sermons. Second Series. Sixth Edition. Crown 8vo, 5s.

BROWN, Rev. J. Baldwin, B.A.—The Higher Life. Its Reality, Experience, and Destiny. Sixth Edition. Crown 8vo, 5s.

Doctrine of Annihilation in the Light of the Gospel of Love. Five Discourses. Fourth Edition. Crown 8vo, 2s. 6d.

The Christian Policy of Life. A Book for Young Men of Business. Third Edition. Crown 8vo, 3s. 6d.

BROWN, Horatio F.—Life on the Lagoons. With two Illustrations and Map. Crown 8vo, 6s.

BROWNE, H. L.—Reason and Religious Belief. Crown 8vo, 3s. 6d.

BURDETT, Henry C.—Help in Sickness—Where to Go and What to Do. Crown 8vo, 1s. 6d.

Helps to Health. The Habitation—The Nursery—The Schoolroom and—The Person. With a Chapter on Pleasure and Health Resorts. Crown 8vo, 1s. 6d.

BURKE, The Late Very Rev. T. N.—His Life. By W. J. Fitzpatrick. 2 vols. With Portrait. Demy 8vo, 30s.

BURTON, Mrs. Richard.—The Inner Life of Syria, Palestine, and the Holy Land. Post 8vo, 6s.

CAPES, J. M.—The Church of the Apostles: an Historical Inquiry. Demy 8vo, 9s.

Carlyle and the Open Secret of His Life. By HENRY LARKIN. Demy 8vo, 14s.

CARPENTER, W. B., LL.D., M.D., F.R.S., etc.—**The Principles of Mental Physiology.** With their Applications to the Training and Discipline of the Mind, and the Study of its Morbid Conditions. Illustrated. Sixth Edition. 8vo, 12s.

Catholic Dictionary. Containing some Account of the Doctrine, Discipline, Rites, Ceremonies, Councils, and Religious Orders of the Catholic Church. By WILLIAM E. ADDIS and THOMAS ARNOLD, M.A. Third Edition. Demy 8vo, 21s.

CHEYNE, Rev. T. K.—**The Prophecies of Isaiah.** Translated with Critical Notes and Dissertations. 2 vols. Third Edition. Demy 8vo, 25s.

Circulating Capital. Being an Inquiry into the Fundamental Laws of Money. An Essay by an East India Merchant. Small crown 8vo, 6s.

CLAIRAUT.—**Elements of Geometry.** Translated by Dr. KAINES. With 145 Figures. Crown 8vo, 4s. 6d.

CLAPPERTON, Jane Hume.—**Scientific Meliorism and the Evolution of Happiness.** Large crown 8vo, 8s. 6d.

CLARKE, Rev. Henry James, A.K.C.—**The Fundamental Science.** Demy 8vo, 10s. 6d.

CLAYDEN, P. W.—**Samuel Sharpe.** Egyptologist and Translator of the Bible. Crown 8vo, 6s.

CLIFFORD, Samuel.—**What Think Ye of the Christ?** Crown 8vo, 6s.

CLODD, Edward, F.R.A.S.—**The Childhood of the World:** a Simple Account of Man in Early Times. Seventh Edition. Crown 8vo, 3s.
  A Special Edition for Schools. 1s.

The Childhood of Religions. Including a Simple Account of the Birth and Growth of Myths and Legends. Eighth Thousand. Crown 8vo, 5s.
  A Special Edition for Schools. 1s. 6d.

Jesus of Nazareth. With a brief sketch of Jewish History to the Time of His Birth. Small crown 8vo, 6s.

COGHLAN, J. Cole, D.D.—**The Modern Pharisee and other Sermons.** Edited by the Very Rev. H. H. DICKINSON, D.D., Dean of Chapel Royal, Dublin. New and Cheaper Edition. Crown 8vo, 7s. 6d.

COLE, George R. Fitz-Roy.—**The Peruvians at Home.** Crown 8vo, 6s.

COLERIDGE, Sara.—**Memoir and Letters of Sara Coleridge.** Edited by her Daughter. With Index. Cheap Edition. With Portrait. 7s. 6d.

Collects Exemplified. Being Illustrations from the Old and New Testaments of the Collects for the Sundays after Trinity. By the Author of "A Commentary on the Epistles and Gospels." Edited by the Rev. JOSEPH JACKSON. Crown 8vo, 5s.

CONNELL, *A. K.*—**Discontent and Danger in India.** Small crown 8vo, 3s. 6d.

The Economic Revolution of India. Crown 8vo, 4s. 6d.

COOK, *Keningale, LL.D.*—**The Fathers of Jesus.** A Study of the Lineage of the Christian Doctrine and Traditions. 2 vols. Demy 8vo, 28s.

CORY, *William.*—**A Guide to Modern English History.** Part I.—MDCCCXV.-MDCCCXXX. Demy 8vo, 9s. Part II.—MDCCCXXX.-MDCCCXXXV., 15s.

COTTERILL, *H. B.*—**An Introduction to the Study of Poetry.** Crown 8vo, 7s. 6d.

COTTON, *H. J. S.*—**New India, or India in Transition.** Third Edition. Crown 8vo, 4s. 6d.

COUTTS, *Francis Burdett Money.*—**The Training of the Instinct of Love.** With a Preface by the Rev. EDWARD THRING, M.A. Small crown 8vo, 2s. 6d.

COX, *Rev. Sir George W., M.A., Bart.*—**The Mythology of the Aryan Nations.** New Edition. Demy 8vo, 16s.

Tales of Ancient Greece. New Edition. Small crown 8vo, 6s.

A Manual of Mythology in the form of Question and Answer. New Edition. Fcap. 8vo, 3s.

An Introduction to the Science of Comparative Mythology and Folk-Lore. Second Edition. Crown 8vo. 7s. 6d.

COX, *Rev. Sir G. W., M.A., Bart., and JONES, Eustace Hinton.*—**Popular Romances of the Middle Ages.** Third Edition, in 1 vol. Crown 8vo, 6s.

COX, *Rev. Samuel, D.D.*—**A Commentary on the Book of Job.** With a Translation. Second Edition. Demy 8vo. 15s.

Salvator Mundi; or, 'Is Christ the Saviour of all Men? Tenth Edition. Crown 8vo, 5s.

The Larger Hope. A Sequel to "Salvator Mundi." Second Edition. 16mo, 1s.

The Genesis of Evil, and other Sermons, mainly expository. Third Edition. Crown 8vo, 6s.

Balaam. An Exposition and a Study. Crown 8vo, 5s.

Miracles. An Argument and a Challenge. Crown 8vo, 2s. 6d.

CRAVEN, *Mrs.*—**A Year's Meditations.** Crown 8vo, 6s.

CRAWFURD, *Oswald.*—**Portugal, Old and New.** With Illustrations and Maps. New and Cheaper Edition. Crown 8vo, 6s.

CROZIER, *John Beattie, M.B.*—**The Religion of the Future.** Crown 8vo, 6s.

CUNNINGHAM, *W., B.D.*—**Politics and Economics:** An Essay on the Nature of the Principles of Political Economy, together with a survey of Recent Legislation. Crown 8vo, 5s.

DANIELL, *Clarmont.*—**The Gold Treasure of India.** An Inquiry into its Amount, the Cause of its Accumulation, and the Proper Means of using it as Money. Crown 8vo, 5s.

Discarded Silver: a Plan for its Use as Money. Small crown, 8vo, 2s.

DANIEL, *Gerard.* **Mary Stuart: a Sketch and a Defence.** Crown 8vo, 5s.

DAVIDSON, *Rev. Samuel, D.D., LL.D.*—**Canon of the Bible:** Its Formation, History, and Fluctuations. Third and Revised Edition. Small crown 8vo, 5s.

The Doctrine of Last Things contained in the New Testament compared with the Notions of the Jews and the Statements of Church Creeds. Small crown 8vo, 3s. 6d.

DAWSON, *Geo., M.A.* **Prayers, with a Discourse on Prayer.** Edited by his Wife. First Series. Ninth Edition. Crown 8vo, 3s. 6d.

Prayers, with a Discourse on Prayer. Edited by GEORGE ST. CLAIR. Second Series. Crown 8vo, 6s.

Sermons on Disputed Points and Special Occasions. Edited by his Wife. Fourth Edition. Crown 8vo, 6s.

Sermons on Daily Life and Duty. Edited by his Wife. Fourth Edition. Crown 8vo, 6s.

The Authentic Gospel, and other Sermons. Edited by GEORGE ST. CLAIR, F.G.S. Third Edition. Crown 8vo, 6s.

Biographical Lectures. Edited by GEORGE ST. CLAIR, F.G.S. Large crown, 8vo, 7s. 6d.

DE JONCOURT, *Madame Marie.*—**Wholesome Cookery.** Third Edition. Crown 8vo, 3s. 6d.

Democracy in the Old World and the New. By the Author of "The Suez Canal, the Eastern Question, and Abyssinia," etc. Small crown 8vo, 2s. 6d.

DENT, *H. C.*—**A Year in Brazil.** With Notes on Religion, Meteorology, Natural History, etc. Maps and Illustrations. Demy 8vo, 18s.

Discourse on the Shedding of Blood, and The Laws of War. Demy 8vo, 2s. 6d.

DOUGLAS, Rev. Herman.—**Into the Deep**; or, The Wonders of the Lord's Person. Crown 8vo, 2s. 6d.

DOWDEN, Edward, LL.D.—**Shakspere**: a Critical Study of his Mind and Art. Eighth Edition. Post 8vo, 12s.

Studies in Literature, 1789-1877. Third Edition. Large post 8vo, 6s.

Dulce Domum. Fcap. 8vo, 5s.

DU MONCEL, Count.—**The Telephone, the Microphone, and the Phonograph.** With 74 Illustrations. Third Edition. Small crown 8vo, 5s.

DURUY, Victor.—**History of Rome and the Roman People.** Edited by Prof. MAHAFFY. With nearly 3000 Illustrations. 4to. 6 vols. in 12 parts, 30s. each vol.

EDGEWORTH, F. Y.—**Mathematical Psychics.** An Essay on the Application of Mathematics to Social Science. Demy 8vo, 7s. 6d.

Educational Code of the Prussian Nation, in its Present Form. In accordance with the Decisions of the Common Provincial Law, and with those of Recent Legislation. Crown 8vo, 2s. 6d.

Education Library. Edited by PHILIP MAGNUS:—

An Introduction to the History of Educational Theories. By OSCAR BROWNING, M.A. Second Edition. 3s. 6d.

Old Greek Education. By the Rev. Prof. MAHAFFY, M.A. Second Edition. 3s. 6d.

School Management. Including a general view of the work of Education, Organization and Discipline. By JOSEPH LANDON. Fifth Edition. 6s.

EDWARDES, Major-General Sir Herbert B.—**Memorials of his Life and Letters.** By his Wife. With Portrait and Illustrations. 2 vols. Demy 8vo, 36s.

ELSDALE, Henry.—**Studies in Tennyson's Idylls.** Crown 8vo, 5s.

Emerson's (Ralph Waldo) Life. By OLIVER WENDELL HOLMES. English Copyright Edition. With Portrait. Crown 8vo, 6s.

Enoch the Prophet. The Book of. Archbishop LAURENCE'S Translation, with an Introduction by the Author of "The Evolution of Christianity." Crown 8vo, 5s.

Eranus. A Collection of Exercises in the Alcaic and Sapphic Metres. Edited by F. W. CORNISH, Assistant Master at Eton. Second Edition. Crown 8vo, 2s.

EVANS, Mark.—**The Story of Our Father's Love,** told to Children. Sixth and Cheaper Edition. With Four Illustrations. Fcap. 8vo, 1s. 6d.

"Fan Kwae" at Canton before Treaty Days 1825-1844. By an old Resident. With Frontispiece. Crown 8vo, 5s.

Faith of the Unlearned, The. Authority, apart from the Sanction of Reason, an Insufficient Basis for It. By "One Unlearned." Crown 8vo, 6s.

FEIS, *Jacob.*—Shakspere and Montaigne. An Endeavour to Explain the Tendency of Hamlet from Allusions in Contemporary Works. Crown 8vo, 5s.

FLOREDICE, *W. H.*—A Month among the Mere Irish. Small crown 8vo. Second Edition. 3s. 6d.

Frank Leward. Edited by CHARLES BAMPTON. Crown 8vo, 7s. 6d.

FULLER, *Rev. Morris.*—The Lord's Day; or, Christian Sunday. Its Unity, History, Philosophy, and Perpetual Obligation. Sermons. Demy 8vo, 10s. 6d.

GARDINER, *Samuel R., and J. BASS MULLINGER, M.A.*—Introduction to the Study of English History. Second Edition. Large crown 8vo, 9s.

GARDNER, *Dorsey.*—Quatre Bras, Ligny, and Waterloo. A Narrative of the Campaign in Belgium, 1815. With Maps and Plans. Demy 8vo, 16s.

GELDART, *E. M.*—Echoes of Truth. Sermons, with a Short Selection of Prayers and an Introductory Sketch, by the Rev. C. B. UPTON. Crown 8vo, 6s.

Genesis in Advance of Present Science. A Critical Investigation of Chapters I.-IX. By a Septuagenarian Beneficed Presbyter. Demy 8vo. 10s. 6d.

GEORGE, *Henry.*—Progress and Poverty: An Inquiry into the Causes of Industrial Depressions, and of Increase of Want with Increase of Wealth. The Remedy. Fifth Library Edition. Post 8vo, 7s. 6d. Cabinet Edition. Crown 8vo, 2s. 6d. Also a Cheap Edition. Limp cloth, 1s. 6d. Paper covers, 1s.

Protection, or Free Trade. An Examination of the Tariff Question, with especial regard to the Interests of Labour. Crown 8vo, 5s.

Social Problems. Fourth Thousand. Crown 8vo, 5s. Cheap Edition. Paper covers, 1s.

GLANVILL, *Joseph.*—Scepsis Scientifica; or, Confest Ignorance, the Way to Science; in an Essay of the Vanity of Dogmatizing and Confident Opinion. Edited, with Introductory Essay, by JOHN OWEN. Elzevir 8vo, printed on hand-made paper, 6s.

Glossary of Terms and Phrases. Edited by the Rev. H. PERCY SMITH and others. Second and Cheaper Edition. Medium 8vo, 7s. 6d.

GLOVER, F., M.A.—**Exempla Latina.** A First Construing Book, with Short Notes, Lexicon, and an Introduction to the Analysis of Sentences. Second Edition. Fcap. 8vo, 2s.

GOLDSMID, Sir Francis Henry, Bart., Q.C., M.P.—**Memoir of.** With Portrait. Second Edition, Revised. Crown 8vo, 6s.

GOODENOUGH, Commodore J. G.—**Memoir of,** with Extracts from his Letters and Journals. Edited by his Widow. With Steel Engraved Portrait. Third Edition. Crown 8vo, 5s.

GORDON, Major-Genl. C. G.—**His Journals at Kartoum.** Printed from the original MS. With Introduction and Notes by A. EGMONT HAKE. Portrait, 2 Maps, and 30 Illustrations. Two vols., demy 8vo, 21s. Also a Cheap Edition in 1 vol., 6s.

Gordon's (General) Last Journal. A Facsimile of the last Journal received in England from GENERAL GORDON. Reproduced by Photo-lithography. Imperial 4to, £3 3s.

Events in his Life. From the Day of his Birth to the Day of his Death, By Sir H. W. GORDON. With Maps and Illustrations. Demy 8vo, 18s.

GOSSE, Edmund.—**Seventeenth Century Studies.** A Contribution to the History of English Poetry. Demy 8vo, 10s. 6d.

GOULD, Rev. S. Baring, M.A.—**Germany, Present and Past.** New and Cheaper Edition. Large crown 8vo, 7s. 6d.

GOWAN, Major Walter E.—**A. Ivanoff's Russian Grammar.** (16th Edition.) Translated, enlarged, and arranged for use of Students of the Russian Language. Demy 8vo, 6s.

GOWER, Lord Ronald. **My Reminiscences.** MINIATURE EDITION, printed on hand-made paper, limp parchment antique, 10s. 6d.

Last Days of Mary Antoinette. An Historical Sketch. With Portrait and Facsimiles. Fcap. 4to, 10s. 6d.

Notes of a Tour from Brindisi to Yokohama, 1883-1884. Fcap. 8vo, 2s. 6d.

GRAHAM, William, M.A.—**The Creed of Science,** Religious, Moral, and Social. Second Edition, Revised. Crown 8vo, 6s.

The Social Problem, in its Economic, Moral, and Political Aspects. Demy 8vo, 14s.

GREY, Rowland.—**In Sunny Switzerland.** A Tale of Six Weeks. Second Edition. Small crown 8vo, 5s.

Lindenblumen and other Stories. Small crown 8vo, 5s.

GRIMLEY, Rev. H. N., M.A.—**Tremadoc Sermons, chiefly on the Spiritual Body, the Unseen World, and the Divine Humanity.** Fourth Edition. Crown 8vo, 6s.

GUSTAFSON, Alex.—**The Foundation of Death.** Third Edition. Crown 8vo, 5s.

GUSTAFSON, Alex.—continued.
> **Some Thoughts on Moderation.** Reprinted from a Paper read at the Reeve Mission Room, Manchester Square, June 8, 1885. Crown 8vo, 1s.

HADDON, Caroline.—**The Larger Life, Studies in Hinton's Ethics.** Crown 8vo, 5s.

HAECKEL, Prof. Ernst.—**The History of Creation.** Translation revised by Professor E. RAY LANKESTER, M.A., F.R.S. With Coloured Plates and Genealogical Trees of the various groups of both Plants and Animals. 2 vols. Third Edition. Post 8vo, 32s.
> **The History of the Evolution of Man.** With numerous Illustrations. 2 vols. Post 8vo, 32s.
>
> **A Visit to Ceylon.** Post 8vo, 7s. 6d.
>
> **Freedom in Science and Teaching.** With a Prefatory Note by T. H. HUXLEY, F.R.S. Crown 8vo, 5s.

HALF-CROWN SERIES :—
> **A Lost Love.** By ANNA C. OGLE [Ashford Owen].
>
> **Sister Dora :** a Biography. By MARGARET LONSDALE.
>
> **True Words for Brave Men :** a Book for Soldiers and Sailors. By the late CHARLES KINGSLEY.
>
> **Notes of Travel :** being Extracts from the Journals of Count VON MOLTKE.
>
> **English Sonnets.** Collected and Arranged by J. DENNIS.
>
> **Home Songs for Quiet Hours.** By the Rev. Canon R. H. BAYNES.

Hamilton, Memoirs of Arthur, B.A., of Trinity College, Cambridge. Crown 8vo, 6s.

HARRIS, William.—**The History of the Radical Party in Parliament.** Demy 8vo, 15s.

HARROP, Robert.—**Bolingbroke.** A Political Study and Criticism. Demy 8vo, 14s.

HART, Rev. J. W. T.—**The Autobiography of Judas Iscariot.** A Character Study. Crown 8vo, 3s. 6d.

HAWEIS, Rev. H. R., M.A.—**Current Coin.** Materialism—The Devil—Crime—Drunkenness—Pauperism—Emotion—Recreation—The Sabbath. Fifth Edition. Crown 8vo, 5s.
> **Arrows in the Air.** Fifth Edition. Crown 8vo, 5s.
>
> **Speech in Season.** Fifth Edition. Crown 8vo, 5s.
>
> **Thoughts for the Times.** Thirteenth Edition. Crown 8vo, 5s.
>
> **Unsectarian Family Prayers.** New Edition. Fcap. 8vo, 1s. 6d.

HAWKINS, Edward Comerford.—**Spirit and Form.** Sermons preached in the Parish Church of Leatherhead. Crown 8vo, 6s.

HAWTHORNE, Nathaniel.—**Works.** Complete in Twelve Volumes. Large post 8vo, 7s. 6d. each volume.

- VOL. I. TWICE-TOLD TALES.
- II. MOSSES FROM AN OLD MANSE.
- III. THE HOUSE OF THE SEVEN GABLES, AND THE SNOW IMAGE.
- IV. THE WONDERBOOK, TANGLEWOOD TALES, AND GRANDFATHER'S CHAIR.
- V. THE SCARLET LETTER, AND THE BLITHEDALE ROMANCE.
- VI. THE MARBLE FAUN. [Transformation.]
- VII. } OUR OLD HOME, AND ENGLISH NOTE-BOOKS.
- VIII. }
- IX. AMERICAN NOTE-BOOKS.
- X. FRENCH AND ITALIAN NOTE-BOOKS.
- XI. SEPTIMIUS FELTON, THE DOLLIVER ROMANCE, FANSHAWE, AND, IN AN APPENDIX, THE ANCESTRAL FOOTSTEP.
- XII. TALES AND ESSAYS, AND OTHER PAPERS, WITH A BIOGRAPHICAL SKETCH OF HAWTHORNE.

HEATH, Francis George.—**Autumnal Leaves.** Third and cheaper Edition. Large crown 8vo, 6s.

Sylvan Winter. With 70 Illustrations. Large crown 8vo, 14s.

HENNESSY, Sir John Pope.—**Ralegh in Ireland.** With his Letters on Irish Affairs and some Contemporary Documents. Large crown 8vo, printed on hand-made paper, parchment, 10s. 6d.

HENRY, Philip.—**Diaries and Letters of.** Edited by MATTHEW HENRY LEE, M.A. Large crown 8vo, 7s. 6d.

HINTON, J.—**Life and Letters.** With an Introduction by Sir W. W. GULL, Bart., and Portrait engraved on Steel by C. H. Jeens. Fifth Edition. Crown 8vo, 8s. 6d.

Philosophy and Religion. Selections from the Manuscripts of the late James Hinton. Edited by CAROLINE HADDON. Second Edition. Crown 8vo, 5s.

The Law Breaker, and The Coming of the Law. Edited by MARGARET HINTON. Crown 8vo, 6s.

The Mystery of Pain. New Edition. Fcap. 8vo, 1s.

Hodson of Hodson's Horse; or, Twelve Years of a Soldier's Life in India. Being extracts from the Letters of the late Major W. S. R. Hodson. With a Vindication from the Attack of Mr. Bosworth Smith. Edited by his brother, G. H. HODSON, M.A. Fourth Edition. Large crown 8vo, 5s.

HOLTHAM, E. G.—**Eight Years in Japan, 1873-1881.** Work, Travel, and Recreation. With three Maps. Large crown 8vo, 9s.

Homology of Economic Justice. An Essay by an East India Merchant. Small crown 8vo, 5s.

HOOPER, Mary.—**Little Dinners: How to Serve them with Elegance and Economy.** Twentieth Edition. Crown 8vo, 2s. 6d.

Cookery for Invalids, Persons of Delicate Digestion, and Children. Fifth Edition. Crown 8vo, 2s. 6d.

Every-Day Meals. Being Economical and Wholesome Recipes for Breakfast, Luncheon, and Supper. Sixth Edition. Crown 8vo, 2s. 6d.

HOPKINS, Ellice.—**Work amongst Working Men.** Sixth Edition. Crown 8vo, 3s. 6d.

HORNADAY, W. T.—**Two Years in a Jungle.** With Illustrations. Demy 8vo, 21s.

HOSPITALIER, E.—**The Modern Applications of Electricity.** Translated and Enlarged by JULIUS MAIER, Ph.D. 2 vols. Second Edition, Revised, with many additions and numerous Illustrations. Demy 8vo, 12s. 6d. each volume.
    VOL. I.—Electric Generators, Electric Light.
    VOL. II.—Telephone: Various Applications: Electrical Transmission of Energy.

HOWARD, Robert, M.A.—**The Church of England and other Religious Communions.** A course of Lectures delivered in the Parish Church of Clapham. Crown 8vo, 7s. 6d.

HUMPHREY, Rev. William.—**The Bible and Belief.** A Letter to a Friend. Small Crown 8vo, 2s. 6d.

HUNTER, William C.—**Bits of Old China.** Small crown 8vo, 6s.

HUNTINGFORD, Rev. E., D.C.L.—**The Apocalypse.** With a Commentary and Introductory Essay. Demy 8vo, 5s.

HUTCHINSON, H.—**Thought Symbolism, and Grammatic Illusions.** Being a Treatise on the Nature, Purpose, and Material of Speech. Crown 8vo, 2s. 6d.

HUTTON, Rev. C. F.—**Unconscious Testimony;** or, The Silent Witness of the Hebrew to the Truth of the Historical Scriptures. Crown 8vo, 2s. 6d.

HYNDMAN, H. M.—**The Historical Basis of Socialism in England.** Large crown 8vo, 8s. 6d.

IDDESLEIGH, Earl of.—**The Pleasures, Dangers, and Uses of Desultory Reading.** Fcap. 8vo, in Whatman paper cover, 1s.

IM THURN, Everard F.—**Among the Indians of Guiana.** Being Sketches, chiefly anthropologic, from the Interior of British Guiana. With 53 Illustrations and a Map. Demy 8vo, 18s.

JACCOUD, Prof. S.—**The Curability and Treatment of Pulmonary Phthisis.** Translated and edited by MONTAGU LUBBOCK, M.D. Demy 8vo, 15s.

Jaunt in a Junk : A Ten Days' Cruise in Indian Seas. Large crown 8vo, 7s. 6d.

JENKINS, E., and RAYMOND, J.—**The Architect's Legal Handbook.** Third Edition, revised. Crown 8vo, 6s.

JENKINS, Rev. Canon R. C.—**Heraldry : English and Foreign.** With a Dictionary of Heraldic Terms and 156 Illustrations. Small crown 8vo, 3s. 6d.

JERVIS, Rev. W. Henley.—**The Gallican Church and the Revolution.** A Sequel to the History of the Church of France, from the Concordat of Bologna to the Revolution. Demy 8vo, 18s.

JOEL, L.—**A Consul's Manual and Shipowner's and Shipmaster's Practical Guide in their Transactions Abroad.** With Definitions of Nautical, Mercantile, and Legal Terms; a Glossary of Mercantile Terms in English, French, German, Italian, and Spanish; Tables of the Money, Weights, and Measures of the Principal Commercial Nations and their Equivalents in British Standards; and Forms of Consular and Notarial Acts. Demy 8vo, 12s.

JOHNSTON, H. H., F.Z.S.—**The Kilima-njaro Expedition.** A Record of Scientific Exploration in Eastern Equatorial Africa, and a General Description of the Natural History, Languages, and Commerce of the Kilima-njaro District. With 6 Maps, and over 80 Illustrations by the Author. Demy 8vo, 21s.

JOYCE, P. W., LL.D., etc.—**Old Celtic Romances.** Translated from the Gaelic. Crown 8vo, 7s. 6d.

KAUFMANN, Rev. M., B.A.—**Socialism : its Nature, its Dangers, and its Remedies considered.** Crown 8vo, 7s. 6d.

Utopias; or, Schemes of Social Improvement, from Sir Thomas More to Karl Marx. Crown 8vo, 5s.

KAY, David, F.R.G.S.—**Education and Educators.** Crown 8vo, 7s. 6d.

KAY, Joseph.—**Free Trade in Land.** Edited by his Widow. With Preface by the Right Hon. JOHN BRIGHT, M.P. Seventh Edition. Crown 8vo, 5s.

** Also a cheaper edition, without the Appendix, but with a Revise of Recent Changes in the Land Laws of England, by the RIGHT HON. G. OSBORNE MORGAN, Q.C., M.P. Cloth, 1s. 6d. Paper covers, 1s.

KELKE, W. H. H.—**An Epitome of English Grammar for the Use of Students.** Adapted to the London Matriculation Course and Similar Examinations. Crown 8vo, 4s. 6d.

KEMPIS, Thomas à.—**Of the Imitation of Christ.** Parchment Library Edition.—Parchment or cloth, 6s. ; vellum, 7s. 6d. The Red Line Edition, fcap. 8vo, red edges, 2s. 6d. The Cabinet Edition, small 8vo, cloth limp, 1s. ; cloth boards, red edges, 1s. 6d. The Miniature Edition, red edges, 32mo, 1s.

*** All the above Editions may be had in various extra bindings.

KETTLEWELL, Rev. S.—**Thomas à Kempis and the Brothers of Common Life.** With Portrait. Crown 8vo, 7s. 6d.

KIDD, Joseph, M.D.—**The Laws of Therapeutics ;** or, the Science and Art of Medicine. Second Edition. Crown 8vo, 6s.

KINGSFORD, Anna, M.D.—**The Perfect Way in Diet.** A Treatise advocating a Return to the Natural and Ancient Food of our Race. Second Edition. Small crown 8vo, 2s.

KINGSLEY, Charles, M.A.—**Letters and Memories of his Life.** Edited by his Wife. With two Steel Engraved Portraits, and Vignettes on Wood. Fifteenth Cabinet Edition. 2 vols. Crown 8vo, 12s.

*** Also a People's Edition, in one volume. With Portrait. Crown 8vo, 6s.

All Saints' Day, and other Sermons. Edited by the Rev. W. HARRISON. Third Edition. Crown 8vo, 7s. 6d.

True Words for Brave Men. A Book for Soldiers' and Sailors' Libraries. Eleventh Edition. Crown 8vo, 2s. 6d.

KNOX, Alexander A.—**The New Playground ;** or, Wanderings in Algeria. New and Cheaper Edition. Large crown 8vo, 6s.

Land Concentration and Irresponsibility of Political Power, as causing the Anomaly of a Widespread State of Want by the Side of the Vast Supplies of Nature. Crown 8vo, 5s.

LANDON, Joseph.—**School Management ;** Including a General View of the Work of Education, Organization, and Discipline. Fifth Edition. Crown 8vo, 6s.

LEE, Rev. F. G., D.C.L.—**The Other World ;** or, Glimpses of the Supernatural. 2 vols. A New Edition. Crown 8vo, 15s.

Letters from an Unknown Friend. By the Author of "Charles Lowder." With a Preface by the Rev. W. H. CLEAVER. Fcap. 8vo, 1s.

Leward, Frank. Edited by CHARLES BAMPTON. Crown 8vo, 7s. 6d.

LEWIS, Edward Dillon.—**A Draft Code of Criminal Law and Procedure.** Demy 8vo, 21s.

Life of a Prig. By ONE. Third Edition. Fcap. 8vo, 3s. 6d.

LILLIE, Arthur, M.R.A.S.—**The Popular Life of Buddha.** Containing an Answer to the Hibbert Lectures of 1881. With Illustrations. Crown 8vo, 6s.

LLOYD, Walter.—**The Hope of the World :** An Essay on Universal Redemption. Crown 8vo, 5s.

LONGFELLOW, H. Wadsworth.—**Life.** By his Brother, SAMUEL LONGFELLOW. With Portraits and Illustrations. 2 vols. Demy 8vo, 28s.

LONSDALE, Margaret.—**Sister Dora :** a Biography. With Portrait. Cheap Edition. Small crown 8vo, 2s. 6d.

George Eliot: Thoughts upon her Life, her Books, and Herself. Second Edition. Small crown 8vo, 1s. 6d.

LOUNSBURY, Thomas R.—**James Fenimore Cooper.** With Portrait. Crown 8vo, 5s.

LOWDER, Charles.—**A Biography.** By the Author of "St. Teresa." New and Cheaper Edition. Crown 8vo. With Portrait. 3s. 6d.

LÜCKES, Eva C. E.—**Lectures on General Nursing,** delivered to the Probationers of the London Hospital Training School for Nurses. Crown 8vo, 2s. 6d.

LYALL, William Rowe, D.D.—**Propædeia Prophetica ;** or, The Use and Design of the Old Testament Examined. New Edition. With Notices by GEORGE C. PEARSON, M.A., Hon. Canon of Canterbury. Demy 8vo, 10s. 6d.

LYTTON, Edward Bulwer, Lord.—**Life, Letters and Literary Remains.** By his Son, the EARL OF LYTTON. With Portraits, Illustrations and Facsimiles. Demy 8vo. Vols. I. and II., 32s.

MACAULAY, G. C.—**Francis Beaumont :** A Critical Study. Crown 8vo, 5s.

MAC CALLUM, M. W.—**Studies in Low German and High German Literature.** Crown 8vo, 6s.

MACHIAVELLI, Niccolò. — **Life and Times.** By Prof. VILLARI. Translated by LINDA VILLARI. 4 vols. Large post 8vo, 48s.

MACHIAVELLI, Niccolò.—**Discourses on the First Decade of Titus Livius.** Translated from the Italian by NINIAN HILL THOMSON, M.A. Large crown 8vo, 12s.

The Prince. Translated from the Italian by N. H. T. Small crown 8vo, printed on hand-made paper, bevelled boards, 6s.

MACKENZIE, Alexander.—**How India is Governed.** Being an Account of England's Work in India. Small crown 8vo, 2s.

MAGNUS, Mrs.—**About the Jews since Bible Times.** From the Babylonian Exile till the English Exodus. Small crown 8vo, 6s.

MAGUIRE, Thomas.—**Lectures on Philosophy.** Demy 8vo, 9s.

MAIR, R. S., M.D., F.R.C.S.E.—**The Medical Guide for Anglo-Indians.** Being a Compendium of Advice to Europeans in India, relating to the Preservation and Regulation of Health. With a Supplement on the Management of Children in India. Second Edition. Crown 8vo, limp cloth, 3s. 6d.

MALDEN, Henry Elliot.—**Vienna, 1683.** The History and Consequences of the Defeat of the Turks before Vienna, September 12th, 1683, by John Sobieski, King of Poland, and Charles Leopold, Duke of Lorraine. Crown 8vo, 4s. 6d.

Many Voices. A volume of Extracts from the Religious Writers of Christendom from the First to the Sixteenth Century. With Biographical Sketches. Crown 8vo, cloth extra, red edges, 6s.

MARKHAM, Capt. Albert Hastings, R.N.—**The Great Frozen Sea:** A Personal Narrative of the Voyage of the *Alert* during the Arctic Expedition of 1875-6. With 6 Full-page Illustrations, 2 Maps, and 27 Woodcuts. Sixth and Cheaper Edition. Crown 8vo, 6s.

MARTINEAU, Gertrude.—**Outline Lessons on Morals.** Small crown 8vo, 3s. 6d.

MAUDSLEY, H., M.D.—**Body and Will.** Being an Essay concerning Will, in its Metaphysical, Physiological, and Pathological Aspects. 8vo, 12s.

Natural Causes and Supernatural Seemings. Crown 8vo, 6s.

McGRATH, Terence.—**Pictures from Ireland.** New and Cheaper Edition. Crown 8vo, 2s.

MEREDITH, M.A.—**Theotokos, the Example for Woman.** Dedicated, by permission, to Lady Agnes Wood. Revised by the Venerable Archdeacon DENISON. 32mo, limp cloth, 1s. 6d.

MILLER, Edward.—**The History and Doctrines of Irvingism;** or, The so-called Catholic and Apostolic Church. 2 vols. Large post 8vo, 25s.

The Church in Relation to the State. Large crown 8vo, 7s. 6d.

MITCHELL, Lucy M.—**A History of Ancient Sculpture.** With numerous Illustrations, including 6 Plates in Phototype. Super royal 8vo, 42s.

MITFORD, Bertram.—**Through the Zulu Country.** Its Battlefields and its People. With Five Illustrations. Demy 8vo, 14s.

MOCKLER, E.—**A Grammar of the Baloochee Language,** as it is spoken in Makran (Ancient Gedrosia), in the Persia-Arabic and Roman characters. Fcap. 8vo, 5s.

MOLESWORTH, Rev. W. Nassau, M.A.—**History of the Church of England from 1660.** Large crown 8vo, 7s. 6d.

MORELL, J. R.—**Euclid Simplified in Method and Language.** Being a Manual of Geometry. Compiled from the most important French Works, approved by the University of Paris and the Minister of Public Instruction. Fcap. 8vo, 2s. 6d.

MORGAN, C. Lloyd.—**The Springs of Conduct.** An Essay in Evolution. Large crown 8vo, cloth, 7s. 6d.

MORRIS, George.—**The Duality of all Divine Truth in our Lord Jesus Christ.** For God's Self-manifestation in the Impartation of the Divine Nature to Man. Large crown 8vo, 7s. 6d.

MORSE, E. S., Ph.D.—**First Book of Zoology.** With numerous Illustrations. New and Cheaper Edition. Crown 8vo, 2s. 6d.

NELSON, J. H., M.A.—**A Prospectus of the Scientific Study of the Hindû Law.** Demy 8vo, 9s.

NEWMAN, Cardinal.—**Characteristics from the Writings of.** Being Selections from his various Works. Arranged with the Author's personal Approval. Seventh Edition. With Portrait. Crown 8vo, 6s.

*** A Portrait of Cardinal Newman, mounted for framing, can be had, 2s. 6d.

NEWMAN, Francis William.—**Essays on Diet.** Small crown 8vo, cloth limp, 2s.

New Truth and the Old Faith: Are they Incompatible? By a Scientific Layman. Demy 8vo, 10s. 6d.

New Social Teachings. By POLITICUS. Small crown 8vo, 5s.

NICOLS, Arthur, F.G.S., F.R.G.S.—**Chapters from the Physical History of the Earth:** an Introduction to Geology and Palæontology. With numerous Illustrations. Crown 8vo, 5s.

NOEL, The Hon. Roden.—**Essays on Poetry and Poets.** Demy 8vo, 12s.

NOPS, Marianne.—**Class Lessons on Euclid.** Part I. containing the First Two Books of the Elements. Crown 8vo, 2s. 6d.

Nuces: EXERCISES ON THE SYNTAX OF THE PUBLIC SCHOOL LATIN PRIMER. New Edition in Three Parts. Crown 8vo, each 1s.

*** The Three Parts can also be had bound together, 3s.

OATES, Frank, F.R.G.S.—**Matabele Land and the Victoria Falls.** A Naturalist's Wanderings in the Interior of South Africa. Edited by C. G. OATES, B.A. With numerous Illustrations and 4 Maps. Demy 8vo, 21s.

O'CONNOR, T. P., M.P.—**The Parnell Movement.** With a Sketch of Irish Parties from 1843. Large crown 8vo, 7s. 6d.

OGLE, W., M.D., F.R.C.P.—**Aristotle on the Parts of Animals.** Translated, with Introduction and Notes. Royal 8vo, 12s. 6d.

O'HAGAN, Lord, K.P.—**Occasional Papers and Addresses.** Large crown 8vo, 7s. 6d.

O'MEARA, Kathleen.—**Frederic Ozanam,** Professor of the Sorbonne: His Life and Work. Second Edition. Crown 8vo, 7s. 6d.

Henri Perreyve and his Counsels to the Sick. Small crown 8vo, 5s.

One and a Half in Norway. A Chronicle of Small Beer. By Either and Both. Small crown 8vo, 3s. 6d.

O'NEIL, *the late Rev. Lord.*—Sermons. With Memoir and Portrait. Crown 8vo, 6s.

Essays and Addresses. Crown 8vo, 5s.

Only Passport to Heaven, The. By One who has it. Small crown 8vo, 1s. 6d.

OSBORNE, *Rev. W. A.*—The Revised Version of the New Testament. A Critical Commentary, with Notes upon the Text. Crown 8vo, 5s.

OTTLEY, *H. Bickersteth.*—The Great Dilemma. Christ His Own Witness or His Own Accuser. Six Lectures. Second Edition. Crown 8vo, 3s. 6d.

Our Public Schools—Eton, Harrow, Winchester, Rugby, Westminster, Marlborough, The Charterhouse. Crown 8vo, 6s.

OWEN, *F. M.*—John Keats: a Study. Crown 8vo, 6s.

Across the Hills. Small crown 8vo, 1s. 6d.

OWEN, *Rev. Robert, B.D.*—Sanctorale Catholicum; or, Book of Saints. With Notes, Critical, Exegetical, and Historical. Demy 8vo, 18s.

OXONIENSIS.—Romanism, Protestantism, Anglicanism. Being a Layman's View of some questions of the Day. Together with Remarks on Dr. Littledale's "Plain Reasons against joining the Church of Rome." Crown 8vo, 3s. 6d.

PALMER, *the late William.*—Notes of a Visit to Russia in 1840-1841. Selected and arranged by JOHN H. CARDINAL NEWMAN, with Portrait. Crown 8vo, 8s. 6d.

Early Christian Symbolism. A Series of Compositions from Fresco Paintings, Glasses, and Sculptured Sarcophagi. Edited by the Rev. Provost NORTHCOTE, D.D., and the Rev. Canon BROWNLOW, M.A. With Coloured Plates, folio, 42s., or with Plain Plates, folio, 25s.

Parchment Library. Choicely Printed on hand-made paper, limp parchment antique or cloth, 6s.; vellum, 7s. 6d. each volume.

The Poetical Works of John Milton. 2 vols.

Letters and Journals of Jonathan Swift. Selected and edited, with a Commentary and Notes, by STANLEY LANE POOLE.

De Quincey's Confessions of an English Opium Eater. Reprinted from the First Edition. Edited by RICHARD GARNETT.

The Gospel according to **Matthew, Mark,** and **Luke.**

Parchment Library—*continued*.

Selections from the Prose Writings of Jonathan Swift. With a Preface and Notes by STANLEY LANE-POOLE and Portrait.

English Sacred Lyrics.

Sir Joshua Reynolds's Discourses. Edited by EDMUND GOSSE.

Selections from Milton's Prose Writings. Edited by ERNEST MYERS.

The Book of Psalms. Translated by the Rev. T. K. CHEYNE, M.A.

The Vicar of Wakefield. With Preface and Notes by AUSTIN DOBSON.

English Comic Dramatists. Edited by OSWALD CRAWFURD.

English Lyrics.

The Sonnets of John Milton. Edited by MARK PATTISON. With Portrait after Vertue.

French Lyrics. Selected and Annotated by GEORGE SAINTSBURY. With a Miniature Frontispiece designed and etched by H. G. Glindoni.

Fables by Mr. John Gay. With Memoir by AUSTIN DOBSON, and an Etched Portrait from an unfinished Oil Sketch by Sir Godfrey Kneller.

Select Letters of Percy Bysshe Shelley. Edited, with an Introduction, by RICHARD GARNETT.

The Christian Year. Thoughts in Verse for the Sundays and Holy Days throughout the Year. With Miniature Portrait of the Rev. J. Keble, after a Drawing by G. Richmond, R.A.

Shakspere's Works. Complete in Twelve Volumes.

Eighteenth Century Essays. Selected and Edited by AUSTIN DOBSON. With a Miniature Frontispiece by R. Caldecott.

Q. Horati Flacci Opera. Edited by F. A. CORNISH, Assistant Master at Eton. With a Frontispiece after a design by L. Alma Tadema, etched by Leopold Lowenstam.

Edgar Allan Poe's Poems. With an Essay on his Poetry by ANDREW LANG, and a Frontispiece by Linley Sambourne.

Shakspere's Sonnets. Edited by EDWARD DOWDEN. With a Frontispiece etched by Leopold Lowenstam, after the Death Mask.

English Odes. Selected by EDMUND GOSSE. With Frontispiece on India paper by Hamo Thornycroft, A.R.A.

Parchment Library—*continued*.
> Of the Imitation of Christ. By THOMAS À KEMPIS. A revised Translation. With Frontispiece on India paper, from a Design by W. B. Richmond.
>
> Poems: Selected from PERCY BYSSHE SHELLEY. Dedicated to Lady Shelley. With a Preface by RICHARD GARNETT and a Miniature Frontispiece.

PARSLOE, Joseph.—Our Railways. Sketches, Historical and Descriptive. With Practical Information as to Fares and Rates, etc., and a Chapter on Railway Reform. Crown 8vo, 6s.

PASCAL, Blaise.—The Thoughts of. Translated from the Text of Auguste Molinier, by C. KEGAN PAUL. Large crown 8vo, with Frontispiece, printed on hand-made paper, parchment antique, or cloth, 12s.; vellum, 15s.

PAUL, Alexander.—Short Parliaments. A History of the National Demand for frequent General Elections. Small crown 8vo, 3s. 6d.

PAUL, C. Kegan.—Biographical Sketches. Printed on hand-made paper, bound in buckram. Second Edition. Crown 8vo, 7s. 6d.

PEARSON, Rev. S.—Week-day Living. A Book for Young Men and Women. Second Edition. Crown 8vo, 5s.

PENRICE, Major J.—Arabic and English Dictionary of the Koran. 4to, 21s.

PESCHEL, Dr. Oscar.—The Races of Man and their Geographical Distribution. Second Edition. Large crown 8vo, 9s.

PHIPSON, E.—The Animal Lore of Shakspeare's Time. Including Quadrupeds, Birds, Reptiles, Fish and Insects. Large post 8vo, 9s.

PIDGEON, D.—An Engineer's Holiday; or, Notes of a Round Trip from Long. 0° to 0°. New and Cheaper Edition. Large crown 8vo, 7s. 6d.
> Old World Questions and New World Answers. Second Edition. Large crown 8vo, 7s. 6d.

Plain Thoughts for Men. Eight Lectures delivered at Forester's Hall, Clerkenwell, during the London Mission, 1884. Crown 8vo, cloth, 1s. 6d; paper covers, 1s.

POE, Edgar Allan.—Works of. With an Introduction and a Memoir by RICHARD HENRY STODDARD. In 6 vols. With Frontispieces and Vignettes. Large crown 8vo, 6s. each.

POPE, J. Buckingham.—Railway Rates and Radical Rule. Trade Questions as Election Tests. Crown 8vo, 2s. 6d.

PRICE, Prof. Bonamy.—Chapters on Practical Political Economy. Being the Substance of Lectures delivered before the University of Oxford. New and Cheaper Edition. Crown 8vo, 5s.

Pulpit Commentary, The. (Old Testament Series.) Edited by the Rev. J. S. EXELL, M.A., and the Rev. Canon H. D. M. SPENCE.

    Genesis. By the Rev. T. WHITELAW, M.A. With Homilies by the Very Rev. J. F. MONTGOMERY, D.D., Rev. Prof. R. A. REDFORD, M.A., LL.B., Rev. F. HASTINGS, Rev. W. ROBERTS, M.A. An Introduction to the Study of the Old Testament by the Venerable Archdeacon FARRAR, D.D., F.R.S.; and Introductions to the Pentateuch by the Right Rev. H. COTTERILL, D.D., and Rev. T. WHITELAW, M.A. Eighth Edition. 1 vol., 15s.

    Exodus. By the Rev. Canon RAWLINSON. With Homilies by Rev. J. ORR, Rev. D. YOUNG, B.A., Rev. C. A. GOODHART, Rev. J. URQUHART, and the Rev. H. T. ROBJOHNS. Fourth Edition. 2 vols., 18s.

    Leviticus. By the Rev. Prebendary MEYRICK, M.A. With Introductions by the Rev. R. COLLINS, Rev. Professor A. CAVE, and Homilies by Rev. Prof. REDFORD, LL.B., Rev. J. A. MACDONALD, Rev. W. CLARKSON, B.A., Rev. S. R. ALDRIDGE, LL.B., and Rev. MCCHEYNE EDGAR. Fourth Edition. 15s.

    Numbers. By the Rev. R. WINTERBOTHAM, LL.B. With Homilies by the Rev. Professor W. BINNIE, D.D., Rev. E. S. PROUT, M.A., Rev. D. YOUNG, Rev. J. WAITE, and an Introduction by the Rev. THOMAS WHITELAW, M.A. Fourth Edition. 15s.

    Deuteronomy. By the Rev. W. L. ALEXANDER, D.D. With Homilies by Rev. C. CLEMANCE, D.D., Rev. J. ORR, B.D., Rev. R. M. EDGAR, M.A., Rev. D. DAVIES, M.A. Fourth edition. 15s.

    Joshua. By Rev. J. J. LIAS, M.A. With Homilies by Rev. S. R. ALDRIDGE, LL.B., Rev. R. GLOVER, REV. E. DE PRESSENSÉ, D.D., Rev. J. WAITE, B.A., Rev. W. F. ADENEY, M.A.; and an Introduction by the Rev. A. PLUMMER, M.A. Fifth Edition. 12s. 6d.

    Judges and Ruth. By the Bishop of Bath and Wells, and Rev. J. MORISON, D.D. With Homilies by Rev. A. F. MUIR, M.A., Rev. W. F. ADENEY, M.A., Rev. W. M. STATHAM, and Rev. Professor J. THOMSON, M.A. Fifth Edition. 10s. 6d.

    1 Samuel. By the Very Rev. R. P. SMITH, D.D. With Homilies by Rev. DONALD FRASER, D.D., Rev. Prof. CHAPMAN, and Rev. B. DALE. Sixth Edition. 15s.

    1 Kings. By the Rev. JOSEPH HAMMOND, LL.B. With Homilies by the Rev. E. DE PRESSENSÉ, D.D., Rev. J. WAITE, B.A., Rev. A. ROWLAND, LL.B., Rev. J. A. MACDONALD, and Rev. J. URQUHART. Fourth Edition. 15s.

Pulpit Commentary, The—*continued.*

1 Chronicles. By the Rev. Prof. P. C. BARKER, M.A., LL.B. With Homilies by Rev. Prof. J. R. THOMSON, M.A., Rev. R. TUCK, B.A., Rev. W. CLARKSON, B.A., Rev. F. WHITFIELD, M.A., and Rev. RICHARD GLOVER. 15s.

Ezra, Nehemiah, and Esther. By Rev. Canon G. RAWLINSON, M.A. With Homilies by Rev. Prof. J. R. THOMSON, M.A., Rev. Prof. R. A. REDFORD, LL.B., M.A., Rev. W. S. LEWIS, M.A., Rev. J. A. MACDONALD, Rev. A. MACKENNAL, B.A., Rev. W. CLARKSON, B.A., Rev. F. HASTINGS, Rev. W. DINWIDDIE, LL.B., Rev. Prof. ROWLANDS, B.A., Rev. G. WOOD, B.A., Rev. Prof. P. C. BARKER, M.A., LL.B., and the Rev. J. S. EXELL, M.A. Sixth Edition. 1 vol., 12s. 6d.

Jeremiah. (Vol. I.) By the Rev. T. K. CHEYNE, M.A. With Homilies by the Rev. W. F. ADENEY, M.A., Rev. A. F. MUIR, M.A., Rev. S. CONWAY, B.A., Rev. J. WAITE, B.A., and Rev. D. YOUNG, B.A. Second Edition. 15s.

Jeremiah (Vol. II.) and Lamentations. By Rev. T. K. CHEYNE, M.A. With Homilies by Rev. Prof. J. R. THOMSON, M.A., Rev. W. F. ADENEY, M.A., Rev. A. F. MUIR, M.A., Rev. S. CONWAY, B.A., Rev. D. YOUNG, B.A. 15s.

Pulpit Commentary, The. (New Testament Series.)

St. Mark. By Very Rev. E. BICKERSTETH, D.D., Dean of Lichfield. With Homilies by Rev. Prof. THOMSON, M.A., Rev. Prof. GIVEN, M.A., Rev. Prof. JOHNSON, M.A., Rev. A. ROWLAND, B.A., LL.B., Rev. A. MUIR, and Rev. R. GREEN. Fifth Edition. 2 vols., 21s.

The Acts of the Apostles. By the Bishop of Bath and Wells. With Homilies by Rev. Prof. P. C. BARKER, M.A., LL.B., Rev. Prof. E. JOHNSON, M.A., Rev. Prof. R. A. REDFORD, M.A., Rev. R. TUCK, B.A., Rev. W. CLARKSON, B.A. Third Edition. 2 vols., 21s.

I. Corinthians. By the Ven. Archdeacon FARRAR, D.D. With Homilies by Rev. Ex-Chancellor LIPSCOMB, LL.D., Rev. DAVID THOMAS, D.D., Rev. D. FRASER, D.D., Rev. Prof. J. R. THOMSON, M.A., Rev. J. WAITE, B.A., Rev. R. TUCK, B.A., Rev. E. HURNDALL, M.A., and Rev. H. BREMNER, B.D. Third Edition. Price 15s.

II. Corinthians and Galatians. By the Ven. Archdeacon FARRAR, D.D., and Rev. Preb. E. HUXTABLE. With Homilies by Rev. Ex-Chancellor LIPSCOMB, LL.D., Rev. DAVID THOMAS, D.D., Rev. DONALD FRASER, D.D., Rev. R. TUCK, B.A., Rev. E. HURNDALL, M.A., Rev. Prof. J. R. THOMSON, M.A., Rev. R. FINLAYSON, B.A., Rev. W. F. ADENEY, M.A., Rev. R. M. EDGAR, M.A., and Rev. T. CROSKERRY, D.D. Price 21s.

Pulpit Commentary, The. (New Testament Series.)—*continued.*

Ephesians, Phillipians, and Colossians. By the Rev. Prof. W. G. BLAIKIE, D.D., Rev. B. C. CAFFIN, M.A., and Rev. G. G. FINDLAY, B.A. With Homilies by Rev. D. THOMAS, D.D., Rev. R. M. EDGAR, M.A., Rev. R. FINLAYSON, B.A., Rev. W. F. ADENEY, M.A., Rev. Prof. T. CROSKERRY, D.D., Rev. E. S. PROUT, M.A., Rev. Canon VERNON HUTTON, and Rev. U. R. THOMAS, D.D. Price 21s.

Hebrews and James. By the Rev. J. BARNBY, D.D., and Rev. Prebendary E. C. S. GIBSON, M.A. With Homiletics by the Rev. C. JERDAN, M.A., LL.B., and Rev. Prebendary E. C. S. GIBSON. And Homilies by the Rev. W. JONES, Rev. C. NEW, Rev. D. YOUNG, B.A., Rev. J. S. BRIGHT, Rev. T. F. LOCKYER, B.A., and Rev. C. JERDAN, M.A., LL.B. Price 15s.

PUNCHARD, E. G., D.D.—**Christ of Contention.** Three Essays. Fcap. 8vo, 2s.

PUSEY, Dr.—**Sermons for the Church's Seasons from Advent to Trinity.** Selected from the Published Sermons of the late EDWARD BOUVERIE PUSEY, D.D. Crown 8vo, 5s.

RANKE, Leopold von.—**Universal History.** The oldest Historical Group of Nations and the Greeks. Edited by G. W. PROTHERO. Demy 8vo, 16s.

RENDELL, J. M.—**Concise Handbook of the Island of Madeira.** With Plan of Funchal and Map of the Island. Fcap. 8vo, 1s. 6d.

REYNOLDS, Rev. J. W.—**The Supernatural in Nature.** A Verification by Free Use of Science. Third Edition, Revised and Enlarged. Demy 8vo, 14s.

The Mystery of Miracles. Third and Enlarged Edition. Crown 8vo, 6s.

The Mystery of the Universe; Our Common Faith. Demy 8vo, 14s.

RIBOT, Prof. Th.—**Heredity:** A Psychological Study on its Phenomena, its Laws, its Causes, and its Consequences. Second Edition. Large crown 8vo, 9s.

RIMMER, William, M.D.—**Art Anatomy.** A Portfolio of 81 Plates. Folio, 70s., nett.

ROBERTSON, The late Rev. F. W., M.A.—**Life and Letters of.** Edited by the Rev. STOPFORD BROOKE, M.A.

    I. Two vols., uniform with the Sermons. With Steel Portrait. Crown 8vo, 7s. 6d.

    II. Library Edition, in Demy 8vo, with Portrait. 12s.

    III. A Popular Edition, in 1 vol. Crown 8vo, 6s.

Sermons. Four Series. Small crown 8vo, 3s. 6d. each.

The Human Race, and other Sermons. Preached at Cheltenham, Oxford, and Brighton. New and Cheaper Edition. Small crown 8vo, 3s. 6d.

ROBERTSON, The late Rev. F. W., M.A.—continued.
 Notes on Genesis. New and Cheaper Edition. Small crown 8vo, 3s. 6d.
 Expository Lectures on St. Paul's Epistles to the Corinthians. A New Edition. Small crown 8vo, 5s.
 Lectures and Addresses, with other Literary Remains. A New Edition. Small crown 8vo, 5s.
 An Analysis of Tennyson's " In Memoriam." (Dedicated by Permission to the Poet-Laureate.) Fcap. 8vo, 2s.
 The Education of the Human Race. Translated from the German of GOTTHOLD EPHRAIM LESSING. Fcap. 8vo, 2s. 6d.
 The above Works can also be had, bound in half morocco.
*** A Portrait of the late Rev. F. W. Robertson, mounted for framing, can be had, 2s. 6d.

ROMANES, G. J.—**Mental Evolution in Animals.** With a Posthumous Essay on Instinct by CHARLES DARWIN, F.R.S. Demy 8vo, 12s.

ROOSEVELT, Theodore. **Hunting Trips of a Ranchman.** Sketches of Sport on the Northern Cattle Plains. With 26 Illustrations. Royal 8vo, 18s.

Rosmini's Origin of Ideas. Translated from the Fifth Italian Edition of the Nuovo Saggio *Sull' origine delle idee*. 3 vols. Demy 8vo, cloth, 16s. each.

Rosmini's Psychology. 3 vols. Demy 8vo. [Vols. I. and II. now ready, 16s. each.

Rosmini's Philosophical System. Translated, with a Sketch of the Author's Life, Bibliography, Introduction, and Notes by THOMAS DAVIDSON. Demy 8vo, 16s.

RULE, Martin, M.A.—**The Life and Times of St. Anselm, Archbishop of Canterbury and Primate of the Britains.** 2 vols. Demy 8vo, 32s.

SAMUEL, Sydney M.—**Jewish Life in the East.** Small crown 8vo, 3s. 6d.

SARTORIUS, Ernestine.—**Three Months in the Soudan.** With 11 Full-page Illustrations. Demy 8vo, 14s.

SAYCE, Rev. Archibald Henry.—**Introduction to the Science of Language.** 2 vols. Second Edition. Large post 8vo, 21s.

SCOONES, W. Baptiste.—**Four Centuries of English Letters:** A Selection of 350 Letters by 150 Writers, from the Period of the Paston Letters to the Present Time. Third Edition. Large crown 8vo, 6s.

SÉE, Prof. Germain.—**Bacillary Phthisis of the Lungs.** Translated and edited for English Practitioners by WILLIAM HENRY WEDDELL, M.R.C.S. Demy 8vo, 10s. 6d.

Shakspere's Works. The Avon Edition, 12 vols., fcap. 8vo, cloth, 18s.; in cloth box, 21s.; bound in 6 vols., cloth, 15s.

SHILLITO, Rev. Joseph.—Womanhood: its Duties, Temptations, and Privileges. A Book for Young Women. Third Edition. Crown 8vo, 3s. 6d.

SIDNEY, Algernon.—A Review. By GERTRUDE M. IRELAND BLACKBURNE. Crown 8vo, 6s.

Sister Augustine, Superior of the Sisters of Charity at the St. Johannis Hospital at Bonn. Authorised Translation by HANS THARAU, from the German "Memorials of AMALIE VON LASAULX." Cheap Edition. Large crown 8vo, 4s. 6d.

SKINNER, James.—A Memoir. By the Author of "Charles Lowder." With a Preface by the Rev. Canon CARTER, and Portrait. Large crown, 7s. 6d.

₊ Also a cheap Edition. With Portrait. Crown 8vo, 3s. 6d.

SMITH, Edward, M.D., LL.B., F.R.S.—Tubercular Consumption in its Early and Remediable Stages. Second Edition. Crown 8vo, 6s.

SMITH, Sir W. Cusack, Bart.—Our War Ships. A Naval Essay. Crown 8vo, 5s.

Spanish Mystics. By the Editor of "Many Voices." Crown 8vo, 5s.

Specimens of English Prose Style from Malory to Macaulay. Selected and Annotated, with an Introductory Essay, by GEORGE SAINTSBURY. Large crown 8vo, printed on handmade paper, parchment antique or cloth, 12s.; vellum, 15s.

SPEDDING, James.—Reviews and Discussions, Literary, Political, and Historical not relating to Bacon. Demy 8vo, 12s. 6d.

Evenings with a Reviewer; or, Macaulay and Bacon. With a Prefatory Notice by G. S. VENABLES, Q.C. 2 vols. Demy 8vo, 18s.

STAPFER, Paul.—Shakespeare and Classical Antiquity: Greek and Latin Antiquity as presented in Shakespeare's Plays. Translated by EMILY J. CAREY. Large post 8vo, 12s.

STATHAM, F. Reginald.—Free Thought and Truth Thought. A Contribution to an Existing Argument. Crown 8vo, 6s.

STEVENSON, Rev. W. F.—Hymns for the Church and Home. Selected and Edited by the Rev. W. FLEMING STEVENSON.
The Hymn Book consists of Three Parts:—I. For Public Worship.—II. For Family and Private Worship.—III. For Children. SMALL EDITION. Cloth limp, 10d.; cloth boards, 1s. LARGE TYPE EDITION. Cloth limp, 1s. 3d.; cloth boards, 1s. 6d.

Stray Papers on Education, and Scenes from School Life. By B. H. Second Edition. Small crown 8vo, 3s. 6d.

STREATFEILD, Rev. G. S., M.A.—Lincolnshire and the Danes. Large crown 8vo, 7s. 6d.

STRECKER-WISLICENUS.—**Organic Chemistry.** Translated and Edited, with Extensive Additions, by W. R. HODGKINSON, Ph.D., and A. J. GREENAWAY, F.I.C. Second and cheaper Edition. Demy 8vo, 12s. 6d.

Suakin, 1885; being a Sketch of the Campaign of this year. By an Officer who was there. Second Edition. Crown 8vo, 2s. 6d.

SULLY, James, M.A.—**Pessimism :** a History and a Criticism. Second Edition. Demy 8vo, 14s.

Sunshine and Sea. A Yachting Visit to the Channel Islands and Coast of Brittany. With Frontispiece from a Photograph and 24 Illustrations. Crown 8vo, 6s.

SWEDENBORG, Eman.—**De Cultu et Amore Dei ubi Agitur de Telluris ortu, Paradiso et Vivario, tum de Primogeniti Seu Adami Nativitate Infantia, et Amore.** Crown 8vo, 6s.

    On the Worship and Love of God. Treating of the Birth of the Earth, Paradise, and the Abode of Living Creatures. Translated from the original Latin. Crown 8vo, 7s. 6d.

    Prodromus Philosophiæ Ratiocinantis de Infinito, et Causa Finali Creationis : deque Mechanismo Operationis Animæ et Corporis. Edidit THOMAS MURRAY GORMAN, M.A. Crown 8vo, 7s. 6d.

TACITUS.—**The Agricola.** A Translation. Small crown 8vo, 2s. 6d.

TAYLOR, Rev. Isaac.—**The Alphabet.** An Account of the Origin and Development of Letters. With numerous Tables and Facsimiles. 2 vols. Demy 8vo, 36s.

TAYLOR, Jeremy.—**The Marriage Ring.** With Preface, Notes, and Appendices. Edited by FRANCIS BURDETT MONEY COUTTS. Small crown 8vo, 2s. 6d.

TAYLOR, Sedley. — **Profit Sharing between Capital and Labour.** To which is added a Memorandum on the Industrial Partnership at the Whitwood Collieries, by ARCHIBALD and HENRY BRIGGS, with remarks by SEDLEY TAYLOR. Crown 8vo, 2s. 6d.

"**They Might Have Been Together Till the Last.**" An Essay on Marriage, and the position of Women in England. Small crown 8vo, 2s.

Thirty Thousand Thoughts. Edited by the Rev. CANON SPENCE, Rev. J. S. EXELL, and Rev. CHARLES NEIL. 6 vols. Super royal 8vo.

                        [Vols. I.-IV. now ready, 16s. each.

THOM, J. Hamilton.—**Laws of Life after the Mind of Christ.** Two Series. Crown 8vo, 7s. 6d. each.

THOMPSON, Sir H.—**Diet in Relation to Age and Activity.** Fcap. 8vo, cloth, 1s. 6d. ; Paper covers, 1s.

TIPPLE, Rev. S. A.—**Sunday Mornings at Norwood.** Prayers and Sermons. Crown 8vo, 6s.

TODHUNTER, Dr. J.—**A Study of Shelley.** Crown 8vo, 7s.

TOLSTOI, Count Leo.—**Christ's Christianity.** Translated from the Russian. Large crown 8vo, 7s. 6d.

TRANT, William.—**Trade Unions: Their Origin, Objects, and Efficacy.** Small crown 8vo, 1s. 6d.; paper covers, 1s.

TREMENHEERE, Hugh Seymour, C.B.—**A Manual of the Principles of Government,** as set forth by the Authorities of Ancient and Modern Times. New and Enlarged Edition. Crown 8vo, 3s. 6d. Cheap Edition, limp cloth, 1s.

TRENCH, The late R. C., Archbishop.—**Notes on the Parables of Our Lord.** Fourteenth Edition. 8vo, 12s.

Notes on the Miracles of Our Lord. Twelfth Edition. 8vo, 12s.

Studies in the Gospels. Fifth Edition, Revised. 8vo, 10s. 6d.

Brief Thoughts and Meditations on Some Passages in Holy Scripture. Third Edition. Crown 8vo, 3s. 6d.

Synonyms of the New Testament. Ninth Edition, Enlarged. 8vo, 12s.

Selected Sermons. Crown 8vo, 6s.

On the Authorized Version of the New Testament. Second Edition. 8vo, 7s.

Commentary on the Epistles to the Seven Churches in Asia. Fourth Edition, Revised. 8vo, 8s. 6d.

The Sermon on the Mount. An Exposition drawn from the Writings of St. Augustine, with an Essay on his Merits as an Interpreter of Holy Scripture. Fourth Edition, Enlarged. 8vo, 10s. 6d.

Shipwrecks of Faith. Three Sermons preached before the University of Cambridge in May, 1867. Fcap. 8vo, 2s. 6d.

Lectures on Mediæval Church History. Being the Substance of Lectures delivered at Queen's College, London. Second Edition. 8vo, 12s.

English, Past and Present. Thirteenth Edition, Revised and Improved. Fcap. 8vo, 5s.

On the Study of Words. Nineteenth Edition, Revised. Fcap. 8vo, 5s.

Select Glossary of English Words Used Formerly in Senses Different from the Present. Fifth Edition, Revised and Enlarged. Fcap. 8vo, 5s.

Proverbs and Their Lessons. Seventh Edition, Enlarged. Fcap. 8vo, 4s.

Poems. Collected and Arranged anew. Ninth Edition. Fcap. 8vo, 7s. 6d.

TRENCH, The late R. C., Archbishop.—continued.

    Poems. Library Edition. 2 vols. Small crown 8vo, 10s.

    Sacred Latin Poetry. Chiefly Lyrical, Selected and Arranged for Use. Third Edition, Corrected and Improved. Fcap. 8vo, 7s.

    A Household Book of English Poetry. Selected and Arranged, with Notes. Fourth Edition, Revised. Extra fcap. 8vo, 5s. 6d.

    An Essay on the Life and Genius of Calderon. With Translations from his "Life's a Dream" and "Great Theatre of the World." Second Edition, Revised and Improved. Extra fcap. 8vo, 5s. 6d.

    Gustavus Adolphus in Germany, and other Lectures on the Thirty Years' War. Second Edition, Enlarged. Fcap. 8vo, 4s.

    Plutarch: his Life, his Lives, and his Morals. Second Edition, Enlarged. Fcap. 8vo, 3s. 6d.

    Remains of the late Mrs. Richard Trench. Being Selections from her Journals, Letters, and other Papers. New and Cheaper Issue. With Portrait. 8vo, 6s.

TUKE, Daniel Hack, M.D., F.R.C.P.—**Chapters in the History of the Insane in the British Isles.** With Four Illustrations. Large crown 8vo, 12s.

TWINING, Louisa.—**Workhouse Visiting and Management during Twenty-Five Years.** Small crown 8vo, 2s.

TYLER, J.—**The Mystery of Being: or, What Do We Know?** Small crown 8vo, 3s. 6d.

VAUGHAN, H. Halford.—**New Readings and Renderings of Shakespeare's Tragedies.** 3 vols. Demy 8vo, 12s. 6d. each.

VILLARI, Professor.—**Niccolò Machiavelli and his Times.** Translated by LINDA VILLARI. 4 vols. Large post 8vo, 48s.

VILLIERS, The Right Hon. C. P.—**Free Trade Speeches of.** With Political Memoir. Edited by a Member of the Cobden Club. 2 vols. With Portrait. Demy 8vo, 25s.

    ** People's Edition. 1 vol. Crown 8vo, limp cloth, 2s. 6d.

VOGT, Lieut.-Col. Hermann.—**The Egyptian War of 1882.** A translation. With Map and Plans. Large crown 8vo, 6s.

VOLCKXSOM, E. W. v.—**Catechism of Elementary Modern Chemistry.** Small crown 8vo, 3s.

WALLER, Rev. C. B.—**The Apocalypse,** reviewed under the Light of the Doctrine of the Unfolding Ages, and the Restitution of All Things. Demy 8vo, 12s.

    The Bible Record of Creation viewed in its Letter and Spirit. Two Sermons preached at St. Paul's Church, Woodford Bridge. Crown 8vo, 1s. 6d.

WALPOLE, *Chas. George.*—**A Short History of Ireland from the Earliest Times to the Union with Great Britain.** With 5 Maps and Appendices. Second Edition. Crown 8vo, 6s.

WARD, *William George, Ph.D.*—**Essays on the Philosophy of Theism.** Edited, with an Introduction, by WILFRID WARD. 2 vols. Demy 8vo, 21s.

WARD, *Wilfrid.*—**The Wish to Believe.** A Discussion Concerning the Temper of Mind in which a reasonable Man should undertake Religious Inquiry. Small crown 8vo, 5s.

WARTER, *J. W.*—**An Old Shropshire Oak.** 2 vols. Demy 8vo, 28s.

WEDDERBURN, *Sir David, Bart., M.P.*—**Life of.** Compiled from his Journals and Writings by his sister, Mrs. E. H. PERCIVAL. With etched Portrait, and facsimiles of Pencil Sketches. Demy 8vo, 14s.

WEDMORE, *Frederick.*—**The Masters of Genre Painting.** With Sixteen Illustrations. Post 8vo, 7s. 6d.

WHITE, *R. E.*—**Recollections of Woolwich during the Crimean War and Indian Mutiny, and of the Ordnance and War Departments**; together with complete Lists of Past and Present Officials of the Royal Arsenal, etc. Crown 8vo, 2s. 6d.

WHITNEY, *Prof. William Dwight.*—**Essentials of English Grammar,** for the Use of Schools. Second Edition. Crown 8vo, 3s. 6d.

WHITWORTH, *George Clifford.*—**An Anglo-Indian Dictionary**: a Glossary of Indian Terms used in English, and of such English or other Non-Indian Terms as have obtained special meanings in India. Demy 8vo, cloth, 12s.

WILLIAMS, *Rowland, D.D.*—**Psalms, Litanies, Counsels, and Collects for Devout Persons.** Edited by his Widow. New and Popular Edition. Crown 8vo, 3s. 6d.

Stray Thoughts from the Note Books of the late Rowland Williams, D.D. Edited by his Widow. Crown 8vo, 3s. 6d.

WILSON, *Lieut.-Col. C. T.*—**The Duke of Berwick, Marshal of France, 1702-1734.** Demy 8vo, 15s.

WILSON, *Mrs. R. F.*—**The Christian Brothers.** Their Origin and Work. With a Sketch of the Life of their Founder, the Ven. JEAN BAPTISTE, de la Salle. Crown 8vo, 6s.

WOLTMANN, *Dr. Alfred, and* WOERMANN, *Dr. Karl.*—**History of Painting.** With numerous Illustrations. Vol. I. Painting in Antiquity and the Middle Ages. Medium 8vo, 28s., bevelled boards, gilt leaves, 30s. Vol. II. The Painting of the Renascence.

YOUMANS, *Eliza A.*—First Book of Botany. Designed to Cultivate the Observing Powers of Children. With 300 Engravings. New and Cheaper Edition. Crown 8vo, 2s. 6d.

YOUMANS, *Edward L., M.D.*—A Class Book of Chemistry, on the Basis of the New System. With 200 Illustrations. Crown 8vo, 5s.

THE INTERNATIONAL SCIENTIFIC SERIES.

I. **Forms of Water**: a Familiar Exposition of the Origin and Phenomena of Glaciers. By J. Tyndall, LL.D., F.R.S. With 25 Illustrations. Ninth Edition. 5s.

II. **Physics and Politics**; or, Thoughts on the Application of the Principles of "Natural Selection" and "Inheritance" to Political Society. By Walter Bagehot. Seventh Edition. 4s.

III. **Foods.** By Edward Smith, M.D., LL.B., F.R.S. With numerous Illustrations. Eighth Edition. 5s.

IV. **Mind and Body**: the Theories of their Relation. By Alexander Bain, LL.D. With Four Illustrations. Seventh Edition. 4s.

V. **The Study of Sociology.** By Herbert Spencer. Twelfth Edition. 5s.

VI. **On the Conservation of Energy.** By Balfour Stewart, M.A., LL.D., F.R.S. With 14 Illustrations. Sixth Edition. 5s.

VII. **Animal Locomotion**; or Walking, Swimming, and Flying. By J. B. Pettigrew, M.D., F.R.S., etc. With 130 Illustrations. Third Edition. 5s.

VIII. **Responsibility in Mental Disease.** By Henry Maudsley, M.D. Fourth Edition. 5s.

IX. **The New Chemistry.** By Professor J. P. Cooke. With 31 Illustrations. Eighth Edition, remodelled and enlarged. 5s.

X. **The Science of Law.** By Professor Sheldon Amos. Sixth Edition. 5s.

XI. **Animal Mechanism**: a Treatise on Terrestrial and Aerial Locomotion. By Professor E. J. Marey. With 117 Illustrations. Third Edition. 5s.

XII. **The Doctrine of Descent and Darwinism.** By Professor Oscar Schmidt. With 26 Illustrations. Sixth Edition. 5s.

XIII. **The History of the Conflict between Religion and Science.** By J. W. Draper, M.D., LL.D. Nineteenth Edition. 5s.

XIV. **Fungi**: their Nature, Influences, Uses, etc. By M. C. Cooke, M.D., LL.D. Edited by the Rev. M. J. Berkeley, M.A., F.L.S. With numerous Illustrations. Third Edition. 5s.

XV. **The Chemical Effects of Light and Photography.** By Dr. Hermann Vogel. With 100 Illustrations. Fourth Edition. 5s.

XVI. **The Life and Growth of Language.** By Professor William Dwight Whitney. Fifth Edition. 5s.

XVII. **Money and the Mechanism of Exchange.** By W. Stanley Jevons, M.A., F.R.S. Seventh Edition. 5s.

XVIII. **The Nature of Light.** With a General Account of Physical Optics. By Dr. Eugene Lommel. With 188 Illustrations and a Table of Spectra in Chromo-lithography. Third Edition. 5s.

XIX. **Animal Parasites and Messmates.** By P. J. Van Beneden. With 83 Illustrations. Third Edition. 5s.

XX. **Fermentation.** By Professor Schützenberger. With 28 Illustrations. Fourth Edition. 5s.

XXI. **The Five Senses of Man.** By Professor Bernstein. With 91 Illustrations. Fifth Edition. 5s.

XXII. **The Theory of Sound in its Relation to Music.** By Professor Pietro Blaserna. With numerous Illustrations. Third Edition. 5s.

XXIII. **Studies in Spectrum Analysis.** By J. Norman Lockyer, F.R.S. With six photographic Illustrations of Spectra, and numerous engravings on Wood. Third Edition. 6s. 6d.

XXIV. **A History of the Growth of the Steam Engine.** By Professor R. H. Thurston. With numerous Illustrations. Third Edition. 6s. 6d.

XXV. **Education as a Science.** By Alexander Bain, LL.D. Fifth Edition. 5s.

XXVI. **The Human Species.** By Professor A. de Quatrefages. Third Edition. 5s.

XXVII. **Modern Chromatics.** With Applications to Art and Industry. By Ogden N. Rood. With 130 original Illustrations. Second Edition. 5s.

XXVIII. **The Crayfish**: an Introduction to the Study of Zoology. By Professor T. H. Huxley. With 82 Illustrations. Fourth Edition. 5s.

XXIX. **The Brain as an Organ of Mind.** By H. Charlton Bastian, M.D. With numerous Illustrations. Third Edition. 5s.

XXX. **The Atomic Theory.** By Prof. Wurtz. Translated by G. Cleminshaw, F.C.S. Fourth Edition. 5s.

XXXI. **The Natural Conditions of Existence as they affect Animal Life.** By Karl Semper. With 2 Maps and 106 Woodcuts. Third Edition. 5s.

XXXII. **General Physiology of Muscles and Nerves.** By Prof. J. Rosenthal. Third Edition. With Illustrations. 5s.

XXXIII. **Sight**: an Exposition of the Principles of Monocular and Binocular Vision. By Joseph le Conte, LL.D. Second Edition. With 132 Illustrations. 5s.

XXXIV. **Illusions**: a Psychological Study. By James Sully. Second Edition. 5s.

XXXV. **Volcanoes: what they are and what they teach.** By Professor J. W. Judd, F.R.S. With 92 Illustrations on Wood. Third Edition. 5s.

XXXVI. **Suicide**: an Essay on Comparative Moral Statistics. By Prof. H. Morselli. Second Edition. With Diagrams. 5s.

XXXVII. **The Brain and its Functions.** By J. Luys. With Illustrations. Second Edition. 5s.

XXXVIII. **Myth and Science**: an Essay. By Tito Vignoli. Second Edition. 5s.

XXXIX. **The Sun.** By Professor Young. With Illustrations. Second Edition. 5s.

XL. **Ants, Bees, and Wasps**: a Record of Observations on the Habits of the Social Hymenoptera. By Sir John Lubbock, Bart., M.P. With 5 Chromo-lithographic Illustrations. Eighth Edition. 5s.

XLI. **Animal Intelligence.** By G. J. Romanes, LL.D., F.R.S. Third Edition. 5s.

XLII. **The Concepts and Theories of Modern Physics.** By J. B. Stallo. Third Edition. 5s.

XLIII. **Diseases of the Memory**; An Essay in the Positive Psychology. By Prof. Th. Ribot. Second Edition. 5s.

XLIV. **Man before Metals.** By N. Joly, with 148 Illustrations. Third Edition. 5s.

XLV. **The Science of Politics.** By Prof. Sheldon Amos. Third Edition. 5s.

XLVI. **Elementary Meteorology.** By Robert H. Scott. Third Edition. With Numerous Illustrations. 5s.

XLVII. **The Organs of Speech and their Application in the Formation of Articulate Sounds.** By Georg Hermann Von Meyer. With 47 Woodcuts. 5s.

XLVIII. **Fallacies.** A View of Logic from the Practical Side. By Alfred Sidgwick. 5s.

XLIX. **Origin of Cultivated Plants.** By Alphonse de Candolle. 5s.

L. **Jelly-Fish, Star-Fish, and Sea-Urchins.** Being a Research on Primitive Nervous Systems. By G. J. Romanes. With Illustrations. 5s.

LI. **The Common Sense of the Exact Sciences.** By the late William Kingdon Clifford. Second Edition. With 100 Figures. 5s.

LII. **Physical Expression:** Its Modes and Principles. By Francis Warner, M.D., F.R.C.P. With 50 Illustrations. 5s.

LIII. **Anthropoid Apes.** By Robert Hartmann. With 63 Illustrations. 5s.

LIV. **The Mammalia in their Relation to Primeval Times.** By Oscar Schmidt. With 51 Woodcuts. 5s.

LV. **Comparative Literature.** By H. Macaulay Posnett, LL.D. 5s.

LVI. **Earthquakes and other Earth Movements.** By Prof. JOHN MILNE. With 38 Figures. 5s.

LVII. **Microbes, Ferments, and Moulds.** By E. L. TROUESSART. With 107 Illustrations. 5s.

MILITARY WORKS.

BRACKENBURY, Col. C. B., R.A.—**Military Handbooks for Regimental Officers.**

I. **Military Sketching and Reconnaissance.** By Col. F. J. Hutchison and Major H. G. MacGregor. Fourth Edition. With 15 Plates. Small crown 8vo, 4s.

II. **The Elements of Modern Tactics Practically applied to English Formations.** By Lieut.-Col. Wilkinson Shaw. Fifth Edition. With 25 Plates and Maps. Small crown 8vo, 9s.

III. **Field Artillery.** Its Equipment, Organization and Tactics. By Major Sisson C. Pratt, R.A. With 12 Plates. Second Edition. Small crown 8vo, 6s.

IV. **The Elements of Military Administration.** First Part: Permanent System of Administration. By Major J. W. Buxton. Small crown 8vo. 7s. 6d.

V. **Military Law:** Its Procedure and Practice. By Major Sisson C. Pratt, R.A. Second Edition. Small crown 8vo, 4s. 6d.

VI. **Cavalry in Modern War.** By Col. F. Chenevix Trench. Small crown 8vo, 6s.

VII. **Field Works.** Their Technical Construction and Tactical Application. By the Editor, Col. C. B. Brackenbury, R.A. Small crown 8vo.

BRENT, Brig.-Gen. J. L.—**Mobilizable Fortifications and their Controlling Influence in War.** Crown 8vo, 5s.

BROOKE, Major, C. K.—**A System of Field Training.** Small crown 8vo, cloth limp, 2s.

CLERY, C., Lieut.-Col.—**Minor Tactics.** With 26 Maps and Plans. Seventh Edition, Revised. Crown 8vo, 9s.

COLVILE, Lieut.-Col. C. F.—**Military Tribunals.** Sewed, 2s. 6d.

CRAUFURD, Capt. H. J.—**Suggestions for the Military Training of a Company of Infantry.** Crown 8vo, 1s. 6d.

HAMILTON, Capt. Ian, A.D.C.—**The Fighting of the Future.** 1s.

HARRISON, Col. R.—**The Officer's Memorandum Book for Peace and War.** Fourth Edition, Revised throughout. Oblong 32mo, red basil, with pencil, 3s. 6d.

Notes on Cavalry Tactics, Organisation, etc. By a Cavalry Officer. With Diagrams. Demy 8vo, 12s.

PARR, Capt. H. Hallam, C.M.G.—**The Dress, Horses, and Equipment of Infantry and Staff Officers.** Crown 8vo, 1s.

SCHAW, Col. H.—**The Defence and Attack of Positions and Localities.** Third Edition, Revised and Corrected. Crown 8vo, 3s. 6d.

STONE, Capt. F. Gleadowe, R.A.—**Tactical Studies from the Franco-German War of 1870-71.** With 22 Lithographic Sketches and Maps. Demy 8vo, 30s.

WILKINSON, H. Spenser, Capt. 20th Lancashire R.V.—**Citizen Soldiers.** Essays towards the Improvement of the Volunteer Force. Crown 8vo, 2s. 6d.

POETRY.

ADAM OF ST. VICTOR.—**The Liturgical Poetry of Adam of St. Victor.** From the text of GAUTIER. With Translations into English in the Original Metres, and Short Explanatory Notes, by DIGBY S. WRANGHAM, M.A. 3 vols. Crown 8vo, printed on hand-made paper, boards, 21s.

AUCHMUTY, A. C.—**Poems of English Heroism**: From Brunanburh to Lucknow; from Athelstan to Albert. Small crown 8vo, 1s. 6d.

BARNES, William.—**Poems of Rural Life, in the Dorset Dialect.** New Edition, complete in one vol. Crown 8vo, 8s. 6d.

BAYNES, Rev. Canon H. R.—**Home Songs for Quiet Hours.** Fourth and Cheaper Edition. Fcap. 8vo, cloth, 2s. 6d.

BEVINGTON, L. S.—**Key Notes.** Small crown 8vo, 5s.

BLUNT, Wilfrid Scawen.—**The Wind and the Whirlwind.** Demy 8vo, 1s. 6d.

BLUNT, Wilfred Scawen—continued.
  The Love Sonnets of Proteus. Fifth Edition, 18mo. Cloth extra, gilt top, 5s.

BOWEN, H. C., M.A.—**Simple English Poems.** English Literature for Junior Classes. In Four Parts. Parts I., II., and III., 6d. each, and Part IV., 1s. Complete, 3s.

BRYANT, W. C.—**Poems.** Cheap Edition, with Frontispiece. Small crown 8vo, 3s. 6d.

Calderon's Dramas: the Wonder-Working Magician — Life is a Dream—the Purgatory of St. Patrick. Translated by DENIS FLORENCE MACCARTHY. Post 8vo, 10s.

Camoens Lusiads. — Portuguese Text, with Translation by J. J. AUBERTIN. Second Edition. 2 vols. Crown 8vo, 12s.

CAMPBELL, Lewis.—**Sophocles.** The Seven Plays in English Verse. Crown 8vo, 7s. 6d.

CERVANTES.—**Journey to Parnassus.** Spanish Text, with Translation into English Tercets, Preface, and Illustrative Notes, by JAMES Y. GIBSON. Crown 8vo, 12s.

  Numantia: a Tragedy. Translated from the Spanish, with Introduction and Notes, by JAMES Y. GIBSON. Crown 8vo, printed on hand-made paper, 5s.

CHAVANNES, Mary Charlotte. — **A Few Translations from Victor Hugo and other Poets.** Small crown 8vo, 2s. 6d.

CHRISTIE, A. J.—**The End of Man.** With 4 Autotype Illustrations. 4to, 10s. 6d.

Chronicles of Christopher Columbus. A Poem in 12 Cantos. By M. D. C. Crown 8vo, 7s. 6d.

CLARKE, Mary Cowden.—**Honey from the Weed.** Verses. Crown 8vo, 7s.

COXHEAD, Ethel.—**Birds and Babies.** Imp. 16mo. With 33 Illustrations. Gilt, 2s. 6d.

DE BERANGER.—**A Selection from his Songs.** In English Verse. By WILLIAM TOYNBEE. Small crown 8vo, 2s. 6d.

DENNIS, J.—**English Sonnets.** Collected and Arranged by. Small crown 8vo, 2s. 6d.

DE VERE, Aubrey.—**Poetical Works.**
  I. THE SEARCH AFTER PROSERPINE, etc. 6s.
  II. THE LEGENDS OF ST. PATRICK, etc. 6s.
  III. ALEXANDER THE GREAT, etc. 6s.

  The Foray of Queen Meave, and other Legends of Ireland's Heroic Age. Small crown 8vo, 5s.

  Legends of the Saxon Saints. Small crown 8vo, 6s.

DOBSON, Austin.—**Old World Idylls** and other Verses. Sixth Edition. Elzevir 8vo, gilt top, 6s.

    At the Sign of the Lyre. Fourth Edition. Elzevir 8vo, gilt top, 6s.

DOMETT, Alfred.—**Ranolf and Amohia.** A Dream of Two Lives. New Edition, Revised. 2 vols. Crown 8vo, 12s.

    Dorothy: a Country Story in Elegiac Verse. With Preface. Demy 8vo, 5s.

DOWDEN, Edward, LL.D.—**Shakspere's Sonnets.** With Introduction and Notes. Large post 8vo, 7s. 6d.

    Dulce Cor: being the Poems of Ford Bereton. With Two Illustrations. Crown 8vo, 6s.

DUTT, Toru.—**A Sheaf Gleaned in French Fields.** New Edition. Demy 8vo, 10s. 6d.

    Ancient Ballads and Legends of Hindustan. With an Introductory Memoir by EDMUND GOSSE. Second Edition, 18mo. Cloth extra, gilt top, 5s.

EDWARDS, Miss Betham.—**Poems.** Small crown 8vo, 3s. 6d.

ELDRYTH, Maud.—**Margaret,** and other Poems. Small crown 8vo, 3s. 6d.

    All Soul's Eve, "No God," and other Poems. Fcap. 8vo, 3s. 6d.

ELLIOTT, Ebenezer, The Corn Law Rhymer.—**Poems.** Edited by his son, the Rev. EDWIN ELLIOTT, of St. John's, Antigua. 2 vols. Crown 8vo, 18s.

    English Verse. Edited by W. J. LINTON and R. H. STODDARD. 5 vols. Crown 8vo, cloth, 5s. each.
      I. CHAUCER TO BURNS.
      II. TRANSLATIONS.
      III. LYRICS OF THE NINETEENTH CENTURY.
      IV. DRAMATIC SCENES AND CHARACTERS.
      V. BALLADS AND ROMANCES.

ENIS.—**Gathered Leaves.** Small crown 8vo, 3s. 6d.

EVANS, Anne.—**Poems and Music.** With Memorial Preface by ANN THACKERAY RITCHIE. Large crown 8vo, 7s.

GOODCHILD, John A.—**Somnia Medici.** Two series. Small crown 8vo, 5s. each.

GOSSE, Edmund W.—**New Poems.** Crown 8vo, 7s. 6d.

    Firdausi in Exile, and other Poems. Elzevir 8vo, gilt top, 6s.

GRINDROD, Charles.—**Plays from English History.** Crown 8vo, 7s. 6d.

    The Stranger's Story, and his Poem, The Lament of Love: An Episode of the Malvern Hills. Small crown 8vo, 2s. 6d.

GURNEY, Rev. Alfred.—**The Vision of the Eucharist,** and other Poems. Crown 8vo, 5s.

A Christmas Faggot. Small crown 8vo, 5s.

HENRY, Daniel, Junr.—**Under a Fool's Cap.** Songs. Crown 8vo, cloth, bevelled boards, 5s.

HEYWOOD, J. C.—**Herodias,** a Dramatic Poem. New Edition, Revised. Small crown 8vo, 5s.

Antonius. A Dramatic Poem. New Edition, Revised. Small crown 8vo, 5s.

HICKEY, E. H.—**A Sculptor,** and other Poems. Small crown 8vo, 5s.

HOLE, W. G.—**Procris,** and other Poems. Fcap. 8vo, 3s. 6d.

KEATS, John.—**Poetical Works.** Edited by W. T. ARNOLD. Large crown 8vo, choicely printed on hand-made paper, with Portrait in *eau-forte*. Parchment or cloth, 12s.; vellum, 15s.

KING, Mrs. Hamilton.—**The Disciples.** Eighth Edition, and Notes. Small crown 8vo, 5s.

A Book of Dreams. Crown 8vo, 3s. 6d.

KNOX, The Hon. Mrs. O. N.—**Four Pictures from a Life,** and other Poems. Small crown 8vo, 3s. 6d.

LANG, A.—**XXXII Ballades in Blue China.** Elzevir 8vo, 5s.

Rhymes à la Mode. With Frontispiece by E. A. Abbey. Elzevir 8vo, cloth extra, gilt top, 5s.

LAWSON, Right Hon. Mr. Justice.—**Hymni Usitati Latine Redditi:** with other Verses. Small 8vo, parchment, 5s.

Lessing's Nathan the Wise. Translated by EUSTACE K. CORBETT. Crown 8vo, 6s.

Life Thoughts. Small crown 8vo, 2s. 6d.

Living English Poets MDCCCLXXXII. With Frontispiece by Walter Crane. Second Edition. Large crown 8vo. Printed on hand-made paper. Parchment or cloth, 12s.; vellum, 15s.

LOCKER, F.—**London Lyrics.** Tenth Edition. With Portrait, Elzevir 8vo. Cloth extra, gilt top, 5s.

Love in Idleness. A Volume of Poems. With an Etching by W. B. Scott. Small crown 8vo, 5s.

LUMSDEN, Lieut.-Col. H. W.—**Beowulf:** an Old English Poem. Translated into Modern Rhymes. Second and Revised Edition. Small crown 8vo, 5s.

LYSAGHT, Sidney Royse.—**A Modern Ideal.** A Dramatic Poem. Small crown 8vo, 5s.

MACGREGOR, Duncan.—**Clouds and Sunlight.** Poems. Small crown 8vo, 5s.

MAGNUSSON, Eirikr, M.A., and PALMER, E. H., M.A.—Johan Ludvig Runeberg's Lyrical Songs, Idylls, and Epigrams. Fcap. 8vo, 5s.

MAKCLOUD, Even.—Ballads of the Western Highlands and Islands of Scotland. Small crown 8vo, 3s. 6d.

MC'NAUGHTON, J. H.—Onnalinda. A Romance. Small crown 8vo, 7s. 6d.

MEREDITH, Owen [The Earl of Lytton].—Lucile. New Edition. With 32 Illustrations. 16mo, 3s. 6d. Cloth extra, gilt edges, 4s. 6d.

MORRIS, Lewis.—Poetical Works of. New and Cheaper Editions, with Portrait. Complete in 3 vols., 5s. each.
  Vol. I. contains "Songs of Two Worlds." Eleventh Edition.
  Vol. II. contains "The Epic of Hades." Twentieth Edition.
  Vol. III. contains "Gwen" and "The Ode of Life." Sixth Edition.
  The Epic of Hades. With 16 Autotype Illustrations, after the Drawings of the late George R. Chapman. 4to, cloth extra, gilt leaves, 21s.
  The Epic of Hades. Presentation Edition. 4to, cloth extra, gilt leaves, 10s. 6d.
  Songs Unsung. Fifth Edition. Fcap. 8vo, 5s.
  The Lewis Morris Birthday Book. Edited by S. S. COPE-MAN, with Frontispiece after a Design by the late George R. Chapman. 32mo, cloth extra, gilt edges, 2s.; cloth limp, 1s. 6d.

MORSHEAD, E. D. A.—The House of Atreus. Being the Agamemnon, Libation-Bearers, and Furies of Æschylus. Translated into English Verse. Crown 8vo, 7s.
  The Suppliant Maidens of Æschylus. Crown 8vo, 3s. 6d.

MOZLEY, J. Rickards.—The Romance of Dennell. A Poem in Five Cantos. Crown 8vo, 7s. 6d.

MULHOLLAND, Rosa.—Vagrant Verses. Small crown 8vo, 5s.

NOEL, The Hon. Roden.—A Little Child's Monument. Third Edition. Small crown 8vo, 3s. 6d.
  The House of Ravensburg. New Edition. Small crown 8vo, 6s.
  The Red Flag, and other Poems. New Edition. Small crown 8vo, 6s.
  Songs of the Heights and Deeps. Crown 8vo, 6s.

OBBARD, Constance Mary.—Burley Bells. Small crown 8vo, 3s. 6d.

O'HAGAN, John.—The Song of Roland. Translated into English Verse. New and Cheaper Edition. Crown 8vo, 5s.

PFEIFFER, Emily.—The Rhyme of the Lady of the Rock, and How it Grew. Second Edition. Small crown 8vo, 3s. 6d.

PFEIFFER, Emily—continued.
 Gerard's Monument, and other Poems. Second Edition. Crown 8vo, 6s.
 Under the Aspens: Lyrical and Dramatic. With Portrait. Crown 8vo, 6s.
PIATT, J. J.—Idyls and Lyrics of the Ohio Valley. Crown 8vo, 5s.
PIATT, Sarah M. B.—A Voyage to the Fortunate Isles, and other Poems. 1 vol. Small crown 8vo, gilt top, 5s.
 In Primrose Time. A New Irish Garland. Small crown 8vo, 2s. 6d.
Rare Poems of the 16th and 17th Centuries. Edited W. J. LINTON. Crown 8vo, 5s.
RHOADES, James.—The Georgics of Virgil. Translated into English Verse. Small crown 8vo, 5s.
 Poems. Small crown 8vo, 4s. 6d.
ROBINSON, A. Mary F.—A Handful of Honeysuckle. Fcap. 8vo, 3s. 6d.
 The Crowned Hippolytus. Translated from Euripides. With New Poems. Small crown 8vo, 5s.
ROUS, Lieut.-Col.—Conradin. Small crown 8vo, 2s.
SANDYS, R. H.—Egeus, and other Poems. Small crown 8vo, 3s. 6d.
SCHILLER, Friedrich.—Wallenstein. A Drama. Done in English Verse, by J. A. W. HUNTER, M.A. Crown 8vo, 7s. 6d.
SCOTT, E. J. L.—The Eclogues of Virgil.—Translated into English Verse. Small crown 8vo, 3s. 6d.
SCOTT, George F. E.—Theodora and other Poems. Small crown 8vo, 3s. 6d.
SEYMOUR, F. H. A.—Rienzi. A Play in Five Acts. Small crown 8vo, 5s.
Shak's Works. The Avon Edition, 12 vols., fcap. 8vo, cloth, 18s.; and in box, 21s.; bound in 6 vols., cloth, 15s.
SHERBROOKE, Viscount.—Poems of a Life. Second Edition. Small crown 8vo, 2s. 6d.
SMITH, J. W. Gilbart.—The Loves of Vandyck. A Tale of Genoa. Small crown 8vo, 2s. 6d.
 The Log o' the "Norseman." Small crown 8vo, 5s.
Songs of Coming Day. Small crown 8vo, 3s. 6d.
Sophocles: The Seven Plays in English Verse. Translated by LEWIS CAMPBELL. Crown 8vo, 7s. 6d.
SPICER, Henry.—Haska: a Drama in Three Acts (as represented at the Theatre Royal, Drury Lane, March 10th, 1877). Third Edition. Crown 8vo, 3s. 6d.
 Uriel Acosta, in Three Acts. From the German of Gatzkow. Small crown 8vo, 2s. 6d.

SYMONDS, *John Addington.*—Vagabunduli Libellus. Crown 8vo, 6s.

Tasso's Jerusalem Delivered. Translated by Sir JOHN KINGSTON JAMES, Bart. Two Volumes. Printed on hand-made paper, parchment, bevelled boards. Large crown 8vo, 21s.

TAYLOR, *Sir H.*—Works. Complete in Five Volumes. Crown 8vo, 30s.
  Philip Van Artevelde. Fcap. 8vo, 3s. 6d.
  The Virgin Widow, etc. Fcap. 8vo, 3s. 6d.
  The Statesman. Fcap. 8vo, 3s. 6d.

TAYLOR, *Augustus.*—Poems. Fcap. 8vo, 5s.

TAYLOR, *Margaret Scott.*—"Boys Together," and other Poems. Small crown 8vo, 6s.

TODHUNTER, *Dr. J.*—Laurella, and other Poems. Crown 8vo, 6s. 6d.
  Forest Songs. Small crown 8vo, 3s. 6d.
  The True Tragedy of Rienzi: a Drama. 3s. 6d.
  Alcestis: a Dramatic Poem. Extra fcap. 8vo, 5s.
  Helena in Troas. Small crown 8vo, 2s. 6d.

TYLER, *M. C.*—Anne Boleyn. A Tragedy in Six Acts. Second Edition. Small crown 8vo, 2s. 6d.

TYNAN, *Katherine.*—Louise de la Vallière, and other Poems. Small crown 8vo, 3s. 6d.

WEBSTER, *Augusta.*—In a Day: a Drama. Small crown 8vo, 2s. 6d.
  Disguises: a Drama. Small crown 8vo, 5s.

Wet Days. By a Farmer. Small crown 8vo, 6s.

WOOD, *Rev. F. H.*—Echoes of the Night, and other Poems. Small crown 8vo, 3s. 6d.

Wordsworth Birthday Book, The. Edited by ADELAIDE and VIOLET WORDSWORTH. 32mo, limp cloth, 1s. 6d.; cloth extra, 2s.

YOUNGMAN, *Thomas George.*—Poems. Small crown 8vo, 5s.

YOUNGS, *Ella Sharpe.*—Paphus, and other Poems. Small crown 8vo, 3s. 6d.
  A Heart's Life, Sarpedon, and other Poems. Small crown 8vo, 3s. 6d.

NOVELS AND TALES.

"**All But:**" a Chronicle of Laxenford Life. By PEN OLIVER, F.R.C.S. With 20 Illustrations. Second Edition. Crown 8vo, 6s.

BANKS, *Mrs. G. L.*—God's Providence House. New Edition. Crown 8vo, 3s. 6d.

CHICHELE, *Mary.*—Doing and Undoing. A Story. Crown 8vo, 4s. 6d.

Danish Parsonage. By an Angler. Crown 8vo, 6s.

HUNTER, Hay.—The Crime of Christmas Day. A Tale of the Latin Quarter. By the Author of "My Ducats and my Daughter." 1s.

HUNTER, Hay, and WHYTE, Walter.—My Ducats and My Daughter. New and Cheaper Edition. With Frontispiece. Crown 8vo, 6s.

Hurst and Hanger. A History in Two Parts. 3 vols. 31s. 6d.

INGELOW, Jean.—Off the Skelligs: a Novel. With Frontispiece. Second Edition. Crown 8vo, 6s.

JENKINS, Edward.—A Secret of Two Lives. Crown 8vo, 2s. 6d.

KIELLAND, Alexander L.—Garman and Worse. A Norwegian Novel. Authorized Translation, by W. W. Kettlewell. Crown 8vo, 6s.

MACDONALD, G.—Donal Grant. A Novel. Second Edition. With Frontispiece. Crown 8vo, 6s.
   Castle Warlock. A Novel. Second Edition. With Frontispiece. Crown 8vo, 6s.
   Malcolm. With Portrait of the Author engraved on Steel. Seventh Edition. Crown 8vo, 6s.
   The Marquis of Lossie. Sixth Edition. With Frontispiece. Crown 8vo, 6s.
   St. George and St. Michael. Fifth Edition. With Frontispiece. Crown 8vo, 6s.
   What's Mine's Mine. Second Edition. With Frontispiece. Crown 8vo, 6s.
   Annals of a Quiet Neighbourhood. Fifth Edition. With Frontispiece. Crown 8vo, 6s.
   The Seaboard Parish: a Sequel to "Annals of a Quiet Neighbourhood." Fourth Edition. With Frontispiece. Crown 8vo, 6s.
   Wilfred Cumbermede. An Autobiographical Story. Fourth Edition. With Frontispiece. Crown 8vo, 6s.

MALET, Lucas.—Colonel Enderby's Wife. A Novel. New and Cheaper Edition. With Frontispiece. Crown 8vo, 6s.

MULHOLLAND, Rosa.—Marcella Grace. An Irish Novel. Crown 8vo.

PALGRAVE, W. Gifford.—Hermann Agha: an Eastern Narrative. Third Edition. Crown 8vo, 6s.

SHAW, Flora L.—Castle Blair: a Story of Youthful Days. New and Cheaper Edition. Crown 8vo, 3s. 6d.

STRETTON, Hesba.—Through a Needle's Eye: a Story. New and Cheaper Edition, with Frontispiece. Crown 8vo, 6s.

TAYLOR, Col. Meadows, C.S.I., M.R.I.A.—Seeta: a Novel. With Frontispiece. Crown 8vo, 6s.
   Tippoo Sultaun: a Tale of the Mysore War. With Frontispiece. Crown 8vo, 6s.
   Ralph Darnell. With Frontispiece. Crown 8vo, 6s.
   A Noble Queen. With Frontispiece. Crown 8vo, 6s.
   The Confessions of a Thug. With Frontispiece. Crown 8vo, 6s.
   Tara: a Mahratta Tale. With Frontispiece. Crown 8vo, 6s.
Within Sound of the Sea. With Frontispiece. Crown 8vo, 6s.

BOOKS FOR THE YOUNG.

Brave Men's Footsteps. A Book of Example and Anecdote for Young People. By the Editor of "Men who have Risen." With 4 Illustrations by C. Doyle. Eighth Edition. Crown 8vo, 3s. 6d.

COXHEAD, Ethel.—**Birds and Babies.** Imp. 16mo. With 33 Illustrations. Cloth gilt, 2s. 6d.

DAVIES, G. Christopher.—**Rambles and Adventures of our School Field Club.** With 4 Illustrations. New and Cheaper Edition. Crown 8vo, 3s. 6d.

EDMONDS, Herbert.—**Well Spent Lives:** a Series of Modern Biographies. New and Cheaper Edition. Crown 8vo, 3s. 6d.

EVANS, Mark.—**The Story of our Father's Love,** told to Children. Sixth and Cheaper Edition of Theology for Children. With 4 Illustrations. Fcap. 8vo, 1s. 6d.

JOHNSON, Virginia W.—**The Catskill Fairies.** Illustrated by Alfred Fredericks. 5s.

MACKENNA, S. J.—**Plucky Fellows.** A Book for Boys. With 6 Illustrations. Fifth Edition. Crown 8vo, 3s. 6d.

REANEY, Mrs. G. S.—**Waking and Working;** or, From Girlhood to Womanhood. New and Cheaper Edition. With a Frontispiece. Crown 8vo, 3s. 6d.

Blessing and Blessed: a Sketch of Girl Life. New and Cheaper Edition. Crown 8vo, 3s. 6d.

Rose Gurney's Discovery. A Story for Girls. Dedicated to their Mothers. Crown 8vo, 3s. 6d.

English Girls: Their Place and Power. With Preface by the Rev. R. W. Dale. Fourth Edition. Fcap. 8vo, 2s. 6d.

Just Anyone, and other Stories. Three Illustrations. Royal 16mo, 1s. 6d.

Sunbeam Willie, and other Stories. Three Illustrations. Royal 16mo, 1s. 6d.

Sunshine Jenny, and other Stories. Three Illustrations. Royal 16mo, 1s. 6d.

STOCKTON, Frank R.—**A Jolly Fellowship.** With 20 Illustrations. Crown 8vo, 5s.

STORR, Francis, and TURNER, Hawes.—**Canterbury Chimes;** or, Chaucer Tales re-told to Children. With 6 Illustrations from the Ellesmere Manuscript. Third Edition. Fcap. 8vo, 3s. 6d.

STRETTON, Hesba.—**David Lloyd's Last Will.** With 4 Illustrations. New Edition. Royal 16mo, 2s. 6d.

WHITAKER, Florence.—**Christy's Inheritance.** A London Story. Illustrated. Royal 16mo, 1s. 6d.

www.ingramcontent.com/pod-product-compliance
Lightning Source LLC
Chambersburg PA
CBHW022104230426
43672CB00008B/1273